THE EXPANDED PANORAMA BIBLE STUDY COURSE

GOD'S IMMUTABLE PLAN AND PURPOSE OF THE AGES

"A PERFECT COMPANY
IN HARMONY WITH HIS
PERFECT WILL · TO
LOVE HIM WITH A
PERFECT LOVE · TO
BE LIKE HIM AND
WITH HIM THROUGH-
OUT A PERFECT
ETERNITY"

The EXPANDED PANORAMA BIBLE Study Course

ALFRED THOMPSON EADE, S.T.D.

Fleming H. Revell
A Division of Baker Book House Co
Grand Rapids, Michigan 49516

CONTENTS

INTRODUCTORY

THE PANORAMA OF THE AGES

THE EXPANDED PANORAMA BIBLE STUDY COURSE
NO. 1 "THE PLAN OF THE AGES"

THE GREAT PLAN and Purpose of God is often spoken of as "the simple Gospel," so simple that "none need err therein," for the entrance of God's Word "bringeth light." And truly, the first revelation that illumes the seeking soul *is* the simple, clear-cut, most familiar truth in the Bible.

For God so loved the world, that he gave his only begotten Son, that whosoever believeth in him should not perish, but have everlasting life. (John 3:16.)

There is enough Gospel, or Good News, in this one declaration of truth to give every last one of Adam's race a Passport to Heaven. But after accepting the simple Gospel, we soon find ourselves in the depth of *Two Great Mysteries:* **"the Mystery of Iniquity"** and **"the Mystery of Godliness."**

The Bible is the most profound book accessible to man. It was not, however, given to us in one great cloudburst of revelation, but as a gradual unfolding of the Divine Plan and Purpose. It took some 1500 years and forty inspired writers, waiting upon God throughout those centuries for the unfolding "panorama" which runs like a Crimson Highway from Genesis to the Revelation.

There is no short cut to profitable Bible Study, for every book is a progressive link in the unfolding revelation. Thus, the meaning of a part or passage can only be rightfully interpreted by comparing Scripture with Scripture; "line upon line," "precept upon precept." Then will the *Spirit* that reveals and the *Word* that is written *agree.*

To get the best out of Bible revelation we must be as "prospectors," ever searching for gems of deeper truth. There is, however, **a basic background** that if once seen, even though dimly, will make the revelation that follows much easier to understand. And although it is a dark background, it throws much light upon the Eternal Plan and Purpose of God.

We usually begin our study of Bible revelation with the Creation of the Material Universe, followed by the most familiar chapter of human history: Adam and Eve in their Paradise home, the Temptation and the tragic Fall. But we are not really prepared for serious study of the Origin, Place, Purpose. and Destiny of Man until we know something of the Origin, Nature, Office and Purpose of another and *earlier order of created spirit beings* known by the familiar name of "Angels."

7

It is important to us to know something of their relation to God, to Man and to this World, for it was through *one of their number*—a fallen, cast-out Angel—that Man was seduced to sin against his Creator, thus causing all the ruin that necessitated the great Eternal Sacrifice, the far-reaching plan of Redemption, which is the whole sum and substance of God's message of hope to a lost and dying world. Therefore, the purpose of this brief introduction is, at least, to sketch in a suggestion of the eternal background *before Man is introduced* into the great panorama of the ages.

In the opening chapter of Man's history we find him in the midst of Paradise and Perfection, and in Holy Communion with his Creator. But into this scene of perfection steps another, an intruder, called Satan, "that old serpent," the Devil (Genesis 3:1; Revelation 20:2).

The first and most natural question that arises is *"Where did he come from,* and with evil in his heart?" Bringing us face to face with a great Twofold Mystery: (1) That another order of created beings already existed before the creation of Man; (2) The greater Mystery, that before Man's perfect creation, Evil, Rebellion, Discord already existed in the Universe that was spoken into being by the perfect Word, the perfect Will and the perfect Purpose of the Immutable God.

It is only against this background of the Mystery of Original Sin that Man's place and part in the whole Bible story can be clearly revealed. This is the aim and objective of *The Expanded Panorama Bible Study Course*—that we might have an understandable, living, thrilling answer to the Blessed Hope within our hearts.

THE AMAZING CHALLENGE OF BIBLE REVELATION

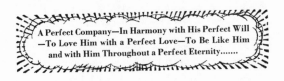

A Perfect Company—In Harmony with His Perfect Will
—To Love Him with a Perfect Love—To Be Like Him
and with Him Throughout a Perfect Eternity.......

To COUNTLESS THOUSANDS of perplexed but honest-hearted mortals in every generation, there has always been a flood of questions regarding the understandable reality of "The Great Plan and Purpose of God"— the Bible revelation generally and universally known as "The Plan of Redemption."

Not only sceptics but sincere seekers of truth have, at some time or other, felt led to open the Bible in an effort to find the answer to "that something" which cannot be answered apart from God.

They have read of the Rebellion of Angels—The Creation of Man— The Entrance of Sin, with its penalty of physical and spiritual Death —The Promise of a Saviour—His Birth, Life, Death, Resurrection and Ascension—The Prophecies of His literal, visible Returning—The Devil's Doom and God's Eternal Triumph. *But what is the meaning and purpose of such tremendous issues?* "What bearing do these mystifying events of Bible revelation have upon the pattern of my humdrum, work-a-day life?" they ask, "or in the affairs of good, but ordinary people like my friends and neighbors—*What is it all about?*"

This question has been asked by millions in every generation, and as startling as the truth may be, "the gates of hell and death" have closed upon millions who never found the answer.

Why Creation? Why Angels?—Earth?—Man?—Manger?—Cross? —Blood?—Open Tomb?—Judgment?—Hell?—Heaven?—Crowns?— Mansions? *Holy Communion* is the answer. **Man getting back to God is the living heartbeat of the Christian Faith;** the whole sum and substance of Bible revelation. Amazing as it is, the Eternal and Immutable Plan and Purpose of God can be told in the two wondrous words *Holy Communion.*

The Longing of God's Heart is the Cause and Purpose of all it is ours to know in the unfolding panorama of Bible revelation. "The heavens declare . . . his handywork" (Psalm 19:1), but ever closer to His heart is a Company of Hell-deserving Sinners brought back into inseparable fellowship and communion with His own great heart of Love. Of all the infinite vastness of God's Creation—"the heavens and the hosts therein," blazing suns, constellations, fathomless galaxies and

9

super-galaxies, universe upon universe—we read, "the Lord's portion [God's particular trophy] is *his people . . .*" (Deuteronomy 32:9).

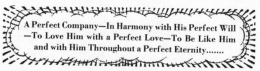

A Perfect Company—In Harmony with His Perfect Will —To Love Him with a Perfect Love—To Be Like Him and with Him Throughout a Perfect Eternity.......

"That in the ages to come he might shew the exceeding riches of his grace in his kindness toward us through Christ Jesus" (Ephesians 2:7).

From the Introduction to the Grand Finale of this Expanded Handbook (studied together with the scenes of unfolding revelation shown in *The New "Panorama" Bible Study Course No. 1,* by the same author) it is our purpose that this treasured gem of revelation shine through its pages again and again, until the understanding of the heart be saturated with the blessed realization and meaning of the Eternal *Oneness* of the Redeemer and the Redeemed.

> *They are those to whom God has planned to give a vision of the full wonder and splendor of His secret plan for the sons of men. And this secret is simply this: Christ in you! (Colossians 1:27,* PHILLIPS.)

That is why God gave His Son as a Ransom for *Sin,* the primary cause that separated us in the beginning and keeps us separated. That is why in making Full Atonement the Redeemer turned the tide of God's wrath that the Redeemed might live Daily and Eternally in inseparable fellowship and Holy Communion with His Maker.

> *That they all may be* one; *as thou, Father, art in me, and I in Thee, that they also may be one in us. . . . I in them, and thou in me, that they may be made perfect in one. . . . (John 17:21-23.)*

When we speak of Holy Communion we immediately think of the table, the linen, the tiny glasses, the elements, the ordinance; but in these two words is enfolded **the Plan and Purpose of God from Eternity to Eternity.** The meaning of "the Sacred Sacrament" goes back far beyond the table—back to the bosom of the Eternal, before man became a living soul.

In the opening chapter of our study we shall see the Longing of God's Heart made manifest before the worlds were made. "God is love"—and love was the first cause and purpose of creation. God first created, or "caused to be," a perfect company of spirit beings: Angels, Archangels, Cherubim and Seraphim. Angelic hosts capable of Understanding, Love and Holy Communion as spirit with spirit—for "God is a Spirit: and they that worship him must worship him in spirit and in truth" (John 4:24).

Had this celestial company been in perfect unison and harmony with the Creator's Perfect Will, the Bible perhaps would never have been written. The Longing of God's Heart would have been perfectly and eternally satisfied. But we soon learn the mystifying truth that the Holy Communion of Heaven was broken. The eternal purpose of the Creator's Will was violated and thwarted by a Creature's will. We learn the solemn truth that when two wills are crossed, instead of Communion there is Conflict. Harmony gives place to Discord, Love to Hate, Obedience to Rebellion, Worship to Enmity.

Casting out the rebellious ones, God purposed another company—"God made Man," and the communion between Creator and Creature was resumed in an even more tender relationship. Whereas the rebel Archangel declared, ". . . I will ascend above the heights of the clouds . . ." (Isaiah 14:14)—God came down "in the cool of the day" (Genesis 3:8) and walked and talked with man whom He had made in His own image and likeness to enjoy the Holy Communion which Angels had rebelliously forfeited.

After the brief record of Man's Creation follows the familiar chapter of "the Adversary's" entrance into the scene of Edenic beauty and Divine companionship. Cast out of Heaven, he enters the earthly scene with one diabolical ambition—to break communion between Man and God. And having accomplished his ungodly aim, he has been working ever since **to keep men out of communion with God.**

We know too well of Satan's triumph. Not by revelation only but by that which is inherent in the very nature of us all—"the seed of rebellion" which that old serpent so soon successfully implanted in the heart of God's first Man.

Holy Communion of Heaven broken! Holy Communion of Earth shattered and marred! But God's Eternal Purpose is as unchanged and unchangeable as His own Eternal Being. In spite of, or better, because of the grievous failure of Angels and of Man, He purposed yet another company—*A New Creation,* that will outlive the ages and outshine the sun, and eternally satisfy the Longing of His Heart.

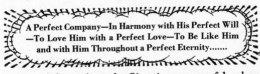

A Perfect Company—In Harmony with His Perfect Will—To Love Him with a Perfect Love—To Be Like Him and with Him Throughout a Perfect Eternity.......

To achieve this mighty triumph, *Sin,* the cause of broken communion, and *Death,* its fearful penalty, must be dealt with and put away once and for all. But who can put away Sin?—Who can conquer Death and in its place give Everlasting Life?—only God. So God came down to do what no one else could do. ". . . the Word became flesh and dwelt among us . . . (John 1:14, RSV). Born of woman but begotten of God, the Redeemer of men in that mystic union of Humanity and Deity took upon Himself man's Nature, man's Sin, man's Guilt, man's Penalty, man's Death.

God yet man. God veiled in a mantle of flesh, and when the veil—that is, His flesh—was rent and He cried, "It is finished," man came face to face with God. No longer need for Altar, Priest, Pope, or Earthly Mediation, the veriest sinner with a broken, contrite heart may come boldly through the rent veil—that is, through His Sacrificial Death, through the Shed Blood—and find *a new and living way back* to the heart of God—to live forever in that blessed and abiding Communion purposed in His great Heart of Love even before Angels sang His praises, or the starry vaults of Heaven declared His glory.

This is a synopsis of the tremendous issues involved in the theme of our study. I have traced them briefly to the beginning because the thought of observing a "Holy Communion Day" has become, in so great a measure, a form throughout Christendom, a day to be remembered on the Church calendar. The Sacrament is remembered but the inner meaning of the Sacrifice is so often veiled by outward form and ritual. Remember the linen, the glasses, the bread, the wine, the words—but Jesus said, "Remember me." Without the conscious presence of the living, risen Christ we have no Communion.

The glorious theme of inseparable fellowship with God—Holy and Eternal Communion—runs like a vein of pure gold throughout the entire structure of Holy Writ, challenging whosoever will to the abiding riches of His Grace. Living, loving, comforting Communion—moment by moment, day by day, in sunshine and shadow. Not only at the Communion Table, but in the kitchen, in the shop, in the everyday program of life—to feel His wondrous presence, and above the confusion of a troubled world to hear "the still small voice" of comforting assurance: "I will never leave you nor forsake you." ". . . if I go and prepare a place for you, I will come again, and receive you unto myself . . ." (John 14:3). *Holy and Eternal Communion* between the Redeemer and the Redeemed is the Glorious Plan and Purpose of Almighty God from Eternity to Eternity.

THE EXPANDED PANORAMA BIBLE STUDY COURSE

THE ORIGINAL CREATION (GEN 1:1) • THE

PREPARED FOR THE

GENESIS

GOD PREPARES THE EARTH FOR THE HABITATION OF MAN PS.104:30.

2ND DAY	3RD DAY	4TH DAY	5TH DAY	6TH DAY	7TH DAY
THE FIRMAMENT • WATERS ABOVE DIVIDED FROM WATERS BELOW GEN 1:6-8	EARTH AND SEAS DIVIDED • GRASS HERBS AND TREES BROUGHT FORTH GEN 1:11:12	SUN AND MOON APPOINTED LIGHT HOLDERS "He made the stars also." GEN 1:14-18	CREATURES OF THE SEA AND EVERY WINGED FOWL GEN 1:20-22	CATTLE BEASTS AND CREEPING THINGS • AND THE FIRST MAN GEN 1:24-30 •	"Thus the heavens and the earth were finished and all the host of them GEN. 2:1

EARTH NOW WASTE AND VOID (GEN 1:2) •

DWELLING PLACE OF MAN •

Chaps 1 – 2

Study 1

"IN THE BEGINNING"

FROM THE CREATION OF THE UNIVERSE
TO THE CREATION OF MAN

In the beginning God created the heaven [Hebrew plural, "heavens"] and the earth. (Genesis 1:1.)

As WE OPEN our Bible and cross the threshold of its sacred pages and read the first majestic sentence, "In the beginning God . . . ," we immediately sense the blessed truth that this Book is different from any other book in the world. And the difference is declared by the One who is the Theme of the Book, the Purpose of the Book, and the Revelation of the Book; the Lord Jesus Christ Himself: ". . . the words that I speak unto you, they are *spirit,* and they are *life*" (John 6:63). The Bible is a Living Message from the heart of a Living, Loving God.

"In the beginning God created the heavens and the earth." The first profound declaration of revelation is complete and conclusive. The Holy Spirit introduces us immediately to God as the Author and Cause of the beginning of all things. "In the beginning *God* . . ."—there is nothing left for human speculation. In spite of all the theories of the ages as to the beginning of the material universe and the origin of life, this is all man has ever known, or ever will know this side of the veil —"In the beginning *God created* . . ."—"Thus the heavens and the earth were finished, and all the host of them" (Genesis 2:1).

The fact of a material universe stares every creature in the face, and the Bible contains the only authoritative and truly acceptable account of its origin. Amazingly brief, but it stands as immutable as its Author. Scientists and geologists may speculate on strata, fossil remains, missing links, and with amazing instruments penetrate farther and farther into the realm "above the blue," and draw aside the veil of the ages from all the previously unknown; but still, "The secret of the Lord is with them that fear him . . ." (Psalm 25:14).

The World's Wisest have written volumes of theories and conjectures (some fascinating and some fantastic) as to how the Universe came into being, but "Through faith we understand that the worlds were framed by the word of God, so that things which are seen were not made of things which do appear" (Hebrews 11:3). The Universe (or better, as the Hebrew correctly states, "The host of heaven" [Deuteronomy 17:3, ASV], for astronomers tell us that we are living in "a

17

universe of universes") was *created*. The word "create" in the Hebrew is *bara,* which means "the divine and sovereign act of bringing into existence that which *was not,*" and is used solely in association with Deity. We use the term "something out of nothing" too loosely; the Universe did not come from "nothing"; it came from "God." Better then to say, "It owes its existence to nothing but God's Will and God's Word alone"—as the Psalmist declares that by the breath of His mouth He commanded and they were *created* (Psalm 104:30). Brought into being by the Divine *fiat* (Latin, "Let it be done"; hence a sanction or decree).

Now comes the question that is asked so simply and naturally, not only in the questioning "why" of a child, or the challenge of the agnostic, but in all sincerity by multitudes of honest-hearted questioners in every generation—"If God *was,* in the beginning, then *who created God?* When and from whence did God have His beginning? Can we explain the eternal existence of God?"

The Bible declares that ". . . *faith* is the . . . evidence of things not seen" (Hebrews 11:1); therefore, no explanation is given or needed to *prove* the existence of God. In the Spiritual Realm, the Realm of the Eternal, "proof" is not sought as evidence—Faith is the evidence. It is neither Reason, Knowledge, nor Wisdom, but Faith alone that puts Man on speaking terms with God. *Faith* is where the whole course of Bible revelation begins—". . . he that cometh to God must believe that *he is*" (Hebrews 11:6). This is the challenge that calls whosoever will to make the Venture of Faith. When a man takes God at His Word and by Faith believes that He *is,* and has an honest desire in his heart to know Him, the Holy Spirit immediately brings about the introduction, and makes God real and understandable to the seeking soul. "If any man will do his will, he shall know of the doctrine, whether it be of God . . ." (John 7:17).

In the Beginning "Elohim"

In the original Hebrew, the One to whom we are immediately introduced is "Elohim," being the first form of the Divine name in the Bible. Although conveying a singular meaning it is plural in form, bringing us immediately to the concept of the Unity of the Godhead. While there is one, and only one, true and living God, there are three persons in the Godhead: the Father, the Son and the Holy Ghost; and these three are *one* (I John 5:7).

The word "Trinity" is not found in the Scriptures. It is a term used to express the threefold unity of the Divine Nature; and though dimly intimated in the Old Testament, it is clearly revealed in the New. Thus, it is very significant that this expressive name, "Elohim," in the plural form, should be used "in the beginning."

Let us pause for a moment to review the manifold Nature; the mighty Work and Persons revealed in this strong name, "Elohim."

(1) "In the beginning was the Word [the Eternal Word, the *Logos*], and the Word was with God, and the Word was God. . . . All things were made by him; and without him was not any thing made that was made" (John 1:1-3). Here is the *Son* in His pre-incarnate Glory as the mighty Creator: Co-existent, Con-substantial, and Co-eternal with the Father.

(2) "Thou sendest forth thy *spirit,* they [all things] are created . . ." (Psalm 104:30). Here is the *Holy Spirit,* the "operative" Power and Person of the Godhead. God in action (also Genesis 1:2). "The Acts of the Apostles" might well be called "The Acts of the Holy Ghost."

(3) Hebrews 9:14 speaks of the *Son* who offered Himself through the *Spirit* to the *Father* before the foundation of the earth. In this revealing passage we see the distinction of persons in the being of the Godhead—the Father, Son and Holy Ghost—preparing ahead of time for the great Eternal Sacrifice which, in their fore-knowledge, must needs be made for the Eternal Redemption of a wrecked and ruined Creation.

"In the Beginning"—When this beginning was we are not told; without doubt it refers to the unfathomable past, when the heavens and the earth were originally created by the Sovereign Act and Will of the Great Creator (the chronological dates found in most Bibles are reckoned from the creation of Adam, not from the creation of the heavens and the earth).

And the earth was without form, and void; and darkness was upon the face of the deep. And the Spirit of God moved upon the face of the waters. (Genesis 1:2.)

As Genesis 1:1 is the record of a conclusive act; the heavens and the earth brought into being by the Divine *fiat* ("Let it be so")—Genesis 1:2 is the record of a subsequent event, not a continued description of the first, complete and conclusive creative act. If, by weight and harmony of subsequent revelation, this fact, with the Holy Spirit's witness, is understood by *faith* (for faith is the evidence), then so many otherwise difficult phases of Bible revelation are clarified, and the continuity of events and Divine purposes dovetail, as it were, in the harmonious unfolding of the Bible panorama.

". . . without form, and void . . ."—These words, *tohu* and *bohu,* mean in the Hebrew "desolation and emptiness," and are found together only in two other passages, both expressing "ruin" caused by God's displeasure (Isaiah 34:11; Jeremiah 4:23). That this verse (Genesis 1:2) is not a description of the original creation is settled forever by the words of Isaiah: ". . . he [God] created it not in vain [not a *tohu,* 'desolation or waste'], he formed it to be inhabited" (Isaiah 45:18). This truth is further substantiated by the correct form of the verb "to be"—"was"—which in the Hebrew reads (as Rotherham correctly translates the passage): "and the earth *became,* or had become, desolation and emptiness." The same word is used in Genesis 19:26, ". . . and she [Lot's wife] became a pillar of salt." She certainly was not so in the beginning. The obvious meaning of the word "became" bears the same strong intimation that the earth was not waste and void in the beginning, but became so, as declared in the second verse of Earth's Primeval History.

Tremendous issues revolve around this simple word "became." If the original creation of the material universe was a shapeless, chaotic mass, "without form and void," gradually developing through successive stages and ages to the present perfect order, then the Theory of Evolution, which has blasted the simple faith of millions, has much to support it. But, in the light of God's Holy Word, and of that "understanding" which "faith alone" can bring to the human heart, just the reverse is true. That "In the beginning" the original creation was a perfect, finished work; and for some reason, greatly veiled to us, but clearly known to God, the Earth was brought to desolation, darkness, emptiness and chaos—it became "waste and void."

God is Absolute Perfection, in Being, in Nature, and in all of His Attributes; therefore, everything that leaves His Hand and Heart must, by the very essence of His Being, be perfect. Be it creation, it is a Perfect Creation, be it redemption, it is a Perfect Redemption. A Perfect God creating a Perfect Chaos is contradictory even to our finite intelligence.

> "Evolution is continuous change from indefinite, incoherent homogeneity, to definite, coherent heterogeneity of structure and function, through successive differentiations and integrations."

But the *Bible,* with simple majesty and absolute authority, declares: "In the beginning God created the heavens and the earth," and "Through faith we understand that the worlds were framed by the word of God . . ." (Hebrews 11:3).

When and Why "Waste and Void"?

The Next Question is—"Do we know when or why the earth became waste and void?" How long a time elapsed between God's Original and Perfect Creation and the scene of desolation and darkness we are not told. But that some great catastrophe took place, greatly changing the earth's physical beauty and reducing it to the Bible description of chaos, is beyond all doubt. The cause of this great cataclysm is all-important in its relation to "The Story of the Ages," and as we search the Scriptures we shall find that God's Word is not without strong intimation that the Earth, in its original beauty, was the dominion of *Lucifer* (correctly translated "light-bearer"), in Isaiah 14:12 named the "son of the morning," or "shining one." He is also referred to as "the anointed cherub that covereth," and when being lifted up with pride he rebelled against his Creator, his beautiful Domain was brought to desolation and ruin by the wrath of God.

Let us take a moment to examine this belief in the light of Scripture. *"God is a Spirit . . ."* (John 4:24). ". . . the Father of spirits . . ." (Hebrews 12:9). What "pure Spirit" is, we can never fathom with our finite minds. In the sublime declaration, "I AM THAT I AM . . ." (Exodus 3:14), God expresses Himself as the self-existing, self-revealing One "Which *is,* and which *was,* and which *is* to come." "I AM THAT I AM" is the self-revelation of changeless existence, personality and eternity. (The word "eternity" is only used once in the Bible: ". . . [He] that inhabiteth eternity . . ." (Isaiah 57:15). It is the Divine revelation of Absolute Existence without the distinction of past, present, or future. God is above and before and beyond all time, and all things that He has created.

How then could God's eternal, invisible, absolute existence as pure Spirit, in essence and being, ever be made known? Out of the silence of the Eternal Ages did God at last reveal Himself? *Yes!*—That is the only answer to the Infinite Mystery. The only way "I AM THAT I AM" could ever be known was for the Eternal Presence to reveal Himself. Revelation means "to disclose," "to communicate." Divine revelation is the means by which God desires to communicate His Nature, His Will and His Purpose to intelligent spiritual beings of His creation and special interest; otherwise the creature could not know of the great end and purpose for which he was created.

The First Revelation of the Presence and Purpose of God, strange to say, is not a declaration of His Eternal Existence, or of His Mighty Power; the creation of a material universe and "the world of Nature" should be enough to satisfy the mind of any intelligent being. But *what caused Him to create* can only be disclosed by a revelation of His *Heart.* God as the Absolute Being must find the End and Cause and Purpose of Creation in Himself. Thus, Creation is God expressing *that which He is.* The First and Greatest Revelation of the Eternal Ages is that **"GOD IS LOVE."** Love is the very essence of His Nature and Being. The sum and substance of Bible revelation from first to last and forever is that *"God is love."* Once we realize the great fundamental truth of the "Nature" of God, His Will and Purpose become clear and understandable. Being, above everything else, Love, His great Heart yearns for Love (even true human love is "an answering to" of hearts); thus, **the first creative act** of God was to create and surround Himself with a company of "spiritual beings" capable of loving Him and understanding the desire of His Heart. Like Him in spirit and in harmony with His Perfect Will—thus, He created the Angelic Hosts.

What Do We Know of Angels?

God's Word clearly teaches that they were the first and highest order of creation. Angels constitute a "Company" or "Host" in distinction from a "Race." That is, they did not, in the beginning, nor do they now, propagate themselves. ". . . a spirit hath not flesh and bones [physical or corporeal bodies] . . ." (Luke 24:39; Matthew 22:30; Hebrews 1:7). The Angelic Hosts—Angels, Archangels, Cherubim and Seraphim —were created "innumerable in number," a perfect and complete Company of Unembodied, Immortal, Celestial, Spirit Beings. Angels are not the spirits of departed loved ones, neither are they Glorified Mortals. "You'll be an Angel by and by," is unscriptural and undesirable; there is something infinitely better for the Redeemed, as the good old Salvation Army song testifies:

> The Angels sing a wondrous song
> But not a song like mine
> For I am washed in Jesus' Blood
> And singing all the time,
> Singing glory be to God on high.

The word "angel" is literally translated "messenger," which suggests the Office rather than the Nature of these Celestial Hosts, called into being by a creative act of God, according to His own Will and Purpose. "Are they [angels] not all ministering spirits . . . ?" (Hebrews 1:14). The answer is clearly realized when over 230 times in the Bible record we find Angels busily engaged in carrying out their office work as "ministering messengers of the Almighty." It will be noticed that Angels are present at every crisis in the unfolding panorama of the Ages.

How long after their creation "God created the heavens and the earth," we do not know. But this we do know—they were present and "shouted for joy" when the foundation of the earth was laid (Job 38:4-7). We do not read of these celestial spectators rejoicing over the creation of any other planet—Mars, Jupiter, Saturn—but over the *Earth*. Perhaps the great Creator revealed to "the multitude of the heavenly hosts" (which was to be so closely associated with this World) that this tiny planet was to be the center of the whole story of Amazing Grace (John 3:16). That in all the Universe, the Earth would be the scene of the poured-out **Love,** the poured-out **Blood,** and the poured-out

Spirit of the *Incarnate God*. "The heavens declare . . . his handywork," but He chose the *Earth* for the Revelation of His *Heart*.

The Rebellion and Fall of Lucifer

When in the veiled ages of eternity the Angel Hosts were created we do not know—the First Recorded Event in Spiritual history is the Apostasy and Fall of a highly conspicuous one of their number. Among the Angelic Beings who sang the Creator's praise was Lucifer, the highest and brightest of the celestial order. The name "Lucifer" is rendered "light-bearer," and Ezekiel 28 undoubtedly tells us more about this mighty one and throws much light upon his relationship to this greatly veiled period of eternity between the first and second verses of Genesis.

Of no other created being in all Bible revelation is such a description written:

> *Thus saith the Lord God; thou sealest up the sum, full of wisdom, and perfect in beauty. Thou hast been in Eden the garden of God; every precious stone was thy covering. . . . Thou art the anointed cherub that covereth; and I have set thee so: thou wast upon the holy mountain of God; thou hast walked up and down in the midst of the stones of fire. Thou wast perfect in thy ways from the day that thou wast created, till iniquity was found in thee. . . . Thou hast sinned: therefore I will cast thee as profane out of the mountain of God: I will destroy thee, O covering cherub, from the midst of the stones of fire. (Ezekiel 28:12-16.)*

The whole context suggests a position of highest authority over the original creation, even in immediate attendance before the Throne of God. The teaching is very plain: God created Lucifer the fairest and wisest of the Angel Hosts. He was not only in the original Eden of God but was there by Divine Appointment: ". . . I have set thee so . . ."; placed in authority as the Anointed Covering Cherub. He was Perfect, we read, in his ways *until,* and in this *until* there is every indication that we might find the cause of Earth's first great catastrophe. The scene of desolation described in Genesis 1:2 is without doubt closely associated with the Fall, Judgment and Doom of this rebellious Angel and the Host that followed him in his unholy insurrection. Losing his Princely Appointment, the Anointed Covering Cherub became "Satan" the Adversary. The grandeur of his high office overwhelmed him with Pride—so reads the Divine Indictment: "Thine heart was lifted up because of thy beauty, thou hast corrupted thy wisdom by reason of thy brightness" (Ezekiel 28:17).

The Prophets were the mouthpiece through which God Himself spoke, as seeing the end from the beginning; thus, the Prophetic range has no bounds. It is not a description but a revelation. The Prophet may be speaking of a conspicuous earthly being or scene, when suddenly the language lifts to the spiritual realm, and God makes it applicable to spiritual truth, or a spiritual being. This is peculiar to prophecy. For instance, much that is spoken of David is actually carried far beyond David to Christ, as in the familiar Twenty-second Psalm. The same principle is here applied toward Satan as toward Christ. The Prophecies of Ezekiel 28:1-17, and Isaiah 14:12-15, are directed toward two Kings, and after revealing and condemning their presumptuous sins, the accusing voice of God lifts the prophecy from the earthly scene to the heavenly **origin** of presumptuous sin and **the original sinner,** declaring his Judgment and Doom. The language cannot possibly rest in the earthly, human scene; God carries it up and draws back the veil of eternal history and reveals an exalted, presumptuous, rebellious "spirit being" close to His own Throne, whom He designates by the name *Lucifer* (light-bearer).

That Pride was the sin that caused Lucifer's downfall is confirmed in the New Testament warning to young Christians: ". . . lest being lifted up with pride he fall into the condemnation of the devil [or share Satan's downfall]" (I Timothy 3:6). The sin of Lucifer is clearly and eternally recorded:

> *For thou hast said in thine heart, I* will *ascend into heaven, I* will *exalt my throne above the stars of God: I* will *sit also upon the mount of the congregation, . . . I* will *ascend above the heights of the clouds; I* will *be like the most High.* (*Isaiah 14:13-15.*)

Five "I *will*'s" are recorded in this amazing revelation. Here, Lucifer is seen as the first created being to set his will against the Will of his Creator. Here, we find **the Origin of Sin.** The Sin of the Ages. The Creature setting his will against the Creator was, and is, *the* Sin that condemns the rebellious, impenitent Creature, be he Angel or Man.

Although the nature of Lucifer's sin is clearly disclosed, it yet remains a mystery *how* the principle of Evil could find welcome in a perfect and uninfluenced spirit being. The Temptation did not come from beyond his own heart, but from within his own heart. The fact is: the Creature, whether Angel or Man, is created to be *God-centered*—to become *self-centered* is *the* contradiction of the very purpose of the Creature's existence. The only way this mighty Arch-Rebel, a created spirit being, endowed with the privilege of choice, could sin (as the Divine Indictment reveals) is by centering his Wisdom and Understanding

upon *himself*. Being held with pride of his own beauty and honor and
diverting the Worship—which he no doubt was ordained to lead toward
God—toward himself.

Thus this original sin is the parent sin, and Lucifer, now Satan, the
Adversary, is "the father" of the lie (John 8:44), the great Temptation
from Eden to the End—". . . ye shall be as gods . . ."—the exalta-
tion of the Creature above the Creator; and sad to say, multitudes "believing the lie" shall share the fate of the presumptuous Angel who first
conceived "the lie" in his own heart. Let us not forget that Lucifer,
although high and mighty, was finite and capable of falling. The Power
of self-determined choice—"free will"—God's own irrevocable "gift,"
places a terrible responsibility upon the creature free to choose, and carries with it the startling thought that one so exalted, and as close to God
as Lucifer, was capable of *wrong self-determination* which led to Apostasy, Judgment and eternal Perdition. ". . . let him that thinketh he
standeth take heed lest he fall" (I Corinthians 10:12).

Since iniquity was found in Lucifer, how will God deal with this first
defiance of His Holy and Perfect Will?—an insurrection which influenced a third of the Angel Hosts (Revelation 12:4)? God Himself
gives the answer: ". . . I *will* cast thee . . . out of the mountain of
God: and I *will* destroy thee, O covering cherub, from the midst of the
stones of fire" (Ezekiel 28:16). Did not Jesus declare to His disciples,
"I beheld Satan as lightning fall from heaven" (Luke 10:18)?

The First Evidence of the "casting down" of Lucifer from Heaven,
and from his appointed office as Covering Cherub—the one in authority
over the Angel Hosts appointed with him in the Original Eden of God—
is seen, as many eminent Bible Scholars believe, when the Earth, en-
hanced in its primal splendor with gold and "every precious stone"
(Ezekiel 28:13), a scene of wondrous beauty that caused Angels to
"shout for joy," was brought to "desolation and emptiness." The once
beautiful domain of the Covering Cherub now "waste and void" and
wrapped in a funeral pall of darkness. A very significant passage in the
Book of Job may have bearing upon such a scene:

> *Which removeth the mountains, and they know not: which
> overturneth them in his anger. Which shaketh the earth out
> of her place, and the pillars thereof tremble. Which com-
> mandeth the sun, and it riseth not; and sealeth up the stars.*
> (*Job 9:5-7.*)

The casting out of Lucifer and the catastrophe that fell upon the Earth,
the realm of his Domain, was only punishment in part; when this exalted
one first lifted up his heart in self-assertion, God at once pronounced

the eternal sentence, ". . . thou shalt be brought down to hell . . ." (Isaiah 14:15). Created an Angel, this mighty one by his own self-will became a Devil, or more correctly "the Devil," for in the kingdom of Satan there is only one "Diabolos." Of the Angels that followed Lucifer in his blasphemous insurrection it is written: ". . . and delivered them into chains of darkness, to be reserved unto judgment" (II Peter 2:4).

To our sorrow we have learned, both by the written word and by personal experience, that although fallen and under sentence, with lies and cunning Satan was successful in retaining much of his influence and power, and even now ". . . as a roaring lion, walketh about, seeking whom he may devour" (I Peter 5:8). His overwhelming influence in the affairs of men cannot be underestimated when three times our Lord refers to him as "the prince of this world," and John admits the awful truth that ". . . the Devil . . . deceiveth the whole world . . ." (Revelation 12:9).

The Bible was written to bring fallen Man back to God, not as a message of hope to apostate Angels. Therefore, all of God's dealings with these celestial creatures are greatly veiled to us, but in reviewing the evidence there is no question as to *Satan's past and present relationship to this earth*. After being cast down from his "first estate" and his heavenly appointment, he enters into the first scene of Human history and becomes an integral part of Bible revelation. From the beginning to the end, his dark, hostile, unholy presence ever looms, throwing into bold relief the Holiness and Righteousness of God's Eternal Purpose. There is no question as to the triumph of Right and Truth, and as the panorama of the ages unfolds we shall rejoice that in God's Time, in God's Way and in God's Power, Satan shall meet his final perdition, "the lake of fire" (Revelation 20:10). But while we rejoice in his anticipated destruction, the great eternal tragedy is the truth that multitudes, not only fallen Angels, but blinded, impenitent men and women will meet the same eternal doom and destiny. The sin that condemns, whether Angels or Man, is the crossing of God's Will and Purpose, and the rejection of His great Love. For the Lord is ". . . not willing that any should perish, but that all should come to repentance" (II Peter 3:9). God granting to Men the mercy that Angels are denied.

The New Beginning

Let us once more refresh our understanding of the Eternal Plan and Purpose of God as simply told in the two all-inclusive and conclusive words *Holy Communion*. It is God receiving unto Himself, from the "free beings" of His special creation and undying Love:

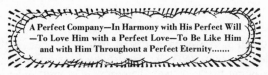

A Perfect Company—In Harmony with His Perfect Will
—To Love Him with a Perfect Love—To Be Like Him
and with Him Throughout a Perfect Eternity.......

The Holy Communion of Heaven broken and marred by the cross-purpose of Lucifer and his attending Angels, whose love and fellowship God so desired—the Great Creator now reveals to the wondering ages an exhibition of Amazing Grace. He purposes to bring forth another Company, made of the very clay which is to be their future home. Made, we read, ". . . lower than the angels . . ." (Psalm 8:5); that is, inferior in might and power and wisdom to God's first order of created beings, but to have the Dominion that Lucifer rebelliously forfeited.

The First Verse of Genesis declares the Creation of the heaven and the earth.

The Second Verse declares the earth (had become) waste and void.

The Third Verse reveals the Great Creator beginning the work of "renewing" the face of the disfigured earth to prepare it for a dwelling place for Man, in whom He now purposes to fulfill the desire of His Heart. Thus, from the Third Verse to the end of the First Chapter of Genesis we find the progressive revelation of **the reconstruction of the Earth** for the presence and the needs of Man, God's new order of free, created beings.

As we follow these events step by step we must note the use of the two words "created" and "made." They are two distinctly different words in the Hebrew text. Create is *bara,* made is *asah.* As already defined, *bara* is the Divine and Sovereign act of bringing into existence that which *was not.* The Divine *fiat* (sanction or decree, "Let it be so"). The word *bara* is used but three times in this chapter of "beginnings": (1) The Creation of the heavens and the earth; (2) Animal, or sentient life; (3) Man. To "make" (*asah*) is to fashion something out of pre-existing material (as a seamstress "makes" a dress).

In the verses that follow, the word "made" (*asah*) is used in connection with the six days' work of "renewing" the earth's surface. As the Psalmist declared: "Thou sendest forth thy spirit, and they [the heavens and the earth, in the beginning] were created: and thou *renewest* the face of the earth" (Psalm 104:30); obviously after Earth "had become" "waste and void."

On the First Day God did not *create* Light, but made it *to appear*.

On the Second Day God did not *create* the Waters, but *divided* the waters.

On the Third Day God did not *create* the Earth, but *gathered the waters* that the dry land be made *to appear.*

On the Fourth Day we do not read that God *created* the Sun, but that He made (or appointed) two light-holders or luminaries (the word used in the original text); as we set apart a man and *make him* a president, we do not *create* the man, but *appoint* him to an office. God created the Sun "in the beginning," together with all the celestial bodies (Genesis 2:1), "all the hosts of them," and on the Fourth Day of the work of "restoration" He appointed the Sun to an office in relation to the renewed Earth and the needs of Man (Genesis 1:16-17).

"Let there be light . . ." (Genesis 1:3)

On the First Day "light" penetrated the darkness at the command of God. Job (38:9) very significantly speaks of a "thick darkness [like] a swaddling band for it [the earth]." The great upheaval, revealed in the second verse, evidently did not affect the heavens; the Earth alone is said to have "become" the scene of desolation and darkness. The rays of the Sun were unable to penetrate the blackness that enveloped the stricken planet, but in God's own Time and Purpose (now to prepare the earth for the abode of Man) the thickly packed layers of darkness were dispersed at His command, "Let there be light. . . ." Everyone that is "born again" or "renewed" in the image of God has the same blessed experience. Into the darkness of Sin and Guilt and Broken Communion "the entrance of thy [God's] words giveth *light* . . ." (Psalm 119:130).

Light on the First Day—the Sun on the Fourth

It has often been asked, "How could there be light on the first day, when the Sun was not made until the fourth day?" On the first day God commanded the already existing light to appear through the thick darkness that surrounded the earth. On the fourth day God concentrated the light at one given point, making the Sun the great "light-holder," and "setting" it in the heavens, in its relation to the earth and its appointed office, to give light for days and for seasons (the measurement of "time"), the actual beginning of our Solar System (Genesis 1:14-19).

Instead of bathing the earth in universal light so that there would be no shadows, God made (or appointed) the Sun to be the "light-holder" and "set it," or focused it, as it were, upon the side of the earth facing it, leaving the other side in darkness or shadow. Proving another scientific fact that the earth rotates; if it did not, the half of the globe facing the Sun would always be in the light (or day), while the shadowed side would always be in the dark (or night). But God, "who doeth all things well," wound it up and set it going, revolving smoothly and faithfully giving us day and night, light and dark, to meet the essential needs of Man, with the added beauty of the "lesser light," using the sun's reflected rays to beautify the night with the serene majesty of "moonlight."

Scientists have long discovered "cosmic" light, light apart from the Sun; and this we know: someday we are going to a City "full of light," yet there will be no sun, nor moon, nor even candle needed there (Revelation 22:5).

"Let there be a firmament . . ." (Genesis 1:6)

And God said, Let there be a firmament in the midst of the waters, and let it divide the waters from the waters.

The simplest definition of Firmament is "expanse," or "a space," literally "a breathing space" for all life, and an habitation for the fowls of the air. It also provides the Waves upon which Light and Sound must travel. When Job of old asked the question, "Where is the *way* where light dwelleth?" (Job 38:19), he was scientifically correct in his question. For light dwelleth not in a "place" but a "way," traveling on waves at the speed of 186,000 miles a second.

Few of us realize how thin is the belt of atmosphere, or ozone, that sustains life on our planet; so vital is the Firmament to our existence that a few thousand feet from the earth's surface Man cannot exist unless he takes his own supply of oxygen. Most scientists and astronomers agree that because of this very Firmament, or atmosphere, the Earth is the only planet capable of sustaining life, at least, life as we know it.

By God's command, "Let it be," this breathing space separated the waters above from the waters below. The waters above (the vapors), carried by the wind, provide God's marvelous system of watering the earth. It is estimated that an average of sixteen million *tons* of water per second falls over the entire earth's surface. Water is eight hundred times heavier than air, yet how easily God holds it in the heavens. The never-ending cycle of evaporation and precipitation is God's wonderful water-works. "He causeth the *vapours* to ascend from the ends of the earth; he maketh lightnings for the *rain;* he bringeth the *wind* out of his treasuries" (Psalm 135:7).

In the account of this day's work, the making of the Firmament, there is an omission which seems very significant. This is the only day's work that did not conclude with the words of approval, "and God saw that it was good." Could it have been that the moment the Firmament was made, the fallen, rebellious spirits who lost their first estate swarmed into the earth's atmosphere, led by Lucifer, now "Diabolos" the Devil and "prince of the powers of the air"? It may well be, for in the day of final reckoning even the Firmament must be purged of every trace of rebellion and discord (II Peter 3:10-12).

Dividing the Earth From the Sea

And God said, Let the waters under the heaven be gathered together unto one place, and let the dry land appear: and it was so. (Genesis 1:9-10.)

On the third day, at God's command, the whole planet must have been the scene of rushing waters pouring into the "receptacles" prepared for them; revealing the mountains and the valleys of the earth, and setting forever the boundaries of the mighty deep. Had the earth been perfectly smooth there would have been no place for the seas to be gathered. In reading the following verses we can but re-echo the words of the Psalmist: ". . . marvellous are thy works . . ." (Psalm 139:14).

He gathereth the waters of the sea together as an heap: he layeth up the depth in storehouses [receptacles]. (Psalm 33:7.)

Who hath measured the waters in the hollow of his hand, . . . and weighed the mountains in scales, and the hills in a balance? (Isaiah 40:12.)

The right depth of the receptacles and the right amount of water carefully weighed and measured; that by the process of "evaporation and rainfall" the Bounds, or Tide, are constantly kept "thus far and no farther."

Plant Life Made to Appear

On the third day God spoke a second time. The dry land was now called to "yield" and cover itself with a garment of Grass, Herbs, and Fruit-bearing Trees, whose ". . . seed is in itself, upon the earth . . ." (Genesis 1:11-12).

And every plant of the field before it was in the earth, and every herb of the field before it grew. . . . (Genesis 2:5.)

There is no reason to believe that the life-bearing seed perished in the earth's first upheaval, any more than in the Flood which devastated the earth in the days of Noah. When the dry earth again appeared, kissed by the warmth and light of the sun, it brought forth vegetation "whose seed was within itself."

The Great Light-holders

The fourth day we have already considered. God setting the Sun in the heavens at the right distance, angle or tilt, and focus to meet the needs of all life upon the earth. Thus, the Earthly Home of Man was finished and prepared for habitation.

The Creation of Sentient Life

On the fifth and sixth days God put forth His Hand once more to "Create" (*bara*), commanding into being all Sentient (conscious) Life. The Waters were commanded to swarm with Living Creatures; the Firmament with every Winged Fowl that fly. Thus, sea and air were filled with life. The Earth was then commanded to bring forth Living Creatures "after their kind": Cattle and Creeping Things, and the Beasts of the Earth. Cattle (domesticated animals), Creeping Things (land reptiles and insects), Beasts, or roaming animals of forest and field—all were granivorous; that is, all were vegetarians; the green herb alone was given for meat. Man's diet also was restricted to herbs and the fruit of the trees. The present state of affairs in which animal flesh is allowed, even deemed necessary to Man and flesh-eating beasts and birds and reptiles, testifies to an unnatural condition, both in the light of God's original order of things and in the Restoration and Final Deliverance from the Curse, when "The wolf also shall dwell with the lamb, and the leopard shall lie down with the kid; . . . and the lion shall eat straw like the ox" (Isaiah 11:6-7).

The Creation of Man

On the sixth day God created *Man,* the Crowning Glory of His Hand and Heart, and on the seventh day God rested from all His work which He had "created" and "made."

INNOCENCE

THE SOUL THAT SINNETH IT SHALL DIE " GEN 2:17
EZK 18:4

THE CREATION OF MAN
GEN 1:27 - 2:7

THE KNOWLEDGE OF GOOD & EVIL

ADAM AND EVE
GEN 2:18-25

GEN 3:
THE TEMPTATION

CREATED IN INNOCENCY
THEY ARE SOLEMNLY
WARNED OF THE
CONSEQUENCE OF SIN
GEN 2:15-17

SIN

Paradise
GEN 2:8-15

ANNO MUNDI — 4004 B.C.

THE CREATION OF MAN • THE TEMPTATION • THE FALL

GENESIS

1ST DISPENSATION
ENDS IN JUDGMENT
"THE EXPULSION"

PARADISE LOST

"HE DROVE OUT
THE MAN"
GEN 3:24

THE TREE OF LIFE

THE
FALL

SIN
BREAKS COMMUNION
WITH GOD

THE
CURSE
GEN 3:14-19

THE
PROMISE
GEN 3:15

THE FALL OF MAN
EMBODIES A CURSE
AND A PROMISE

"THE SEED OF THE WOMAN"
TO REDEEM FALLEN MAN
FROM THE CURSE GEN 3:15

AND PUNISHMENT • THE PROMISE • THE EXPULSION •

Chaps 2–3

Study 2

THE DISPENSATION OF INNOCENCE

FROM THE CREATION OF MAN
TO THE FALL AND EXPULSION

THE ACCOUNT OF Man's Creation is given twice in Genesis, the book of beginnings. The first brief account is the climax of the order of the creation of all sentient life (life capable of sensation, able to experience the senses), creatures of the sea and air, cattle and creeping things, beasts of the field.

The Creation of Man

The waters teemed with life from the mighty Leviathan to the myriad Minnows. Birds of every song and plumage. Living creatures after their kind in flocks and herds. Insects in uncountable hosts; and over the Earth a carpet of verdant beauty. The Palace designed for God's Vicegerent was wonderfully fitted and furnished for his reception.

> *So God created man in his own image, in the image of God created he him; male and female created he them. (Genesis 1:27.)*

In the second account of Man's Creation more details are revealed. The record is extremely brief but of vital importance for it forms the only basis of Sound Doctrine regarding the Origin and Nature of Man. Countless volumes have been written in an attempt to explain "the Origin of Life," but God, the Author and Cause of Man's Creation, declares it in twenty-seven words:

> *And the Lord God* [Jehovah Elohim] *formed man of the dust of the ground, and breathed into his nostrils the breath of life* [Hebrew, *"lives"*]; *and man became a living soul* [Hebrew, nephesh, *"creature"; here translated "soul"*]. (Genesis 2:7.)

There are profound depths in the brief Bible description of the Creation of Man. We are first told that God "formed" Man (the word is *yatzah*), meaning to "shape" or "mold," as a potter molds the clay.

34

The material molded was "the dust of the ground" watered by "a mist" —"But there went up a mist from . . . the face of the ground . . ." (Genesis 2:6). The word translated "ground" is *adamah,* of some association with *ēdlom* (Genesis 25:30), meaning "red," from which Adam seems to have derived his name. Whether the association comes from the redness of the ground, or the ruddiness of the man, is uncertain. There are many conjectures as to the root meaning of the Hebrew word, as "creature," "ruddy one," "earthborn." The word "Adam" occurs some 560 times in the Old Testament, with the meaning "man" or "mankind" in all but a few instances.

Man was formed "of the dust of the ground," giving truth to the words spoken of the body without the breath: ". . . dust thou art, and unto dust shalt thou return" (Genesis 3:19). Man in his now inflated ego would have chosen rather "gold dust" or "diamond dust" for the manufacture of his frame—but God chose the common "dust of the ground." He purposed His Treasure in earthen vessels, ". . . that the excellency of the power may be of God, and not of us" (II Corinthians 4:7).

After molding the frame or form of Man, God breathed into his nostrils "the breath of life." "Nostrils" suggesting, now, not a mold of clay, but the Creative Mystery of "earth" becoming "flesh and blood." "Flesh" which, while living, continues to be "earth" in its basic elements, and when dead returns to "earth" again—and "blood," for ". . . the life of the flesh is in the blood . . ." (Leviticus 17:11). The "blood" is the vehicle that carries the physical life, and life is the resultant of God's breath: "man became a living soul." Although Man is both a physical and a spiritual being, he is not primarily a body with a spirit, but spirit clothed with a body, and when the two separate (at death), each returns from whence it came. The spirit goes back to God, the body goes back to the dust (Ecclesiastes 12:7).

Body—Soul—Spirit

The fine dividing line of Soul and Spirit can be distinguished with a careful reading of Genesis 2:7; yet, it seems, with all of the scholarly research on the subject much remains an infinite mystery. Amazing as it may be, the three words "dust, breath, and soul" are actually all that is known of the Origin of Life. By its infusion into the physical form, "the breath of life" became "the spirit of Man."

The spirit of God hath made me, and the breath of the Almighty hath given me life. (Job 33:4.)

. . . I also am formed out of the clay. (Job 33:6.)

The material used in the Creation of Man was "dust" for the body and "breath" (Greek, *pneuma,* "spirit") for the life. Two elements, the physical (of the earth, earthy), and the spiritual; thus, Man is aligned with two worlds, Earth and Heaven. With "the inbreathing of God," the combination of the physical and the spiritual, the body and "the breath of God" produced a third element: "Man became a living soul." He did not merely possess it, he became it. Thus, we do not rightly say "Man has a Soul"; he *is* a Soul. Therefore, the simplest definition of soul is *you,* the personal consciousness that thinks, wills, decides and is responsible for the affairs of both body and spirit. Briefly then: The Spirit is the quickening, animating, life-principle inbreathed by God. The Body is the tabernacle of the Spirit, which is the life and support of it. The Soul is the conscious result of the two, a living, personal being. The Soul of Man is his proper being, his truest self, the *Man* within the man.

The Creation of Eve

> . . . *but for Adam there was not found an help meet for him.* (*Genesis 2:20.*)

There was a higher order of Angels and a lower order of the Animal Creation, and Man was created between the two. The creatures of neither world could suit the nature of his soul, nor satisfy its just desires, or be "the answering to" of his heart's affections, for Man is a special creation, and "there was not found an help meet for him."

> *And the Lord God caused a deep sleep to fall upon Adam,* . . . *and he took one of his ribs,* . . . *and* . . . *made he a woman.* . . . (*Genesis 2:21-25.*)

Thus, woman was made of a rib out of the side of Adam; as Matthew Henry graciously describes the Divine operation: "Not made out of his head to rule over him, nor out of his feet to be trampled upon by him, but out of his side to be equal with him, under his arm to be protected, and near his heart to be loved." Individual in personality and tendencies, yet **the answering to each other** in love's true longing; the essential meaning of **mating** and **marriage.** A beautiful type of the Church, the Bride of Christ, formed from the riven side of the Second Adam.

Two names are given the created helpmeet. The first name, "Woman," *Ishshah* (literally, "man-ess"). *Ishshah* because she was taken out of *Ish,* "Man" (Genesis 2:23). "Woman" is not strictly a given name but a generic name, as later she is designated "the mother of all living." The second name given to her by her mate was "Eve" (Hebrew, *hawwah*), "life" (Genesis 3:20). Given after the transgression and fall, with its sentence of death, some scholars see "faith" on Adam's part in giving his wife the new name Eve, meaning "life." Remembering, perhaps, the promise accorded to her seed, ". . . it shall bruise thy [the serpent's] head . . ." (Genesis 3:15), for indeed the Prophecy did refer to her unique function in Spiritual history, of which she was the beginning.

Adam and Eve, the Parents of Mankind

There has always been much controversy, curiosity and perplexity regarding the common parentage of all Mankind. That the White, Black, Red and Yellow races have a common origin in Adam and Eve. Even the profoundest scholars, both believers and non-believers, maintain that there is nothing in the various groupings of color, stature or physiognomy to prove that they did not descend from the same common stock. In the *Encyclopaedia Britannica* there is an article on "complexion" which presents a most logical theory, the greatest factor being that of climate.

God's Word, however, is the final court of inquiry. ". . . [God] hath made of one blood all nations of men for to dwell on all the face of the earth . . ." (Acts 17:26), and although "blood" is omitted in some translations, science corroborates the fact that there is no difference; the same "life" is in the blood no matter what the color of the skin may be.

Original and Hereditary Sin

The question, "Why am I held responsible for the sin and depravity of Adam?" is answered in this very question of the common parentage of all Mankind. God "created" only one man, Adam, and God "breathed into his nostrils the breath of life. . . ." In the Hebrew text the word translated "life" is in the plural form, "lives." This undoubtedly referred to the revelation that the inbreathing of God produced a twofold life— Physical and Spiritual. But the meaning also refers to the God-endowed physical miracle of Procreation. That the "inbreathing" of life actually meant the beginning of "lives"—the fountain spring of all future generations of Mankind. For in Adam was contained the self-perpetuating life cell of the race. ("Cell," capable of uniting with one of opposite sex prepared to receive it, to produce a New Living Organism—the process of procreation.) Endowed with the power of reproduction, Adam was commanded to "be fruitful and multiply," the whole future of the race being contained in his life-perpetuating seed. Even as every herb contained within itself the germ of life representative of its kind (Genesis 1:11).

Adam was not only the Federal, or representative head of the race, but the Seminal head. Therefore, the infection of Sin and Depravity, the result of his Disobedience and Apostasy, was received by hereditary transmission to his "seed," the Adamic race; the "lives" contained in him and through his posterity. Hence the meaning of Genesis 5:3, ". . . Adam . . . begat a son in his own likeness, after his image . . ." —not in the image and likeness of *God,* in which he himself was "created," but in his own sinful, fallen and depraved likeness. Having lost the pure and holy likeness of God, he could not convey it to his children. Therefore, ". . . by *one man* sin entered into the world . . ." (Romans 5:12). Consequently, the sinful or depraved **nature** of that "One Man" (Adam) is inherent in his seed, or posterity, begotten in his image and likeness.

We are all "sons of Adam" by birth and by nature, and as long as we remain "in Adam" there is no way out of the consequences of the sin that separated him (and us "in him," for he is both Federal and Seminal head of the race) from Holy and Eternal Communion with God. We cannot change our Adamic nature; no matter how we try we ". . . come short of the glory of God" (Romans 3:23). But Hallelujah! for the "Good News," as the panorama of Divine revelation unfolds it, tells the wondrous story that God has made a way *"out of Adam* into Christ." Out of spiritual Death into spiritual and everlasting Life. Out of Separation into Communion. ". . . as in Adam all die, even so in Christ shall all be made alive" (I Corinthians 15:22). Although Sin and Death are ours "in Adam," Righteousness and Life are ours "in Christ."

The Image and Likeness

We cannot but notice that the events which took place on the days previous to Man's creation were accomplished by the Divine *fiat* "Let it be so," "Let the waters," "Let the earth"; but in the appointed time for the creation of Man, there was a counsel of the Godhead—"Let us make man in our image." Here was a special creation, a creation different from all others. The Father, Son and Holy Ghost have a kindred interest in the body, soul and spirit of Man. The triune pattern of Man's original and perfect creation (though now marred by sin) shall be eternal in God's perfect purpose—a Redeemed Spirit, a Perfected Soul and a Glorified Body.

When God said, "In our own image and likeness," it could not have been physical resemblance, for "God is a Spirit," invisible and incorporeal (having no material or bodily existence). "Pure spirit" without form or substance is beyond the comprehension of our finite minds. The definition of the word "spirit" gives us little help. In Hebrew, *ruach,* in Greek, *pneuma*—"breath, wind, air." Simply expressing "a breathing forth" known only by its resultant effects, as illustrated in Christ's discourse on "the spirit" to Nicodemus (John 3:8).

The measure and meaning of Man being created "in the likeness of God" consisted in that Man was created intelligent, immortal, with power of forethought and full choice; at the same time pure, holy and undefiled. A personal, moral being; that is, **one who is conscious of right and wrong.** Man is not a moral being by habit, or fear of consequences, but by Nature; herein lies "the likeness." The Personality of God was reflected in the full depth of Man's personality at his creation, and Behold! "it was very good." But alas! how sadly the imprint of God's image has been defaced by the sorrows and scars of Sin, and only in *Regeneration,* **"The New Birth,"** can that image be restored.

Before the Fall

The question is often asked, "What was the appearance of Adam and Eve before their tragic Fall?" There is no doubt that they were clothed with the Shekinah Glory of God. When Moses came down from the Mount after communing with God, we read: ". . . the skin of his face shone; and they were afraid to come nigh him. . . . and Moses put the veil upon his face . . ." (Exodus 34:30, 35). The people could not see his physical features for the Glory that hid them. It was not until after their separation from God that Adam and Eve realized they were no longer clothed upon with God's Shekinah; the effulgent Glory of His Light and Life had lifted and they realized that they were naked. Not destitute of clothes, as we think of nakedness, but destitute of God. And that is the sad condition of every one of Adam's race that is still out of communion with his Maker.

Thus, after the Rebellion and Fall of Angels—in full accord with His perfect and eternal purpose—God made Man.

> *Thou madest him a little lower than the angels; thou crownedest him with glory and honour, and didst set him over the works of thy hands.* (*Hebrews 2:7.*)

Lower than Angels in might and wisdom, but crowned with a signal honor and endowed with the right of choice and personal decision. For those who love God, and are ". . . the called according to his purpose . . ." (Romans 8:28), must choose to love Him with a spontaneous devotion of heart and will.

Created in Innocency, Man was placed in a perfect environment, a garden of God's own planting called Eden, or "delight." Fruitful and rich in every gift that Heaven could bestow to meet the need of Man, and all was freely theirs and to their "seed" forever. Not to sit at ease in their paradise home, but to "dress and keep the garden." Occupied in mind, body and soul in worshipful devotion and unquestioning obedience toward their Creator and their God. Some scholars see in this command "to keep" the garden the suggestion of guardianship, as though the Creator anticipated an intruder. And such was actually the case when Satan entered subtly disguised within the serpent's form.

In this state of Innocence our first parents were not only innocent of Sin, but completely innocent of the presence of Evil, which already existed in God's Universe. The very Heavens above were tainted with pride, self-exaltation and rebellion. Adam and Eve were innocent of the knowledge that there existed unseen "spirit beings" wiser and mightier than they.

They had no knowledge of the tragic history of the earth from which they were made. At first perfect in its primal splendor, reduced to darkness, "waste and void," and from that tumultuous mass of moving gloom again to be restored and made beautiful and fitting for their own habitation.

They were innocent of the fact that the very firmament, or expanse above them, was occupied by rebellious spirits, cast out of their first estate and led by a fallen Archangel, now the Adversary of God, themselves and all their seed. When we realize how little they knew apart from the simple limitation of their own surroundings, and, indeed, even of themselves, the prohibition placed upon them regarding "the Tree of Knowledge" perhaps explains to a degree their vulnerability to the Devil's subtle temptation.

Innocent—Sinless—Undefiled in body, mind and spirit—with God's direct blessing upon them, earth's new custodians assumed their appointed responsibility to "multiply and replenish the earth" with God's new order called "Mankind." The word "replenish" obviously tells the story of former habitation, suggesting that Adam's seed was to supplant a previous order. Even as Noah was later given the same Divine commission to "replenish the earth"—Noah's seed to supplant the obliterated antediluvians.

Not attempting a scientific discourse—the discoveries of geology prove the earth to have existed in a remote period long before the creation of man; that is, before the six days' work described in the early verses of the book of beginnings. A time not determined by chronology or Bible revelation. These geological discoveries attest the fact of an undeterminable interval between the original act of the creation of the material universe and the six days' work described in brief, but purposeful detail in the Mosaic record.

During this interval the planet may have been the scene of many catastrophes, and may have been occupied by a pre-Adamic order, or by as many prehistoric creatures as our museums and fossil hunters may declare. Many scholars, however, believe that the earth in its original beauty was "the abode of Angels," with Lucifer the anointed and appointed Leader and God's Vicegerent over the terrestrial domain (as reviewed in Study 1). But exactly what happened during this remote period of Earth's history, science doesn't know and Moses doesn't say—therefore, we shall do well to keep within the confines of Divine revelation, from which we are assured beyond doubt that **Adam was the First Man**—the progenitor of the human race.

It is the unquestionable meaning of the word "replenish" that links the story of Earth's early history and Man's Creation, with God's original charge to Lucifer, thrice-named "prince of this world." And, although once named "the god of this world" (II Corinthians 4:4), it by no means implies that he has overthrown the Almighty, but that in Paul's day he was recognized as the god of this present "world system."

Appointed at his creation as "the Anointed Covering Cherub," with the Firmamental Heaven his throne, and the Earth the sphere of his Dominion—he dared his unholy revolt; and being stripped of his appointment and cast out of his Dominion, the command to Adam to "replenish the earth" can have only one meaning, namely, "to renew, to fill again, as with a stock of goods" (Webster).

The Edenic Covenant

And God blessed them, and God said unto them, Be fruitful, and multiply, and replenish the earth, and subdue it: and have dominion over . . . every living thing that moveth upon the earth. (Genesis 1:28.)

And the Lord God planted a garden eastward in Eden; . . . And out of the ground made the Lord God to grow every tree that is pleasant to the sight, and good for food; the tree of life also in the midst of the garden, and the tree of knowledge of good and evil. (Genesis 2:8.)

And the Lord God took the man, and put him into the garden of Eden to dress it and to keep it. And the Lord God commanded the man, saying, Of every tree of the garden thou mayest freely eat: But of the tree of the knowledge of good and evil, thou shalt not eat of it: for in the day that thou eatest thereof thou shalt surely die. (Genesis 2:15-17.)

This is the First of the Great Covenants between God and Man. In their state of original probation God did not place them under a sovereign Law, although, of course, basically all rational creatures are under a law requiring love and obedience to God—the Edenic Covenant was a special and decisive test of that love and obedience.

The Covenant was a stipulation, or better, an agreement, promising reward to the creature if certain conditions were faithfully fulfilled, and threatening penalty if the conditions were violated. The conditions of the Edenic Covenant rest upon one word—**Obedience.** This was the agreement between the Creator and His Sinless Creature, and we know there was perfect accord, for man's will was in perfect unison with the Will of his Creator, for he was made in the image and likeness of God.

As a recompense for their labor of loving obedience and keeping the garden, God gave them to eat freely of all the fruit of every tree (including "the tree of life")—every tree with one exception—and God so designed that one exception to be the simple test of their loyalty and love. Being obedient to this one reasonable and simple condition would assure Adam, and the whole race contained in his seed, Holy and inseparable Communion with God, the whole Earth a paradise, and the joyous blessing of Never-Ending Life, for we are told in Genesis 3:22 that with access to "the tree of life" they might have lived forever. The gift of a blessed immortality was within man's reach; the immortal, life-sustaining qualities of the "tree of life" was the reward of Obedience. On the other hand, God solemnly warned that Disobedience would mean the loss of Holy Communion with all of its attendant blessings, and the sorrowful evils linked irrevocably with the fearful penalty—Death.

This subject has long been the scorn of unregenerate men. "How could a loving God condemn a race, just because its progenitor ate an apple?" they say.

"In the beginning," the one prohibition "thou shalt not" was the great object lesson to remind Adam of the truth that although he was appointed "lord of creation," he was in subjection to the Authority of his Maker, and that Obedience would be the open witness before Heaven, and Earth and the Ages, of unquestioning, proven loyalty and love.

The guilt of Sin lay not in the trivial act of eating the fruit, but the principle of Rebellion against God's Will. Doubting the Word and Authority of God's government, and believing and accepting the word of a fallen, malignant, Apostate Spirit.

The Temptation and Fall of Man

The Opening Chapter of Man's History begins with God's Eternal and Immutable Purpose:

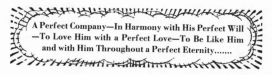

A Perfect Company—In Harmony with His Perfect Will —To Love Him with a Perfect Love—To Be Like Him and with Him Throughout a Perfect Eternity.......

Thus, in full accord with His own Perfect Will and Benediction, God's Plan and Purpose for Man begins, as it must, with Perfection: *Perfect God—Perfect Creation—Perfect Man—Perfect Environment—Perfect Communion.* Yet the presence of evil already lurking in the universe casts its ominous shadow over Eden's beauty and God's Eternal Purpose.

Into this scene of Perfection steps one with whom we are already familiar (both by experience and in our former study)—Lucifer, the once-Anointed Cherub, now Satan, the Slanderer, the Adversary of God and of God's Man. He knew that he was not mighty enough to contend with his Creator, but here was the opportunity to strike back at God through Man, the potential fulfillment of "the longing of God's heart."

War Declared!

If he could plant the seed of his own unholy desire in the mind and heart of Man, he could even yet defeat God's perfect purpose. So, here in the garden, the Devil declared war for the greatest treasure on earth— **the Soul of Man in Communion with God.**

And this we know by personal experience, that although fallen, cast-out and sentenced to Hell, Satan still retains much wisdom and power though using it to his own diabolical end. This power, thanks be to God, is limited to the mysterious and beguiling influence called "temptation." And with all the wisdom, cunning and might that he still retains, let us ever remember, the Devil cannot force transgression. He cannot make any one of us sin against our will. He can only tempt. But beware! For with this subtle weapon he made shipwreck of the human race and is still using it successfully to damn the souls of men.

This same Satan begged the opportunity to tempt Job, and God permitted the test, to Satan's defeat and God's triumph. Jesus said to Peter, ". . . Satan hath desired to have you, that he may sift you as wheat . . ." (Luke 22:31), and God permitted the sifting. So here, in the garden, enraged against God and envious of Man, Satan's one desire is to tempt and sift Adam. To sow the seed of doubt, to blast his confidence, to make shipwreck of his innocence, and to prove to the Creator that Man is too weak and unworthy of the Dominion entrusted to him.

Here in the garden, the three-cornered battle of wills began: Satan's will—against God's Will—and Man's will must be the deciding factor. God declared, ". . . the soul that sinneth, it shall die" (Ezekiel 18:4). Satan declared, "Ye shall not surely die" (Genesis 3:4)—and Man, being endowed with a will of his own, which neither God nor the Devil can invade or violate, must choose between the Word of the Almighty and the word of the Adversary—then he alone is responsible for the choice with its eternal consequences.

The old question, "If God is a God of love, why does He send men to Hell?" is surely answered in this initial test of Obedience against Disobedience. God never has, nor will He ever SEND anyone to Hell. On the contrary, since the very beginning He has done, and is doing, all that Heaven can do **to keep men from Hell** and eternal separation from God's heart of love.

If anyone goes to Hell it will be by virtue of his own choice, and a very determined choice, for all along the broad way "that leadeth to destruction" God has planted substantial Barriers. The Voice of Conscience—Parental Correction—the Striving of the Spirit—the Bible—the Church—the Cross—and every agency of Heaven is working to keep men from Hell's awful embrace. God cannot and will not violate the free will of His creatures; Man alone can make the decision that determines his eternal destiny.

The Tempter's Tactics

Now, let us watch Satan's tactics. He is far too wise to use violence, for rather than separating Adam and Eve from the One in whom they ". . . live, and move, and have [their] being . . ." (Acts 17:28), which is his objective, such an approach would drive the innocent ones closer to their Companion and Creator. He would present himself to them in a familiar and disarming form, through a familiar creature in whom they would suspect nothing that was contrary to the Creator's Will.

We shall do well to remember that the man-invented conception of the Devil as a monster with cloven hoofs and a pitchfork is part of Satan's own cunning. In reality he is a mighty, wise, malignant, fallen spirit. Nowhere in the Scriptures is he recognized merely as an evil influence—but **a personality** to be reckoned with, having power second only to the Godhead. The embodiment of evil, clothed as "an angel of light."

The Animal Creation before the fall of man was evidently docile, harmless and unharmed. The fawn with the leopard, the kid with the lion, and we read, ". . . the serpent was more subtil than any beast of the field . . ." (Genesis 3:1). The word "subtil" or "subtle" has many shades of meaning. The word "serpent" in Hebrew is *nachash,* of which the root, according to *The Standard Encyclopedia,* denotes "mental properties," that is, "to search or scrutinize." This gives support to various meanings of the word "subtle" given by Webster: "mentally keen"; and "subtile"—"rare, slender." Rather a thing of beauty than cunning. This thought would give a better understanding of the serpent being used as an instrument of deception, but in Genesis 3:1 there is no mistaking the meaning of the Hebrew word *arūm*—"crafty."

The name "Lucifer" is actually misapplied as we often use it in common speech referring to Satan in his present state. Lucifer in his original splendor is likened to "the morning star." "How art thou fallen from heaven, O Lucifer [bright star, light-bearer], son of the morning!" (Isaiah 14:12). This truly beautiful name "Lucifer" is the Latin equivalent to the Greek *phosphorus*—from *phos*—"light." It thus seems significant that, disguised within the serpent's form, the Tempter did appear to Eve as "an angel of light."

Naturally, she did not suspect that beneath such a pleasing and attractive form lurked the Adversary of her Creator, bent on Man's downfall and ruin—any more than the Disciples realized that **this same Devil** had entered into the body of Judas Iscariot as they sat together at the Last Supper.

Such an impression of rare attractiveness with the added charm of soft speech would certainly impress Eve with the idea that surely this creature was wiser than she. Especially as he boldly discounted the Word of God. Eve had not heard the command and its conditions directly from God, but indirectly from Adam. And when this "shining one" said, "it shall not be so," she was cunningly led to doubt: (1) her understanding of the given command; (2) the truth of God's spoken Word.

The miracle of "a speaking serpent" is not so amazing when we realize that God permitted Balaam's ass to speak with a human voice. Neither is it difficult to believe that God would allow a creature to be the tabernacle of Satan. The Devil's demons occupied the demoniac at Gadarea and spoke through him, and the same Devil gives utterance through men even today, posing as an "angel of light" but denying the Virgin Birth of our Lord, blasting faith in the Deity of Christ, and the supernatural Work and Person of the Holy Ghost.

Satan's Appeal

The approach Satan chose was an appeal to the most vulnerable part of human nature:

> *And when the woman saw that the tree was good for food, and that it was pleasant to the eyes, and a tree to be desired to make one wise, she took of the fruit thereof, and did eat. . . . (Genesis 3:6.)*

(1) It was good to eat—gratification of the appetite.
(2) Beautiful, or pleasant to look upon—the pride of the eye.
(3) Power to make one wise—the pride and ambition of life.

This, taken as a whole, was a temptation upward rather than downward. A temptation appealing to man's natural ego: "ye shall be as gods" (Hebrew, *Elohim*). The natural appetite—the love of beauty—the desire for knowledge are natural characteristics of man, and, as such, there is nothing wrong with these desires. In fact, God so ordained it (Genesis 2:9). But when given first place in the heart's desire, ruling out altogether the holy impulse of obedience, loyalty and devotion to God—then these natural desires become inordinate desires and agents of evil.

Eve "took" the forbidden fruit, clearly teaching that sin is the willful choice of a free-born soul. Adam soon followed, though not deceived as was Eve (I Timothy 2:14); that is, with no cloud upon his understanding. Sinning willfully against the clearest light, the choice was made and Satan triumphed.

Thus, the First Chapter of Earth's History closes with "the Entrance of Sin" and its eternal consequences. Out from the silent ages of eternity "Spiritual History" began with the Bible revelation of the Creation, Rebellion and Fall of Angels—and the Creation, Probation and Fall of Man. So soon in our study we have learned the first and fearful truth—"Whether it be Men or Angels, it is *Sin* that breaks Communion with God."

The Fall of Man Embodies a Curse and a Promise

And the Lord God said unto the serpent, Because thou hast done this, thou art cursed above all cattle, and above every beast of the field; upon thy belly shalt thou go, and dust shalt thou eat all the days of thy life: And I will put enmity between thee and the woman, and between thy seed and her seed; it shall bruise thy head, and thou shalt bruise his heel. (Genesis 3:14-15.)

The First Part of the Curse falls upon the Serpent. What this creature looked like before the Fall of Man we do not know; we can only venture a contrast—that of its original subtle beauty, upright in form, and perhaps the most graceful, as well as the wisest of the animal kingdom— and the sliding, writhing reptile we now look upon with loathing, whose very hiss is a terrifying echo of Man's tragic Fall.

The curse upon the serpent was an everlasting curse. First—". . . thou art cursed above [or more than] . . . every beast of the field. . . ." Implying that the whole animal creation fell under the curse, as did the very earth itself and all creation (Romans 8:22), only to be delivered from its bondage when "the seed of a woman" shall come to bruise the serpent's head, that is, forever to nullify and destroy the usurper's headship, power and authority in the earth and in the hearts of men. In that day of millennial blessedness the curse shall be forever lifted from the groaning creation.

*The wolf and the lamb shall feed together, and the lion shall
eat straw like the bullock: and* dust shall be the serpent's meat.
(*Isaiah 65:25.*)

That a creature of the field, not endowed with a rational, moral nature, be subjected to Sin's penalty is a mystery—but like the rest of the
animal creation, it was made for the service of man—and it is clearly
taught in the Scriptures that the Devil's instruments must share the
Devil's penalty. As to the Tempter himself, disguised within the serpent's form, sentence had already been pronounced: ". . . thou shalt
be brought down to hell, to the sides of the pit" (Isaiah 14:15).

The Woman
The Second Part of the Curse fell upon the Woman. She sought to
gratify her "pleasure and pride," and she reaped the opposite, "sorrow
and subjection." She came under the judgment of violating God's Will,
as being one with her husband—but because she led in the transgression
she is subjected to bear a special curse:

*I will greatly multiply thy sorrow; . . . in sorrow [travail]
thou shalt bring forth children; and thy desire shall be to
thy husband, and he shall rule over thee. (Genesis 3:16.)*

Thus, everyone born of Woman—every one of Adam's race—is born
in labor, pain and travail. Born not in God's image, but in the sinful
likeness of fallen Man and the deceived and sorrowful Woman. Every
groan of a woman's birth pangs is a grim reminder that *Sin,* the transgression of God's Perfect Law of Love, gave birth to a flood of sorrow
that has deluged the earth and every successive generation of mankind.

The guilty Adam was not cursed directly as was the Serpent and the
Woman, but indirectly. The Earth, Man's paradise, his province and
dominion, his earthly mansion, fitted and furnished by God's own Hand,
the very ground from which he was Created—*cursed.*

*. . . cursed is the ground for thy sake; in sorrow shalt thou
eat of it all the days of thy life; Thorns also and thistles shall
it bring forth; . . . In the sweat of thy face shalt thou eat
bread, till thou return unto the ground; . . . for dust thou
art, and unto dust shalt thou return. (Genesis 3:17-19.)*

The Earth that had yielded so-abundantly and spontaneously would
no longer "bring forth" in plenty. Man "by the sweat of his brow"
would be compelled to force from a cursed and reluctant Earth his daily

bread. Even to this day the struggle for existence is a universal problem. There are millions of Adam's race who never know what it means to have a full stomach, or to appease the ever-present pangs of hunger. Exhaustion and decay taking its daily toll until, at last, as God declared, Man returns to the dust from whence he came.

In Adam there is nothing but certain death. It is the surest thing in life. The only hope for dying men is *to get out of Adam,* and that means being "born again." Out of Adam into Christ. Out of Death into Life. To become "a new creature" in Christ Jesus (Romans 8:14-17; II Corinthians 5:17; John 1:12-13; John 3:7; John 3:16).

The Wages of Sin Is Death

In solemn warning God had announced to Adam the conditions of the Covenant. Obedience would bring continued Life and Blessing—Disobedience would bring both Physical and Spiritual Death. Therefore, the moment Man made the fateful decision in Satan's favor, Death took effect immediately.

(1) Physical Death: the dissolution of the physical body. Now denied the fruit of "the tree of life," which was ordained to be the natural means of sustaining the body in imperishable, undecaying preservation, Man is now subject to exhaustion, decay, the wastings of disease; finally death and commitment "back to the dust." When a branch is severed from the trunk of a tree it may "appear" to have life for some time, but "death set in" the moment it was separated from the trunk, the source of its nourishment and life. Thus it was with Man. Although Adam existed over nine hundred years, "death set in" the moment Communion with God, "Who only hath immortality . . ." (I Timothy 6:16), was broken. Decay and disease is "death at work" in all Mankind.

(2) Spiritual Death: ". . . in the day that thou eatest thereof thou shalt surely die" (Genesis 2:17). The very day, the very moment Adam partook of the forbidden fruit in disobedience to God's gracious Covenant, he became spiritually dead. Spiritual Death is the separation of the soul from God, the Fountainhead, the Source of Spiritual Life. God withdrew from the soul of Adam and Spiritual Life immediately ceased. Thus, the seed of Adam, born "in his likeness," are said to be "born in sin," born spiritually dead.

Spiritual Death carries even a far more dreadful penalty in its full measure. It is Eternal Death. An eternal state of separation from the light and life and love of God, and nothing but an intervention of undeserved mercy great enough and eternal enough to satisfy Divine Justice (God's wrath against sin) could ever "redeem" the guilty from the eternal doom which the Bible calls "the Second Death."

What amazing grace! The sinner is greater than the sin. God loves those who are separated from Him in all of their ruin and shame, but

He hates Sin, which is the cause of the separation. And thanks to His undying love and long-suffering mercy, there is One who has met and satisfied the claims of Divine Justice. One who has bridged the gulf of separation between sinful man and a Holy God. One who has paid the debt that all men might be free. Taking upon Himself "the sins of the world." Drinking the bitter cup of Physical and Spiritual Death, sin's twofold penalty, "for every man." Manifesting the glorious truth that ". . . as in Adam all die, even so **in Christ shall all be made alive"** (I Corinthians 15:22). All that Man lost "in Adam" is more than gained "in Christ."

The Token of Redemption

Unto Adam also and to his wife did the Lord God make coats of skins, and clothed them. (Genesis 3:21.)

Before God expelled the guilty pair from Paradise He gave them an unmistakable token of Redeeming Grace, which is unmerited favor. We often wonder if in their original innocence the threat of Death struck terror to their hearts. Could they fully understand its meaning? Death had no part in God's perfect plan and purpose—they had never seen Death. Therefore, now, God brought before them an object lesson that would be remembered throughout their generations—without the Shedding of Blood there is no Remission (covering) of Sin (Hebrews 9:22; Matthew 26:28)—"God made coats of skins and clothed them."

As the vicarious sacrifice was slain—whose death was to provide a covering for the guilty ones—**The First Gospel Sermon** was preached by God Himself, both in symbol and in action. *The Gospel of Substitution*—an innocent victim offered in the stead of the guilty was thus made real and understandable when the serpent of Sin first lifted its ugly head in the garden, bringing the penalty of Death upon all of Adam's race. Even before the sentence of punishment was pronounced upon the deceived Woman and the guilty Adam, a Revelation, a Prophecy, a Promise of a Redeemer was given them—"the seed of a woman," although Himself bruised in the conflict, would utterly destroy the Adversary and restore to penitent Man all that was lost by the ravages of Sin (Genesis 3:15).

The last verse of Genesis 3 tells the tragic story of "Paradise Lost"— "So he [God] drove out the man. . . ." The expulsion from the garden was, however, not only part of the punishment, but in God's infinite love and mercy their "protection." God placed a Cherubim with flaming sword ". . . to keep the way of the tree of life" (which had not been denied them). The better rendering is "to guard the way" lest they eat of its life-sustaining fruit and live forever in their fallen, sinful depravity

(Genesis 3:22-24). Protecting them from their own eternal guilt made way for a plan of Amazing Grace—God's great Plan of Redemption for Adam and all of his generations.

Paradise was lost, and now begins the sorrowful cycle of the ages until Paradise is regained, and "the tree of life" once more is accessible to all who have been Redeemed by the Blood of the Lamb.

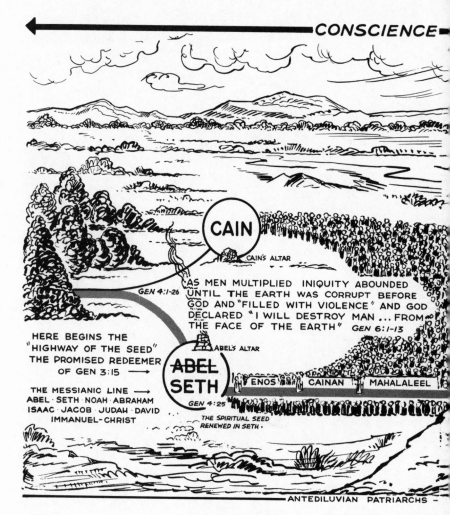

CONSCIENCE

CAIN

CAIN'S ALTAR

GEN 4:1-26

AS MEN MULTIPLIED INIQUITY ABOUNDED UNTIL THE EARTH WAS CORRUPT BEFORE GOD AND "FILLED WITH VIOLENCE" AND GOD DECLARED "I WILL DESTROY MAN ... FROM THE FACE OF THE EARTH" GEN 6:1-13

HERE BEGINS THE "HIGHWAY OF THE SEED" THE PROMISED REDEEMER OF GEN 3:15 →

ABEL'S ALTAR

ABEL
SETH

GEN 4:25

ENOS   CAINAN   MAHALALEEL

THE SPIRITUAL SEED RENEWED IN SETH

THE MESSIANIC LINE →
ABEL · SETH · NOAH · ABRAHAM
ISAAC · JACOB · JUDAH · DAVID
IMMANUEL-CHRIST

— ANTEDILUVIAN PATRIARCHS —

CAIN AND ABEL • GENERATIONS OF

• SEED OF THE RIGHTEOUS

GENESIS

SETH • WICKEDNESS OF THE WORLD

PRESERVED • THE FLOOD

Chaps 3-7

THE DISPENSATION OF CONSCIENCE

FROM THE EXPULSION FROM EDEN TO THE FLOOD

AFTER THE DECEPTION of Eve by Satan, God declared His intention to intervene:

> . . . *I will put enmity between thee and the woman, and between thy seed and her seed; it shall bruise thy head, and thou shalt bruise his heel.* (*Genesis 3:15.*)

This prophetic declaration is the beginning, the "germ" of all Bible Prophecy. The First Promise of a Coming Redeemer. This first prophecy not only gave hope of a personal Deliverer, but also a warning of never-ceasing "enmity"; a state of perpetual conflict between the two opposing seeds: the seed of the woman and the seed of the serpent.

It is not difficult to identify "the seed of the woman," for in the strict, literal sense of the prophecy none but the Lord Jesus Christ could be called "the woman's seed," He alone fulfilled the prophecy of Isaiah: "Behold, a virgin shall conceive, and bear a son, and shall call his name Immanuel [meaning 'God with us']" (Isaiah 7:14). In announcing the miraculous birth of the promised Redeemer, the Angel declared:

> *And, behold, thou shalt conceive in thy womb, and bring forth a son, and shalt call him JESUS. . . . Then said Mary unto the angel, How shall this be, seeing I know not a man? And the angel answered and said unto her, The Holy Ghost shall come upon thee; . . . therefore also that holy thing which shall be born of thee shall be called the Son of God.* (*Luke 1:31-35.*)

Thus, "the seed of a woman" is declared to be "JESUS"—"the Son of God." Neither is it difficult to identify "the seed of the serpent." It was not long before this "seed" first appeared in the person of Cain, the first-born son of Adam, whom we read, ". . . was of that wicked one . . ." (I John 3:12). In spite of the fact that Eve said, "I have gotten a man from the Lord" (Genesis 4:1), it would seem from Cain's spirit and conduct that the Lord had little to do with him.

Neither did Jesus, "the seed of the woman," fail to recognize "the seed of the serpent" in His day. Declaring to the hostile and unregenerated Pharisees, "Ye are of your father the devil . . ."; in other words, the seed of ". . . that old serpent . . ." (John 8:44; Revelation 20:2).

The Enmity, however, is not confined to the serpent and the woman in the garden, but is a state of perpetual conflict throughout the generations of their seed. Just as there are those who manifest the spirit of pride and rebellion; the spirit of their father, the Devil—so there are those in every generation that are reckoned as "one with Christ"—spiritual seed.

In the final analysis the enmity, or never-ceasing conflict, of which every generation of mankind has been conscious, is a warfare not against flesh and blood, but against unseen forces of evil in the spiritual realm. The Kingdom of God versus the kingdom of Satan. Cain and Abel, the first two sons born to Adam and Eve, were clearly representative of the opposing seeds. We read that ". . . Abel . . . was righteous . . ." (Hebrews 11:4); while ". . . Cain, who was of that wicked one, and slew his brother. . . . Because his own works were evil, and his brother's righteous" (I John 3:12).

The enmity between the righteous and the unrighteous is thus manifested in the very beginning, and runs like a treacherous, turbulent stream from Genesis to Revelation; until the promised Redeemer returns, and His Adversary, "that wicked one," meets his final and eternal doom.

All of the sorrow, conflict, hatred, war, bloodshed, persecution and tyranny in the world goes back far beyond the ungodly tyrants of history; back to the garden, where God declared a state of war existing between the Righteous and the Unrighteous in the earth. The Second Psalm clearly indicates that the ranting and raving and sword-rattling of war lords and would-be world conquerors throughout the centuries is no temporary rage of crack-pot dictators—but the deep-seated, age-old hostility of the Devil and his seed against God and His Christ. The battle is still raging, but there is no question as to the outcome. The Devil shall go down to Hell and God and the Lamb shall triumph!

How Can Sinful Man Approach a Holy God?

Our last study ended with Cherubim guarding "the tree of life" as Adam and Eve were expelled from the garden. Now comes the vital question: "How can Sinful Man approach a Holy God?" for God cannot look upon Sin in any degree of allowance.

In the garden there was Holy Communion between God and Man.

Dressing and keeping the garden was a labor of love; exercising body, mind and soul in obeying and serving the Creator and Benefactor. Tilling the soil was not the heartache and the backache as we know it today, for there were no blight, no weeds, no thorns, no devouring hosts, and the sweat of exhaustion was unknown.

There is no reason to believe that the renewed earth was less beautiful than the original earth—for God pronounced it "very good." With nourishing fruits and herbs for food, Adam's and Eve's perfect bodies knew no sickness, disease or physical fatigue; the animal creation docile and harmless; no need to pray "give us our daily bread," for every need was abundantly cared for; with the crowning joy of Holy Communion with their Maker.

But alas!—because of Sin, which is the deliberate crossing of God's Holy Will, it is all different now, even as God had warned them in the beginning: *Holy Communion broken! Fire of Judgment kindled! Eternal Punishment instituted!* Something has gone wrong! This is not the Plan and Purpose of God, who first created Angels, then Man "in His image" —that He might have a company that would live forever in the blessed and inseparable "oneness" of Holy Communion!

One of the most assuring and comforting truths of Bible revelation is that God's purpose is eternal and immutable. ". . . I am the Lord, I change not . . ." (Malachi 3:6). O! what an immovable rock of promise in the shifting sands of time! Even in the gross darkness of sin and separation there was a star of hope. God had made a promise to Man; and had given a token of that promise by the way of "shed blood." The Lord God made coats of skins and clothed them. This was to be the great object lesson from the gates of Paradise to Calvary's Cross—". . . without shedding of blood is no remission [covering]" (Hebrews 9:22), and "Blessed is he . . . whose sin is covered" (Psalm 32:1).

The Bloody Sacrifice

The origin of "the bloody sacrifice" has been much disputed for generations, but it seems very clear that God Himself instituted it immediately after the fall of man, as a medium by which men were to express to Him their sense of sin and need of redemption.

The First recorded attempt of Sinful Man to approach a Holy God, after Adam's expulsion from the garden, was that of Cain and Abel, the first sons of fallen humanity:

> . . . *Cain brought of the fruit of the ground an offering unto the Lord. And Abel, he also brought of the firstlings of his flock. . . . And the Lord had respect unto Abel and to his*

offering: But unto Cain and to his offering he had not respect.
(*Genesis 4:3-5.*)

These two boys had grown up in the same environment, received the same early parental guidance and influence; but, in the process of time, each having formulated his own ideas about religion, they were moved to make an approach to God by the way of an offering. Cain, we read, "brought the fruit of the ground." There was evidently no sense of guilt or need of atonement; the offering was no more than the satisfying results of his own labor, in acknowledgment of God as the Creator of the earth from which such fruit came forth. But, we read, "By faith Abel offered unto God a more excellent sacrifice [a lamb] than Cain, by which he obtained witness that he was righteous . . ." (Hebrews 11:4).

This raises the question—"How did Abel know of 'the blood way' of approach to God to accept it by faith?"

The first and most reasonable answer would be: no doubt, Adam and Eve, the parents of these two boys (whose natures were so opposed to each other), had told them often of their Paradise home and of the sweet Communion they enjoyed with the Great Creator, of the Tree of Life, the Serpent, their temptation and Fall, and of God's great displeasure at their disobedience, and of the curse upon the serpent, themselves, and the very earth from which they were made. And as the two boys listened in wide-eyed wonder there was many a "why?" (still the most familiar word in the vocabulary of a child). At the end of the story no doubt their parents told them of the token of redemption— that, although not understanding its full meaning, they had seen *BLOOD* shed for the first time, and that God had made for them "coats," or coverings, of the skins of the animals slain. And, although driven from the garden, they felt an "inner assurance" that their sin and guilt was covered. (Expressive of this confidence, Adam immediately gave his wife—their mother—a new name, "Eve," meaning "Life.")

There is no doubt that Abel was deeply impressed with the idea, the mental impression that in God's act of mercy He had revealed His Will. By the way of "a life forfeited"—the way of "shed blood"—sin and guilt are covered, and man may again have fellowship with God.

In the process of time, when Abel felt the inner impulse to seek God, he no doubt remembered the innocent victim whose death provided a covering for his parents' guilt; and "by faith" he accepted it as "the way of approach to God," and God immediately gave him the witness that he had come the right way.

"The blood-sprinkled way" is still the right way—**the only way**—that brings witness to the heart of penitent men that they are on "the right track" and acceptable to God. Every lamb slain on the altars of the Old Testament for four thousand years was a shadow—a token—a pledge—a promise—a prophecy—a signpost—a God-ordained object lesson—pre-figuring "the Spotless Lamb" slain on God's own altar to provide a covering for "the sins of the world."

But Cain, with indifferent heart, and with no sense of guilt or need of atonement, came his own way bringing "the fruit of the ground"—products of a cursed earth—as an offering to God. The Scriptures speak of "the way of Cain," and, sad to say, millions even today are still trying to approach God by "the way of Cain," offering their good works, gifts, charities, philosophies, even pompous religious ceremonies, or "a form of Godliness," which at best, can be but the products or accomplishments of a life under the curse of sin and death. Cain came with his hands full of "offering," but Abel came with his heart full of "faith."

The Gospel of Substitution

The Gospel of Substitution—the innocent taking the place of the guilty, as witnessed in Abel's offering of a sacrificial lamb—man's first recorded approach to God after the Fall and expulsion from Paradise—meant just this: Abel no doubt knew by his parents' warning that ". . . the soul that sinneth, it shall die" (Ezekiel 18:4), and remembering the life that was taken—the blood shed to provide a covering for his guilty parents—he, "by faith," brought a lamb for an offering. That act of faith was his confession to God—"I am a sinner, I feel my guilt—I realize that I am under the penalty of separation which means 'spiritual death,' for I am born in my father's sinful image and likeness—therefore, I am offering the life of this innocent lamb as a substitute for my life which is under condemnation. Is this the right way, dear God, to come back to your heart of love and to enjoy the Holy Communion which my father, Adam, forfeited when he deliberately transgressed thy Law of Light and Love?" As he waited for God's witness of approval or disapproval, undoubtedly, fire fell from heaven and consumed the sacrifice; thus Abel knew in his heart that he had come the right way.

Realizing that God had "no respect" for his offering, and seeing the unmistakable evidence of God's favor for Abel and for his bloody sacrifice, Cain was so overcome with anger and bitter resentment that he slew his righteous brother "Because his own works were evil . . ." (I John 3:12).

Seeing Cain's anger, God exhorted him to bring the right kind of offering to find favor in His sight. "If thou doest well, shalt thou not be accepted? [even as Abel was accepted] and if thou doest not well, sin lieth at the door" (Genesis 4:7). Many scholars believe the word "sin" to be understood as "sin offering"—in Hebrew the same word signifies "sin" and "a sacrifice for sin"—thus, "if thou doest not well, the sin offering lieth at the door," close at hand—"take the benefit of it." There are others who interpret God's exhortation as: "if thou will not do well, [that is, 'if you persist in your wrath, and hardening of your heart against God's grace'] sin lieth at the door"—that is, now that **anger** is in your heart, **murder** is close at hand. Each thought is unquestionably true.

"Thy Seed and Her Seed"—Enmity

Turning a deaf ear to God's entreaty, Cain, with rebellious heart, went out and slew his brother, Abel. Here we see the first and violent outbreak of **enmity** between the two opposing seeds, and since the blood of Abel was spilled millions of the Godly have been slain by the Ungodly throughout their generations. The Cains will slay the Abels until the end of the world. So soon were Adam and Eve doomed to harvest the first fruits of their transgression. Their first son a murderer, their second son a victim of the God-predicted "enmity."

God took immediate steps of retribution as the voice of earth's first martyr "cried to Him from the ground." Cain was straightaway tried, condemned and sentenced. "Vengeance is mine; I will repay, saith the Lord" (Romans 12:19). Rejected of God; "cursed from the earth," to be a fugitive and a perpetual reproach among men, ". . . Cain went out from the presence of the Lord . . ." (Genesis 4:9-16).

This record of Cain's departure, told in one short sentence, leaves the inference that after the expulsion of Adam and Eve from the enclosure of their garden home, in all probability they lingered with longing as near as possible to its forbidden gates. For there seems to have been "a place" (perhaps within the eastern gate where the Cherubim stood), marked by a visible symbol of the Divine Presence, or Shekinah, like the glory that later filled the Temple denoting the presence of God. We do not know. But such references as "from thy face shall I be hid," and "Cain went out from the presence of the Lord," suggest a sense of God's nearness, and it may have been before this celestial Presence that Cain and Abel erected their altars, and from which place Cain departed in shame and reproach. Though his life was spared he wandered eastward, a haunted, branded, cursed fugitive.

And Cain knew his wife; and she conceived, . . . and he builded a city, and called the name of the city, after the name of his son, Enoch. (Genesis 4:17.)

"Where did Cain get his wife?" is a natural question, but it is so often asked in cynicism that I often refer the cynic to I Peter 4:15: ". . . let none of you suffer as a . . . busybody in other men's matters." But seriously—the wife of Cain must have been his sister. There is no other possible answer. Coming from common parents, marriage with a sister was indispensable at the beginning of the race. After such necessary intermarriage had accomplished the primary purpose of God's command to Adam to "multiply and replenish the earth" (which could only mean by the process of compound multiplication—their children, their children's children, and children's children's children, *ad infinitum*), that the generations could be established and assured in the earth. Then, in His own appointed time, God instituted the law of strict prohibition regarding family intermarriage.

The Righteous Seed

After the death of Abel, God gave Adam and Eve another son, and in him the righteous seed was renewed. In the birth of Seth, at last, Abel had a successor who also walked by faith and pleased God. In Seth begins "the Highway of the Righteous" whose seed must be preserved in the earth that the two great Messianic promises, Genesis 3:15 and Isaiah 7:14, be gloriously fulfilled.

The rapidly increasing population of the world seems to have attached itself to the way of Cain, who "went out from the presence of the Lord," or Seth in whom men began ". . . to call upon the name of the Lord" (Genesis 4:26). Like a great flowing river the human family divided into two (by no means equal) branches. The line of Cain excelling in worldly achievements: the arts, industry and craftsmanship. Long a nomad people, Jabal introduced tents, or movable dwellings; Jubal was the father of musical instruments; Tubal-cain excelled in the working of brass and iron, all of which was the beginning of cultural life in the early civilization.

Whereas in the line of Seth no mention is made of any such accomplishments. The glory of this branch of the stream of humanity was the testimony of such men as Enoch, who walked with God and never tasted death, and Noah, the perfect man who became the second father of the human race. (See Study 3—*The New "Panorama" Bible Study Course* Charts.)

Seth, Enos, Cainan, Mahalaleel, Jared, Enoch, Methuselah, Lamech, Noah. What do these names mean to you? We know nothing about the majority of these antediluvian celebrities, these links in the Bible history of the righteous seed. What do you know about Methuselah? He was the oldest man, everybody knows that. But did you know that he was the grandfather of Noah, and undoubtedly had much to do with the shaping of a young life—of whom, later, God could declare he was ". . . perfect in his generations . . ." (Genesis 6:9)? Methuselah lived for 969 years, but it isn't the years that count, it's what we do with them; what kind of monument we leave behind. This principle holds true in the long line of Bible history. Know anything about Og, the King of Bashan? His name is mentioned many times—Oh yes! his bedstead was over thirteen feet long!—but that's the only testimony he left behind. Here's a man, nobody knows his name, but he is given space in Bible revelation. He didn't do anything, but he did have six fingers on each hand and six toes on each foot. Twenty-four digits— quite a record—but that is all he is remembered by. When men shall say, "Did you know—(just whisper your name here)?" what will be the outstanding memory and lasting influence? Will it be as the little old lady standing at the casket of Catherine Booth, with tears of gratitude and love flowing down her wrinkled cheeks? The policeman gently explained, "You must move on, Mother, there are thousands in line behind you"—but gently wiping her tears, she said, "Just a moment more, I've traveled so far to look upon her precious face, she saved my boy from a drunkard's grave." What better monument could anyone leave behind than a life well spent for God—and good—and others?

It's a long journey from Adam to Noah; a whole chapter is given to the family register. Names and more names, but only one bright star of immortal testimony in the gathering gloom of the centuries: ". . . Enoch walked with God: and was not; for God took him" (Genesis 5:24).

The longevity of these antediluvians (before-the-deluge people) is amazing when we try to visualize men living for almost a millennium (a thousand years). Adam, for instance (although committed to return to dust from whence he came), lived 930 years—almost to the time of the building of the Ark. It has been estimated that Adam lived to see a possible population of nearly twenty millions, and if Cain lived to the average age of his contemporaries (nine hundred years), he could have lived to see a possible population of over 136 millions. (Our thanks to the patient mathematician who figured it out.)

The Seed of Cain

The Godless branch of the great river of humanity multiplied, not only in numbers, but in wickedness and corruption for almost 130 years before Seth, "the appointed" seed, was born. It seems that in civilizations past, even as today, corruption of moral and spiritual life advanced more rapidly where the greatest so-called progress had been made in worldly achievement and material gain. These "advancements" have no power to purify the heart or preserve mankind from corruption and moral suicide.

So great and contagious was the influence of evil that it spread over the whole habitable earth, contaminating all men with every wicked imagination of the heart, until God, deeming all other measures of moral restraint too inadequate for universal corruption, resolved to destroy the whole wicked race with a flood of waters (Genesis 6:5).

The Deluge, so often spoken of as Judgment, was an act of moral surgery—cutting out the cancer of corruption, violence and wickedness that threatened to engulf all humanity; for even those born in the line of promise and hope, the descendants of Seth, were giving up the struggle and drifting by marriage and intermarriage into the stream of ungodliness.

"The Sons of God and the Daughters of Men."

Different views are taken of the passage in Genesis 6:1-4:

> *There were giants* [nephilim] *in the earth in those days; and also after that, when the sons of God came in unto the daughters of men, and they bare children to them, the same became mighty men which were of old, men of renown.*

The word *nephilim* is translated "giants." One view is that this passage applied to the higher spirits in their unholy desire for flesh, and that a race of giants sprang from this union of angelic beings with human wives. But this theory, apart from the careful study of the context by learned scholars of Hebrew, finds no support in the simple, but careful reading of the passage. First of all, nothing is said in verse 4 of a race of giants springing from angels and woman—or that the violence which is mentioned along with the corruption of the world (vss. 5-13) refers to the sin of these giants.

"There were giants [*already existing*] on the earth **in those days**" (the days of the three preceding verses), **also after** "the sons of God came in unto the daughters of men." This plainly infers that the giants *were not* the offspring of such an unholy union—they already existed before and continued to exist after "the sons of God saw the daughters of men that they were fair; and they took them wives of all they chose" (Genesis 6:2). The phrase "took wives" supports the ethical view, being always used to signify real and permanent marriages, which could not be said of visiting angels. Rather than **identifying** the giants as the offspring of angelic beings and the daughters of men, it **distinguishes them from such a union.** Most eminent critics are agreed that the passage refers to the intermarriage of the pious race descended from Seth and the daughters of the worldly race of men descended from Cain. Adam and Gray's *Commentary* suggests that these daughters of wicked and worldly men were "the city dames" of that early time.

Verse 4 clearly refers to two different and distinct categories of men: (1) Giants who already existed and continued in the land; (2) the Children of the union in question, who became mighty men, men of renown. The description "mighty men" referring chiefly to their tyranical use of force and violence. As, for instance, Nimrod, called "a mighty one," is described by the writers of the Septuagint as "a hunting giant," and in Arabic as "a terrible tyrant," a "mighty hunter," the violent invader of the person and rights of men. Such, evidently, was the application used of the resultant offspring in the breaking down of the bulwark of separation between the godly and the ungodly seed, which ended in the violent corruption of "all flesh"—"through them [mankind]" (Genesis 6:11-13).

The postponement of the Deluge for 120 years was God's forbearance, giving man a designated time and opportunity to repent, seeing, as Moffatt renders verse 3, "**Human creatures** are but flesh . . . ," or the Septuagint version, "My Spirit shall not dwell in man forever, in his errors he is flesh." That God's forbearance is toward the Antediluvian world, Mankind, Human Beings, Flesh, is the clear and logical meaning and purpose of the entire context of Genesis 6.

Nothing is said, implied, or inferred, that the reason for God's judgment upon the Antediluvian world was the union of angels and the daughters of men, with a resultant race of monstrosities. The reason for the Deluge is plainly stated: "And God saw that the wickedness of *man* was great in the earth . . ." (Genesis 6:5); ". . . all flesh [all mankind] had corrupted his way. . . . and the earth is filled with violence" (Genesis 6:12-13).

The Preservation of the Righteous Seed

In the midst of universal wickedness could there be found any whose lives were still uncontaminated by the corruption of the world?

> . . . *the eyes of the Lord run to and fro throughout the whole earth, to shew himself strong in the behalf of them whose heart is perfect toward him. (II Chronicles 16:9.)*

A Perfect Man in a world of utter corruption, violence and depravity would be like the proverbial "needle in a haystack"—but God knew His man. We read, ". . . *Noah found grace in the eyes of the Lord. . . .* [he] was a just man and perfect in his generations, and Noah walked with God." What a blessed testimony! They were already traveling companions (Genesis 6:8, 9).

In every crisis of the ages, God has always had a witness in the earth. A faithful one among the faithless. In Israel's darkest hour God had His Moses; when Moses was taken, God had His Joshua; Saul failed, but God had His David. In the dark ages, God had His Luther, Calvin, Knox. The first Adam failed, but God had His second Adam. To this righteous man, Noah, God announced His resolve to destroy all flesh upon the earth, and commanded him to build an Ark for the preservation of the Righteous Seed, and the perpetuation of life upon the earth.

And the Lord said unto Noah, Come thou and all thy house into the ark; for thee have I seen righteous before me in this generation. (Genesis 7:1.)

It should be well noted that before God revealed His determination to make an end of the degenerate generation before Him in the earth, He gave a solemn warning—at once merciful and dreadful: "My spirit shall not always strive with man, . . . his days shall be an hundred and twenty years" (Genesis 6:3).

First, as evidence of His great displeasure, He threatened to withdraw from them His Spirit. Dreadful—because it is the Holy Spirit that strives with the sinner to turn from his sin to God. Merciful—because the words "shall not always" shed even yet a ray of hope in the Divine determination. It infers that not until hope is utterly exhausted will God release man from the limits of His limitless love.

God never brings Judgment without first a condition of mercy. No sooner was Eden's perfection blasted by sin, than God gave a promise of hope and redemption. The Death Angel swept over Egypt slaying the first-born, but not before "the blood" had been sprinkled on Israel's dwellings. The wicked city of Sodom was destroyed by fire, but not until God sent Angels to warn of coming Judgment. The wages of sin is death, but not until Heaven has exhausted every agency of mercy and grace on behalf of the sinner.

God Grants a Reprieve

. . . his days shall be an hundred and twenty years. (Genesis 6:3.)

Before the final reckoning, in wrath God remembered mercy, and gave the whole wicked world a reprieve. He would defer Judgment, giving all carnal and sensuous flesh a long, last chance of 120 years to repent and turn from their reckless, degenerate, Godless way of life.

During the time of delayed destruction Noah followed God's instructions and built the Ark, while pleading, warning, admonishing and preaching righteousness (II Peter 2:5). But violence, corruption and debauchery continued unrestrained until it grieved God ". . . that he had made man on the earth" (Genesis 6:6). Grieved—because Man, made in His own image and likeness, had missed the mark, the Great End and Purpose for which he was created. It was now that God declared His resolve: "I will destroy man whom I have created from the face of the earth . . ." (Genesis 6:7).

"Make thee an ark . . ."

Taking God at His Word with unquestioning faith regarding the Deluge, Noah set to work to build the Ark even as God had commanded him. The Blueprint of the colossal undertaking is given in three verses: Genesis 6:14-16. A three-storied vessel waterproofed with bitumen, or asphalt. Not unlike a huge house on a raft, divided into rooms (nests or cells). Its given cubit measurements are estimated to be about 450 feet long, seventy-five feet wide, forty-five feet high. Taking the cubit at eighteen inches, or the distance from the elbow to the end of the middle finger (standards varied in places and periods; some put the cubit at twenty-two inches, making the Ark 562 feet long). Taking the latter figure, calculation shows that the vessel contained a space of about 3,500,000 cubic feet. After storing enough food to support several thousand pairs of animals on an ocean voyage for a year, there would remain more than fifty cubic feet per pair. Some smaller, some larger, the giraffe, for instance, would have need for a lot more head room than the guinea pig. What a colossal task to prepare accommodations for such a mixed multitude!

In the selfsame day entered Noah, and Shem, and Ham, and Japheth, the sons of Noah, and Noah's wife, and the three wives of his sons with them into the ark. (Genesis 7:13.)

God also commanded Noah to take into the Ark animals and birds of every specie (the fishes could take care of themselves), a male and a female of all flesh ". . . wherein is the breath of life . . ." (Genesis 6:17), for the perpetuation of the species. Also "clean animals," that is, animals for sacrifice, seven of each, male and female.

And the Lord said unto Noah, Come thou and all thy house into the ark; for thee have I seen righteous before me in this generation. (Genesis 7:1.)

Before Noah set foot on the gangplank there was already a passenger on board extending the gracious invitation, "Come thou and all thy house into the ark. . . ." What a precious picture of refuge in Christ, our Ark of safety, who gently bids "all who are weary and heavy laden" to "come" and in Him find shelter and rest in the time of storm.

In Hebrews 11:7, we read, "By faith Noah, being warned of God of **things not seen as yet,** moved with fear, prepared an ark to the saving of his house. . . ." "Things not seen as yet . . ."; nearly two thousand years had passed since Adam "kept the garden" and the earth was "watered by a mist"—since that time there seems to be no record of "a rainfall," but now God speaks of *a Deluge,* "things not seen as yet." And although the storm did not break for an hundred and twenty years, the coming judgment was so real and certain to Noah that he was moved with fear for the safety of his house.

If God's declared revelation of coming judgment was as real and as certain to us as to this righteous man, we, too, would be "moved with fear" for "things not seen as yet"—but as certain as God's prophetic Word so solemnly declares.

After God revealed to Noah His resolve to send a flood of waters over the earth to wipe out both the wickedness and the wicked, the Sun went on blazing in the heavens for over a century. The unbelieving, reckless and indifferent revelers, absorbed not only in eating and drinking, marrying and giving in marriage, but indulging in "every wicked imagination of the heart," no doubt laughed Noah and his fantastic enterprise to scorn—"He's crazy!"—"He's seeing things!"—How true, he was seeing things that only the eye of faith could see. Throughout the world, even today, there are a faithful few who have caught up Noah's telescope of faith, and are seeing "things not seen as yet" by a blinded, indifferent, unbelieving world—for God declares, ". . . as the days of Noe were, so shall also the coming of the Son of man be" (Matthew 24:37).

If it were possible to lift the veil of the near future—hours, days, or even months from this moment, we, too, perhaps like Noah, would be moved with fear to make our "calling and election *sure*"—and to have the blessed assurance that our loved ones, and as many as we can possibly reach with the warning message, are safe within the Ark—before the Flood of Judgment breaks upon an indifferent Christ-rejecting world. For even now are "Men's hearts failing them for fear, and for looking after those things which are coming on the earth . . ." (Luke 21:26).

". . . the Lord shut him in"

After the passenger list was completed and all that God had commanded were safely aboard—Noah and his family, eight souls in all, the animals to perpetuate their kind and those for sacrifice—we read the words (both faithful and fearful) ". . . and the Lord shut him in" (Genesis 7:16). The shutting of the door of the Ark had a twofold meaning and purpose—righteous Noah was shut in, but the whole wicked world of men was shut out.

> . . . *so shall also the coming of the Son of man be. Then shall two be in the field; the one shall be taken, and the other left. Two women shall be grinding at the mill; the one shall be taken, and the other left. Watch therefore: for ye know not what hour your Lord doth come.* (*Matthew 24:39-42.*)

Noah and his family were within the safety of the Ark for seven days before the storm broke. Seven days of patient faith that brought even more ridicule from those outside the Ark. Unquestioning faith always looks ridiculous to unbelief. But Noah's faith, at last, turned to sight. The heavens grew dark—the storm broke—the fountains of the deep burst in relentless fury—the floodgates of Heaven opened—the laughter outside of the Ark turned to cries of anguish. Noah would have opened the door if he could—but God had shut it—and when God shuts the door, no Man, nor Angel, nor Devil can open it—and when God opens the door, none can shut it. Just as "in the coming of the Son of man," when the foolish virgins shall knock frantically upon the door of the Bridal Chamber—so God was saying to those shut out of the Ark, "I know you not."

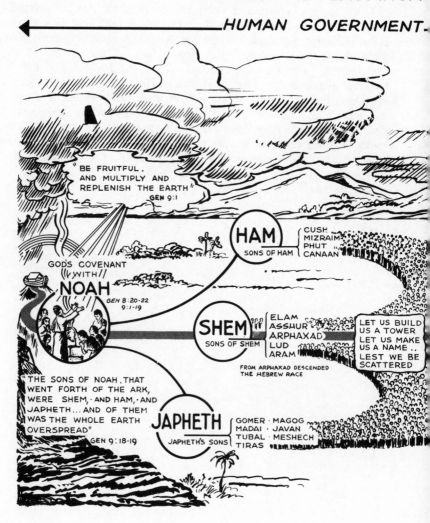

"BE FRUITFUL, AND MULTIPLY AND REPLENISH THE EARTH" GEN 9:1

GOD'S COVENANT WITH NOAH GEN 8:20-22 9:1-19

HAM — SONS OF HAM — CUSH MIZRAIM PHUT CANAAN

SHEM — SONS OF SHEM — ELAM ASSHUR ARPHAXAD LUD ARAM

FROM ARPHAXAD DESCENDED THE HEBREW RACE

LET US BUILD US A TOWER LET US MAKE US A NAME .. LEST WE BE SCATTERED

"THE SONS OF NOAH, THAT WENT FORTH OF THE ARK, WERE SHEM, AND HAM, AND JAPHETH... AND OF THEM WAS THE WHOLE EARTH OVERSPREAD" GEN 9:18-19

JAPHETH — JAPHETH'S SONS — GOMER · MAGOG MADAI · JAVAN TUBAL · MESHECH TIRAS

GOD'S COVENANT WITH NOAH • REPEOPLING THE EARTH

GENESIS

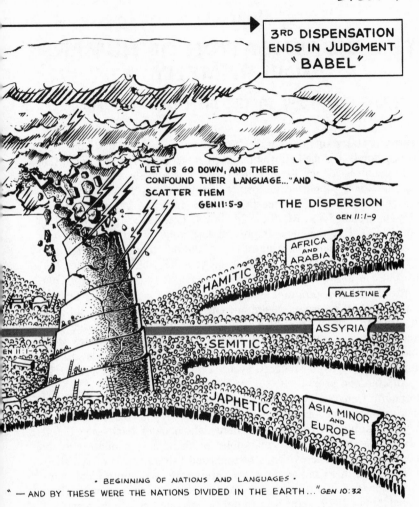

3RD DISPENSATION
ENDS IN JUDGMENT
"BABEL"

"LET US GO DOWN, AND THERE
CONFOUND THEIR LANGUAGE..." AND
SCATTER THEM
GEN 11:5-9

THE DISPERSION
GEN 11:1-9

AFRICA
AND
ARABIA

HAMITIC

PALESTINE

ASSYRIA

SEMITIC

JAPHETIC

ASIA MINOR
AND
EUROPE

· BEGINNING OF NATIONS AND LANGUAGES ·
" — AND BY THESE WERE THE NATIONS DIVIDED IN THE EARTH..." GEN 10:32

THROUGH HAM,- SHEM AND JAPHETH · BABEL · DISPERSION ·

Chaps 8~11

THE DISPENSATION OF HUMAN GOVERNMENT

FROM THE FLOOD TO THE DISPERSION AT BABEL

ALTHOUGH MANY OF the world's learned ones discredit the story of a universal flood, it is well substantiated in Revelation, History, Tradition and Physical Evidence. The Genesis account of the Deluge doesn't stand alone; it is supported by inspired Bible writers, who testified hundreds of years later of the earth's second universal catastrophe: Job 22:15-16; Isaiah 54:9; Matthew 24:38-39; Luke 17:27; II Peter 2:5; I Peter 3:20. But the most important testimony of all is that of our Blessed Lord Himself, speaking of ". . . the day that Noe entered into the ark, and the flood came, and destroyed them all" (Luke 17:27). Thus, those who deny the Flood deny the testimony of the Son of God.

Not only do the Scriptures give undisputed testimony of the Deluge, but almost all of the races of the ancient world have a traditional story built around "a great flood of waters." While many of the stories have become legendary, even mythical traditions, the central features, such as the wickedness of man, the displeasure of God, or the gods, a boat, a mountain, birds as messengers, even the rainbow, testify to a universal story of common origin.

Not only from Scripture and Tradition, but from all over the earth comes unmistakable physical evidence. The Clay Tablets unearthed at Nineveh bearing the Chaldean account, which dates back long before the Bible was written, are remarkable for their close similarity to the Genesis narrative. The evidence of fossilized fish and beds of sea shells deposited high upon mountain passes; well-preserved subtropical mammoths embedded in the icy wastes of Siberia; the excavation at Ur of the Chaldees in 1929, showing stratum of deposited clay eight feet deep, and beneath it the remains of a civilization older than Ur, built above it; these, and numerous other familiar evidences, to which there is no answer but a sudden and violent upheaval that at some time swept the earth and overtook all life upon it.

The terrifying violence with which the Flood swept the earth is beyond our wildest imagination. The fountains of the deep with their pent-up fury bursting through the crust of the earth; while the windows of the firmament above were opened to discharge their torrents of destruction —and when we realize that two-thirds of the earth's surface is water, what tremendous power must have crashed over the earth as the mighty oceans leaped their bounds in thundering, angry billows.

The Bible does not describe the dreadful scene that followed. It merely tells us that the tops of the mountains were covered, and that every living creature that moved on the earth died (Genesis 7). A frightful scene of man and beast struggling against the raging storm from high ground to higher ground, but never to escape the relentless, rising tide. The drifting bodies of earth's wicked millions, and the lifeless carcasses of the animal creation caught and tossed in the swirling debris of the devastated earth, must have been a terrifying sight to those in the safety and security of the God-provided shelter and refuge. ". . . Noah only remained alive and they that were with him in the ark" (Genesis 7:23). The same Flood that carried Judgment in its angry billows lifted the Ark and bore it safely on its heaving bosom. So shall it be at the coming of the Son of man—". . . taking vengeance on those that know not God . . ." (II Thessalonians 1:8)—but "catching away" those that love His appearing.

For seven months the Ark floated on the restless waters. No sail to carry it, no rudder to guide it, seemingly at the mercy of the unleashed elements; but having accepted God's invitation to "Come into the ark," Noah had sublime confidence that the One who shut the door against the storm was mighty to save and faithful to deliver those who put their trust in Him.

At last, the water subsided and the Ark settled ". . . upon the mountains of Ararat" (Genesis 8:4), and ". . . the waters were dried up from off the earth . . ." (Genesis 8:13). After a period of five months and ten days the trusting old Patriarch, his sons and their wives, received instructions from God to leave the strange vessel which had been their home for **one year and ten days.**

Upon leaving the Ark, before turning to the empty, desolated earth to begin to rebuild a new world of men, Noah's first act was to build, not a home, but an *Altar*. Even as later, the remnant returning to Jerusalem to rebuild the demolished Temple first set up the Altar before the foundation of the House of God was laid (Ezra 3). This is the Divine blueprint of life—". . . seek ye first the kingdom of God, and his righteousness . . ." (Matthew 6:33). "God first" should be the rule and principle in every venture, every plan, every decision, in every department of our lives; thus it was with Noah.

Although his stock of cattle, beasts and fowl were small to begin life anew on the earth, Noah offered an abundant burnt offering, gladly giving the most and the best that he had with praise and thanksgiving unto the Lord. The spirit and savor of the offering pleased God. We read, ". . . the Lord smelled a sweet savour . . ." (Genesis 8:21), or, as it is rendered in the Hebrew text, "He smelt a savour of rest." After His outpoured wrath upon a wicked world of violence and sinful disregard for everything sacred to His heart—God caused His love "to rest" upon this little band, "accounted righteous" for the righteousness of Noah.

Pleased with Noah's spontaneous offering of praise, thanksgiving and unquestioning acknowledgment of His sovereignty, God made a Covenant (Hebrew, *berithi,* usually "a mutual compact," here "a solemn promise") with the faithful Patriarch and all the generations of his seed. Never again would He ". . . curse the ground . . . for man's sake . . ." (or, because of man), neither would He ". . . smite any more every living thing . . ." as He had done (Genesis 8:20-22).

The Noahic Covenant (Genesis 9:1-19)

With God's blessing and the command "Be ye fruitful, multiply, and replenish the earth"—with the whole desolated world before them— Noah and his sons set out upon the incredible task: (1) to re-people the earth; (2) subdue the animal creation; (3) keep respect for human life sacred; (4) and as God's witness in the earth to keep the testimony of True Religion pure and undefiled.

God's Covenant with Noah gave the human race *A New Beginning,* with the institution of Human Government. The government of man under God. Whereas before the Flood the earth was filled with violence, now the sacredness of life was stressed by the institution of capital punishment. "Whoso sheddeth man's blood, by man shall his blood be shed: for in the image of God made he man" (Genesis 9:6).

The flesh of animals is now, under certain restrictions, permitted for food. The earth's immediate productiveness had been so impaired by the great upheaval, that God permitted animal flesh to be eaten to augment man's physical need. The blood of the flesh, however, was not to be eaten, for the life is in the blood (Genesis 9:3-4). This prohibition was intended to give a peculiar sacredness to life. Even the blood of beasts, having been appointed as an expiatory (means of atonement) substitute for man's forfeited life, was not to be treated as common. The explanation and sanctity of the blood was given later in impressive detail and command to God's people in the Ceremonial Law (Leviticus 17: 10-14).

God's Covenant with Noah also assured the earth against another universal judgment by a flood of waters. ". . . neither shall all flesh be cut off any more by the waters of a flood . . ." (Genesis 9:11). To confirm His Covenant God set a **Rainbow** in the heavens as a reminder of His promise, "for perpetual generations" (Genesis 9:9-19). The Hebrew *kesheth* is the ordinary word for "bow," there being no special word for "rainbow." The Glory of the Lord is likened to

". . . the appearance of the bow that is in the cloud in the day of rain . . ." (Ezekiel 1:28). The Rainbow is dramatically mentioned in the Apocalyptic vision (Revelation 4:3), and has become a chosen symbol of Peace returning after Tempest, or Grace after Wrath.

Noah and his family settled in the district of Ararat, a mountainous region in Armenia often referred to as "The Cradle of the Race." Noah and his sons went forth from the Ark to re-populate the earth, in the region where Adam and Eve went forth from Eden, with the same Divine command to "replenish the earth." The district is well suited to have been the center from which the human race first spread; it is fertile, furnishing good pasture, crops, and where the vine is indigenous. A radius of a few hundred miles would embrace Eden and Ararat, the birthplace of the race; Babylon and Nineveh, the early seat of civilization; Mesopotamia, from whence Abraham was called; Palestine, the scene and center of earth's most momentous events: the Birth, Death, Resurrection and Ascension of our Lord and Saviour Jesus Christ.

The Shame of Noah and the Sin of Ham

"And Noah began to be an husbandman, and he planted a vineyard" (Genesis 9:20). Of necessity Noah must turn his first effort to coaxing and cultivating a cursed, desolated and reluctant earth to yield their daily bread. He became a husbandman and planted a vineyard, and to his humiliation and shame he succumbed to the intoxicating qualities of the fruit of the vine.

There have been many conjectures regarding the example set by Noah's act of folly, but it is unlikely that he was the first to discover the intoxicating effects of fermented grape juice. Surely this quality was known by the depraved generations before the Flood, and may have been a contributing factor to the violence and degeneracy of the antediluvian age. Noah's previous way of life was far removed from such excesses, for God regarded him as "righteous" and "perfect in his generation"—now, of necessity as a husbandman, he had an experimental acquaintance with the vine and its potential, and the humiliating fact remains that it made him drunk.

While under the intoxicating effect, his youngest son, Ham, discovered his father lying helpless and uncovered in his tent. Instead of having respect and sorrow for his father's shame, he called his brothers to come and enjoy the humiliating spectacle. But his brothers honored their father and respectfully took a garment and went backwards into the tent and covered the old man's nakedness and shame (Genesis 9:20-23).

What a Blessing it would be even today if by a gracious act of Christlike compassion—instead of exposing and criticizing and denouncing the faults and shame of others, to cover them with humility and anxious prayer. True Christ-like love covers a multitude of sins—not only seven, but "seventy times seven." To "cover" doesn't mean to "condone"—but with a spirit of meekness, "lest we ourselves should fall," with the words of the good old Gospel song, "Take it to the Lord and leave it there."

Upon awakening, Noah, knowing what his younger son had done, in the spirit of prophecy assigned to his three sons "a blessing" or "a curse" according to their respective behavior:

> Cursed be Canaan; a servant of servants shall he be unto his brethren. . . . Blessed be the Lord God of Shem; and Canaan shall be his servant. God shall enlarge Japheth, and he shall dwell in the tents of Shem; and Canaan shall be his servant. (Genesis 9:24-27.)

(1) Cursed be Canaan. It will be noticed that the guilty one, Ham, who actually dishonored his father, was not cursed directly, but his son Canaan. It has often been suggested that the colored race, sometimes referred to as "the sons of Ham," were destined to be a servile people because of Noah's prophetic denunciation of Ham. This, however, is not directly so. Noah, not desiring to curse his son, cursed only one branch of that son's descendants, the Canaanites, who were later the constant enemies of the Israelites, and finally became their servants as the prophecy predicted. Of the nationalities descending from the sons of Ham, the darkest in color is Cush (Ethiopia), Mizraim (Egypt), Phut (Libya), and Canaan, last, upon whom the curse was directed. (See Studies 4 and 5—*The New "Panorama" Bible Study Course.*)

The early Church father, Origen, mentions, as a tradition among the Jews, that Canaan first saw the shame of his grandfather and told his father, Ham, to "come and see." Ham, however, was to suffer in the knowledge that his youngest son, Canaan, was to bear the punishment of a curse that he himself had provoked, and although the Canaanites were for a time a prosperous and powerful people, there came at last a day of reckoning. Eight hundred years passed before the curse upon Canaan took its full and final toll. "The mills of God grind slowly but they grind exceeding sure." Suffering, slaughter, slavery, driven or destroyed, because of their abominations, from the land called by their name; to give place to the Hebrews, the descendants of Shem.

(2) "Blessed be the Lord God of Shem. . . ." In this benediction of blessing it will be noticed that the Covenant name *Lord God (Jehovah Elohim)* is used, but not with the blessing to Japheth, which was related to natural and material things, progeny (seed) and territory. The blessing of Shem, by its association with the Covenant name, suggested "spiritual" blessing, for it was through the line of Shem that the Covenant promise of the coming Messiah would be fulfilled. Noah did not direct his blessing immediately to Shem, but said, "Blessed be the LORD God of Shem," giving the glory of Shem's honorable behavior to Shem's God—he praises the Author not the instrument. A wondrous lesson re-echoed by our Lord Himself in Matthew 5:16: "Let your light so shine before men, that they may see **your good works,** and glorify **your Father** which is in heaven."

(3) **"God shall enlarge Japheth. . . ."** His descendants (as history now confirms) to spread over the greatest portion of the globe. ". . . and he shall dwell in the tents of Shem. . . ." Some scholars take the view that the word "he" may refer to either God or Japheth. ". . . let him [Japheth] dwell in the tents of Shem . . ." (RSV); that is, ultimately to "dwell together" in the sense of partaking of Shem's spiritual blessings; Jews (descendants of Shem) and Gentiles (descendants of Japheth) united together in "the Church fold."

Many Jewish authorities, with other eminent scholars, however, make the compound name *Lord God* the subject of the verb, more naturally interpreting the words as two acts of God. He (God) will enlarge Japheth, but He will dwell in the tents of Shem. Shem is the habitation of God. The double portion of the birthright (the right of the first-born, in this instance, Shem) seems to have been given to Japheth, whom God would enlarge, both in seed and in territory. But the priesthood, the "spiritual" privilege, is given to Shem.

Shem, the eldest son of Noah, from whom the Jews as well as the Semitic (*Shemitic*) nations in general have descended, is called "the father of all the children of Eber." The word *Eber* means "the other side," "a crossing over," and the word *Hebrew* which is derived from it, denotes those who migrated from the other side of the river (Euphrates), from Haran from whence Abram and his descendants made their way into Canaan.

Thus, in Noah's prophecy concerning his three sons, the historic effect on the whole family of mankind is foreshadowed: (1) The curse upon Canaan, which in some measure affected most of Ham's descendants. (2) The spiritual blessing associated with Shem, in whose descendants, after the flesh, is recorded the genealogy of the Messiah. (3) The enlargement of Japheth in posterity and territory. *Shem, Ham,* and *Japheth,* "These are the three sons of Noah, and of them was the whole earth overspread" (re-populated).

The Postdiluvian (After the Flood) Generations

Noah, who has been called "the second father of the race," with his family, eight souls in all, charged with the same commission given to Adam and Eve in the beginning, to "replenish the earth," did not start out in the state of "innocency" as did our first parents, but with a full knowledge of *Sin* and its dreadful consequences; as well as a knowledge of God's Mercy and Grace. Will they do better than God's first family?

The nucleus of "the new world" had been witnesses of God as a Punisher of the Wicked, and a Saviour of the Obedient; surely the unforgettable terrors of the Deluge, the turbulent history behind them which climaxed with the fearful judgment of God upon the defiant and disobedient children of men, would have caused the postdiluvians to stand in Holy awe and heartfelt gratitude as recipients of God's Grace. But, in spite of the fact that at first their testimony may have been fearless and faithful, as the first family and their children's families increased in the earth, it was not long before the warning was disregarded and even despised, as the generations grew more and more indifferent to the God of their patriarchal father, Noah.

In Earth's Second Great Catastrophe, the Deluge (Genesis 1:2 being first), the tree of humanity was cut down to the very root, and in the unfolding panorama, following the new beginning of the race, we learn the unescapable truth: the root itself must be cured if the branches are to live and be fruitful to the unfading glory of God's perfect purpose.

We look upon the scene before us as past history, but it is continuous truth. Destroy all flesh upon the earth in any seven generations—save one family with three sons and their wives, and in another seven generations reap the same harvest—all that is inherently wicked in the human heart. Water cannot drown transgression, nor the unleashed elements blot out inherent sin. The Flood is now history, but history is no "schoolmaster" to lead us to God's "Ark of Refuge"—men must have a personal revelation and realization that judgment is not only climactic, but continual, and the salvation of the righteous is eternal truth.

The Tower of Babel

It was God's purpose, even from creation, that the whole earth be populated. ". . . he created it not in vain, he formed it to be inhabited" (Isaiah 45:18), that the great human family should gradually and naturally disperse itself over the earth; that all mankind might benefit by the gifts of God's universal providence. But instead of following God's natural order, the spirit of proud and obstinate resistance, the old "enmity" again possessed them with an insane defiance of God's purpose.

Contrary to God's plan of natural and gradual occupation of all the earth, they determined to settle down and make a name for themselves. They had long since decided that they did not need the God of Noah; they needed a permanent headquarters with a great tower to mark the center of their unity, lest they be continually "pushed around" (if they had such phraseology in those days); the Bible says ". . . lest we be scattered. . . ."

. . . the whole earth was of one language, and of one speech. . . . They found a plain in the land of Shinar; and they dwelt there. And they said one to another, Go to, let us make brick, and burn them thoroughly. And they had brick for stone, and slime had they for morter. And they said, Go to, let us build us a city and a tower, whose top may reach unto heaven; and let us make us a name, lest we be scattered abroad upon the face of the whole earth. (Genesis 11:1-4.)

"Let us, let us, let us" sounds like the echo of Lucifer's "I will, I will, I will," and just as God declared to Lucifer, "Thou shalt be brought down," so He deals with Lucifer's rebellious seed; they too shall be brought down, confounded and scattered.

Shinar was the name given, in the earliest Hebrew records, to Babylonia, or the land of Babel, later called Chaldea by the Greeks. In Genesis 10:10, Shinar is the district wherein lay Babel, Erech, Accad and Calneh, cities which were the nucleus of Nimrod's Kingdom. In Genesis 10 (sometimes called "the table of the nations"), we find the brief record of the abovementioned Nimrod and the beginning of his Kingdom:

And Cush begat Nimrod: he began to be a mighty one in the earth. He was a mighty hunter before the Lord. . . . And the beginning of his kingdom was Babel, and Erech, and Accad, and Calneh, in the land of Shinar. (Genesis 10:8-10.)

Nimrod, a notable character in early history, is described as "a mighty one." Not merely a hunter of game, however, but an aggressive invader; the conquest of the early Babylonian cities and their federation into one great kingdom is ascribed to this "mighty one." Early writers believed him to be the first to wear a crown. In his great hunting prowess he probably gathered a number of men under his command, finally making himself their master and soon bringing the land under his subjection. There is an old poem that reads: "Proud Nimrod first his bloody race began, a mighty hunter and his prey was man."

There is no record that he had the right to rule by birth, but somehow or other he got into power and laid the foundation of mighty Babylon, later to be described in Daniel's great prophecy as "the head of gold," the first World-Empire (Daniel 2:37-38). Nimrod was a great builder, probably the architect of the unholy project in the land of Shinar, but when the ambitious scheme was frustrated by Divine intervention, he sought further fields of conquest. "Out of that land went forth Asshur, and builded Nineveh . . ." (Genesis 10:11), literally, "he [Nimrod] went forth into Assyria and builded Nineveh." Assyria is a Greek name formed from Asshur, the primitive capital of the land.

There is no doubt that Idolatry was already prevalent in the land of Shinar, when Nimrod first established his cities and laid the foundation of his kingdom. The building of the tower was prompted, not so much perhaps by the idea of actually reaching Heaven (the language suggests "an exceeding high tower"), but having long neglected, even forsaken the God of their fathers, if Babylon was to be their dwelling place they would do honor to the gods of the land and build a monument high enough to challenge the very God of Heaven. There is no stone in this region and the building material discovered in the ruins of like erections was well-burnt brick. The "slime" used for mortar was bitumen or asphalt, a natural product of the region with a peculiarly adhesive nature.

The actual ruins of the tower, called Babel, have not been positively identified. There is, however, a great mound called *Birs Nimrood,* near the site of ancient Babylon, that some authorities believe to be the remains of the tower of Babel. It is rectangular in form, measuring about two thousand feet around, and over 150 feet high. If not the actual ruins it could well have been an erection of similar architectural pattern. According to an inscription deciphered by Sir Henry Rawlinson, the original tower consisted of seven stages, each diminishing in size, the top stage being a temple, or sanctuary, the bottom platform having six gates admitting to temples, or small chapels, dedicated to the various gods of Babylonia.

The account of the building of the tower of Babel has always been branded as a fantastic and ridiculous enterprise; we cannot but recognize the fact, however, that men are doing pretty much the same thing the world over, even today. Our present world-system is still "in the land of Shinar," building its towers of ways-and-means, both fascinating and frightening philosophies and Godless Ideologies, using unstickable doctrines for brick, and the "slime" of propaganda, instead of truth, for mortar. The result is ever the same, "Therefore is the name of it called *Babel* [confusion heaped upon confusion] . . ." (Genesis 11:9).

Throughout the centuries men have tried to build their own way to Heaven, using the best and the worst that earth's brains and brawn could conceive and propagate. When God made the way, the *Only Way* to Heaven, it took the Almighty's best—His Own Beloved and Only Begotten Son. There is no other name—no other way back to God but the way He Himself has provided in His Son—and man's Saviour—the Lord Jesus Christ (John 10:1-18).

The Confusion of Tongues

And the Lord came down to see the city and the tower,
which the children of men builded. (Genesis 11:5.)

". . . the Lord came down. . . ." When we read such expressions as God walking, coming down, laying His hand upon, and the eye, the ear, the hand, the arm of God, we must realize such expressions are used in a human sense to bring the infinite within the understanding of the finite. The use of language within the realm of human understanding is the only way we could ever conceive of God as a Person, with all the attributes of personality.

God is not only Omnipotent (having all power), and Omniscient (having all knowledge, wisdom and understanding), but He is also Omnipresent (always and everywhere present, and all things are present to Him). The Lord coming down "to see" what was going on in the plain of Shinar reveals the fact that "Building Inspection" is an ever-occurring part and purpose of God's interest in the affairs of those whom He originally created in His "own image." ". . . all things are naked and opened unto the eyes of him with whom we have to do" (Hebrews 4:13). Not only the inspection of our ledger books, but the motives and the intent of the heart. God saw through the defiant motive in the building of a tower that would reach to Heaven, and He declared, ". . . now nothing will be restrained from them, which they have imagined to do. . . . let *us* go down, and there confound their language, that they may not understand one another's speech" (Genesis 11:6-7).

The way God chose to defeat the rebellious conspiracy was not with lightning bolts of wrath, but by a very simple, yet amazingly effective method—He confounded their speech. Until this time ". . . the whole earth was of one language, and of one speech" (Genesis 11:1). What the original language was when Adam and Eve first conversed together, we do not know, but now, God caused men to speak many, new, strange and confusing languages, that they might not understand one another. As language is the medium of intercourse with man to man, the confusion and bewilderment among them caused them to separate themselves into groups whose language they had been supernaturally given to speak and understand. This Divine intervention caused them to stop building the tower and depart in defeated and frustrated companies ". . . after their families, after their tongues . . ." (Genesis 10:20).

So the Lord scattered them abroad from thence upon the
face of all the earth: and they left off to build the city. There-
fore is the name of it called Babel; because the Lord did there

confound the language of all the earth. . . . (Genesis 11: 8-9.)

This scattering was the beginning of the nations and languages into which the generations of the sons of Noah were divided in the earth (Genesis 10:32).

TABLE SHOWING HOW THE EARTH WAS REPEOPLED
BY THE DESCENDANTS OF NOAH.

The sons of Noah were: SHEM, HAM, JAPHETH.

SHEM'S SONS:	*The principal nations which sprang from them were:*	*They settled in:*
Elam, Asshur, Arphaxad, Lud, Aram,	Persians, Assyrians, Chaldeans—Hebrews— Lydians, Armenians, Syrians.	Assyria, Syria, Persia, Northern Arabia Mesopotamia.
HAM'S SONS: Cush Mizraim, Phut, Canaan.	Ethiopians, Egyptians, Libyans, Canaanites.	*The continent of Africa and Arabia.*
JAPHETH'S SONS: Gomer, Magog, Madai, Javan, Tubal, Meshech, Tiras.	Russians, Germans, Britons. Scythians, Medes, Ionians and Athenians, Iberians, Muscovites, Thracians.	Asia Minor, Armenia, Caucasus, Europe.

The Confusion of Tongues marked the dividing of nations in the earth. Nations are still divided, and ever will be, in spite of the numerous and ambitious schemes of man to unite them. Not until the rightful King returns to the troubled and hopelessly divided world will there be Unity and Peace—One King and One Kingdom in all the earth. With all the noble intents of honest representatives of the peoples of the earth, "United Nations" is a most unfortunate misnomer, and surely marks the end-time of the present world-system. "For when they shall say, Peace and safety; then sudden destruction cometh upon them, . . . and they shall not escape" (I Thessalonians 5:3).

In the beginning, Lucifer said, "I will ascend into heaven"—but he is on his way to Hell.

In the garden, Satan said, "Ye shall not surely die"—but they did die, and are still dying.

At Babel, they said, "Lest we be scattered"—but they were scattered. And all the way through the panorama of Divine revelation we learn the solemn lesson—*God's Word Is the Final Authority* in all the vital issues of life—in Time and Eternity.

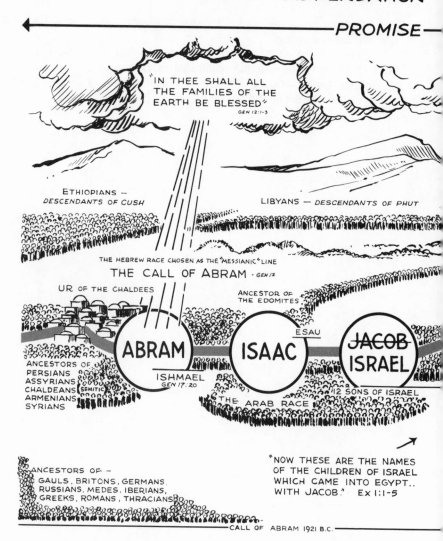

PROMISE—

"IN THEE SHALL ALL THE FAMILIES OF THE EARTH BE BLESSED"
GEN 12:1-3

ETHIOPIANS — DESCENDANTS OF CUSH

LIBYANS — DESCENDANTS OF PHUT

THE HEBREW RACE CHOSEN AS THE "MESSIANIC" LINE

THE CALL OF ABRAM - GEN 12

UR OF THE CHALDEES

ANCESTOR OF THE EDOMITES

ABRAM   ISAAC   ESAU   JACOB ISRAEL

ANCESTORS OF
PERSIANS
ASSYRIANS
CHALDEANS (SEMITIC)
ARMENIANS
SYRIANS

ISHMAEL
GEN 17:20

THE ARAB RACE

12 SONS OF ISRAEL

ANCESTORS OF —
GAULS, BRITONS, GERMANS,
RUSSIANS, MEDES, IBERIANS,
GREEKS, ROMANS, THRACIANS

"NOW THESE ARE THE NAMES OF THE CHILDREN OF ISRAEL WHICH CAME INTO EGYPT.. WITH JACOB." Ex 1:1-5

CALL OF ABRAM 1921 B.C.

CALL OF ABRAM • ISAAC • JACOB • CHILDREN OF

GENESIS Chaps

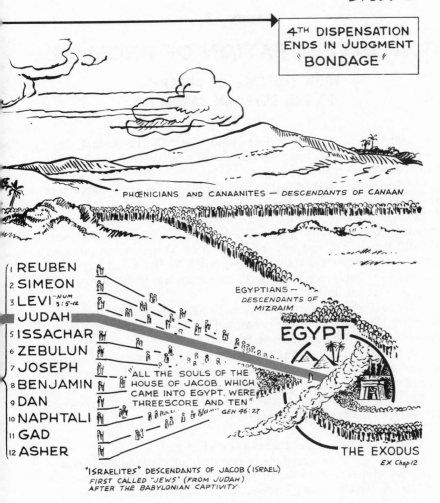

4TH DISPENSATION
ENDS IN JUDGMENT
"BONDAGE"

PHŒNICIANS AND CANAANITES — DESCENDANTS OF CANAAN

1 REUBEN
2 SIMEON
3 LEVI -NUM 3:5-12
4 JUDAH
5 ISSACHAR
6 ZEBULUN
7 JOSEPH
8 BENJAMIN
9 DAN
10 NAPHTALI
11 GAD
12 ASHER

EGYPTIANS —
DESCENDANTS OF
MIZRAIM

EGYPT

"ALL THE SOULS OF THE
HOUSE OF JACOB, WHICH
CAME INTO EGYPT, WERE
THREESCORE AND TEN"
GEN 46:27

THE EXODUS
EX Chap 12

"ISRAELITES" DESCENDANTS OF JACOB (ISRAEL)
FIRST CALLED "JEWS" (FROM JUDAH)
AFTER THE BABYLONIAN CAPTIVITY.

THE EXODUS - 1491 B.C.

ISRAEL (JACOB) • EGYPT • BONDAGE • THE EXODUS •

12-40 • EXODUS 1-12

THE DISPENSATION OF PROMISE

FROM THE CALL OF ABRAHAM
TO THE EGYPTIAN BONDAGE

WE REFER TO this period of Bible history as "The Patriarchal Age"; the Patriarch being the founder and ruler of a family or clan. Thus, the Patriarch was recognized as:

(1) The Father of the Clan; holding the place of supreme importance and authority.

(2) The Ruler of the Family; controlling all of the affairs of the children, even after they were married and had children of their own. The old Patriarch's word was law. Genesis 11:31 may be an example: Terah took Abram (and all the household) to Haran, and upon his "say-so," no doubt, they dwelt there, for Abram was under Divine command to proceed farther.

(3) The Patriarch was the Military Leader; when trouble arose between the Clans, he armed his sons and servants and led them in the skirmish, as did Abram (Genesis 14:14-16).

(4) He was also the Family Priest. The regular line of priests had not yet been chosen nor the priesthood instituted; hence, the father erected the Altar, made the sacrifices, and led in worship.

(5) In matters of Religion the Patriarch was the family's representative to God, and God's representative to the family.

The Patriarchal Age

As a setting for the beginning of our study of the Patriarchal Age—two great empires were already the center of early civilization: the *Babylonian* (or Chaldean) Empire, and the *Egyptian* Empire.

In the Genesis account of the dispersion from the plains of Shinar, the record says, ". . . they left off to build the city." The building of the city would automatically stop by the confusion of tongues and the departure of the greater part of the families and groups from the scene; but when the population of the region increased again the building was resumed, with the result that Babylon ultimately became the greatest city of the then known world—the center and capital of the first "World-Empire."

The great builder, Nimrod, who laid the foundation of the kingdom, migrated to Assyria, there to build the city of Nineveh. Among others to leave Shinar, at the time of the dispersion, was a son of Ham named MIZRAIM, the ancestor of a number of peoples, including the Philistines (Genesis 10:13-14). (The word *Mizraim* in Hebrew is translated "Egypt" in many instances.) Migrating southward, Mizraim, with his company, settled on the banks of the River Nile, there to lay the foundation of the great Egyptian Empire. In Psalm 105:23, Egypt (Mizraim) is referred to as "the land of Ham"; i.e. Ham's descendant.

With the phenomenal progress in culture, literature, art, material wealth and splendor, and temporal achievements, both in Babylon and in Egypt, there was a rapid decline in moral standards and religious life; the natural result of the nauseous spread of Idolatry throughout the land. It seems that wherever the descendants of men found themselves they forsook the worship of the one True and Living God, and soon invented religious rituals and gods of their own. Even in this our own day of so-called "enlightenment," there are more "religions" than at any time in history; but a man may be "religious" and go to Hell. There is only one Salvation: ". . . by the name of Jesus Christ of Nazareth. . . . Neither is there salvation in any other: for there is none other name under heaven given among men, whereby we must be saved" (Acts 4:10-12).

God so loves the world that He is forever meeting crisis after crisis to stop every irresponsible, rebellious generation from moral, spiritual and eternal suicide. Had it not been for the intervention of the Almighty, for man's eternal good and the glory of His own eternal purpose, the world would have been de-populated long, long ago.

No sooner had man left the Creator's hand than trouble began and God met the crisis—"The cherubim with flaming sword" guarding our first parents' steps from everlasting guilt. He met the crisis when the degeneracy of the antediluvians threatened all flesh with total corruption. And again, when Babel's tower of defiance threatened God's purpose of the orderly and natural habitation of the earth. And now, another appalling crisis must be met—*Idolatry*—fast spreading over all the world, a dishonor to God and a curse to man. Unless God intervened, the knowledge, the influence, even the memory of pure religion and the one True God would be forever blotted out in the earth.

The scourge of religious corruption came about not because men wished to live without a form of worship altogether, for religious sentiment is inherent in man; even the most savage and barbaric peoples have an intuition of a power greater than themselves, and a sense of guilt and appeasement. But the True Living God had revealed Himself, and godly men of old had borne witness to their children's children—why then did men make images, or worship the sun, the moon, animals, or call upon the dead to make intercession for them? It is because, even from the beginning, when Adam hid himself from God in Eden's Paradise because of his sense of guilt (the God-implanted faculty called "conscience"), men are fearful of **direct dealing** with a Righteous and Holy God. They prefer to approach God through some intermediate process. It has been truly said, "man would rather deal with creation, or the creature, than the Creator."

Thus, the idolatrous system of Polytheism (many gods) soon became an almost universal blight, and the true purpose of worship—to associate the worshiper with the True and Living God, and with purity, goodness, and holiness—was defeated. And in our self-righteousness let us not hold ourselves guiltless of the scourge of Idolatry; for an Idol is anything which usurps God's place in the heart. It may, in itself, be a sinful thing; or a questionable thing, a seemingly innocent thing, or even a sacred thing—but if it takes first place and God is given a secondary place in the heart—it is an Idol.

The Call of Abram

To meet the crisis, God chose to separate One Family from all the families of the earth—that in and through them He might preserve pure, undefiled religion, and the knowledge and worship of the one True and Living God. The one chosen was a man named *Abram,* born in the Chaldean city of Ur; and from that city Abram was called to be a chosen vessel unto the Lord.

Recent archaeological research revealed a startling commentary of the life and times of ancient Babylon, or Chaldea. Although luxurious living was undoubtedly the highlight of their social life, the amazing degree of culture in the land of Abram's early years is very evident. There were great Cities, Temples, Libraries, impressive ruins of a great Hall of Justice, examples of highly skilled craftsmanship; sun dials were used to mark the time of day; there existed a great system of canals, dikes and harbors for sea-going ships; and the pyramids of Egypt were already old when Abram was called from the city of Ur to be a channel through whom, at last, ". . . all families of the earth [would] be blessed" (Genesis 12:3).

The ancient city of Ur was undoubtedly dedicated to the moon-god Ur, hence the name "the city of Ur." The glory of Babylon was truly a veneer of outward splendor—but within it moral corruption was hastening both Babylon and Egypt to ruin, decay and final dissolution. Out of such a time and place, and an idolatrous people, Abram was called of God to be the instrument in the founding of *A New Nation,* separate and distinct from all other peoples of the earth:

(1) A Nation called to be a witness of the One True and Living God, in the midst of universal Idolatry:

Ye are my witnesses, saith the Lord, and my servant whom I have chosen: that ye may know and believe me, and understand that I am he: before me there was no God formed, neither shall there be after me. (Isaiah 43:10.)

(2) To Receive, Protect and Preserve the Divine Revelation:

. . . unto them were committed the oracles of God. (Romans 3:2.)

(3) To Bring Forth the Promised Redeemer:

. . . it shall bruise thy head, and thou shalt bruise his heel. (Genesis 3:15.)

Behold, a virgin shall conceive, and bear a son. . . . (Isaiah 7:14.) . . . and shalt call him JESUS. (Luke 1:31.)

. . . Jesus Christ, the son of David, the son of Abraham. (Matthew 1:1.)

(4) To be a Living Testimony of the Wisdom and Blessing of serving a Living God who hears and answers the prayers of His people:

Behold, I have taught you statutes and judgments. . . . Keep therefore and do them; for this is your wisdom and your understanding in the sight of the nations, which shall hear all these statutes, and say, Surely this great nation is a wise and understanding people. For what nation is there so great, who hath God so nigh unto them, as the Lord our God is in all things that we call upon him for? (Deuteronomy 4:5-8.)

The Abrahamic Covenant

Now the Lord had said unto Abram, Get thee out of thy country, and from thy kindred, and from thy father's house, unto a land which I will shew thee: And I will make of thee a great nation, and I will bless thee, and make thy name great. . . . And I will bless them that bless thee, and curse him that curseth thee: and in thee shall all families of the earth be blessed. (Genesis 12:1-3. Also, Genesis 13:14-18; 15:1-21; 17:4-8; 22:15-18; 26:1-5; 28:10-15.)

The Abrahamic Covenant embodied a Command and a Promise. THE COMMAND: "Get thee out of thy country, and from thy kindred, and from thy father's house, unto a land which I will shew thee." THE COVENANT PROMISE: A great nation, a great name, a limitless posterity, everlasting possession of the promised land, and the ultimate blessing of "all families of the earth"; the great Messianic promise to be fulfilled in Abram's Seed, Christ Jesus (Galatians 3:16; John 8:56-58). The Covenant concludes with God's irrevocable decree, ". . . I will bless them that bless thee, and curse him that curseth thee. . . ." This decree has been honored of God throughout the whole turbulent history of the descendants of Abram; every would-be destroyer has been destroyed on his own gallows, even as Haman of old (Esther 7:10), and the decree will be consummated at the Judgment of the Nations at the Second Coming of Christ, the Lion of the Tribe of Judah, Earth's Rightful King.

The Dispensation of Promise

We refer to this period of Bible revelation as "the Dispensation of Promise," for it was Abraham's faith in the Divine Promise, unsupported by any evidence of the senses, which established that type of faith that leads to Justification. "Abraham *believed* GOD, and it was counted unto him for righteousness" (Romans 4:3). All that Abraham received was through Divine Election, by the Covenant made with him by God— ". . . God gave it [inheritance] to Abraham by promise" (Galatians 3:18); therefore, his descendants (in whom the Covenant was confirmed) are distinctly "the heirs of promise" (Galatians 3:6-9; 3:29).

We are first introduced to Abram in the record of his ancestry, being traced through Terah (his father) back to Shem (Genesis 11:10-27); the brief announcement of his marriage to Sarai, and the fact that Sarai was barren. In this simple remark, however, is enfolded tremendous issues in the sequence of events that followed in God's great Plan and Purpose. Before "the call" of Abram, mentioned in the first of the next chapter (Genesis 12:1), it is important to read the two concluding verses of Chapter 11:

> *And Terah [Abram's father] took Abram his son, and Lot . . . his son's son, and Sarai . . . Abram's wife; and they went forth with them from Ur of the Chaldees, to go into the land of Canaan; and they came unto Haran, and dwelt there. . . . and Terah died in Haran. (Genesis 11:31-32.)*

The company of Terah's household journeyed to Haran and *dwelt there* until Terah died. Now, we can pick up the threads of the story and go back *five years* to the Command and the Covenant that God "had given" to Abram five years before Terah died in Haran (cf. Acts 7:1-5).

*Now the Lord had said [five years before] unto Abram, get
thee out of thy country, and from thy kindred, and from thy
father's house, unto a land which I will shew thee. (Genesis
12:1.)*

When God had thus commanded Abram, he *did* leave his country but
he did *not* leave his kindred, nor his father's house—he took them all
with him—in fact, we read, "Terah took Abram," and the whole household, to Haran "and dwelt there."

The specific Covenant Promises given to Abram depended, primarily,
upon Abram's obedience to the command, "Leave thy country, thy
kindred, thy father's house, etc." No further revelation was given him,
neither did he realize the Covenant Promises until he was obedient to
the original condition of the Covenant (Genesis 12:1). Once the primary condition was met the Covenant was reaffirmed, unconditionally.
God declared it an "everlasting covenant." Israel often lost the Covenant
blessings, but the Covenant itself remains irrevocable.

". . . a land that I will shew thee"

Changing circumstances have contributed a great variety of names to
the country unto which Abram was called. The most familiar name was
Canaan: derived from Canaan, a son of Ham, and brother of Mizraim
(Egypt). Palestine is another familiar name, derived from the Philistines.
The Egyptians were holding the south part of the country about the
time of the Exodus, and were expelled by the Philistines, who probably
made themselves masters of the land, thus causing the name of Philistia
or Palestine to become synonymous with Canaan, as "O Canaan, the
land of the Philistines . . ." (Zephaniah 2:5).

The name "Israel" was given to the land after the conquest under
Joshua, who divided it among the tribes of Jacob (Israel). From that
time until the time of Christ the land was generally known as "the land
of Israel" (Matthew 2:20). There is no record of any official decree
changing the name back to Palestine, yet after the predicted scattering
of the nation to the ends of the earth (Deuteronomy 28:64), for the
past eighteen centuries the land has been known by the old name
"Palestine." But, according to prophecy, in the end-time Israel shall be
regathered and restored to her homeland, which is again called "the
land of Israel" (Ezekiel 38:18). How significant, that in our day—the
beginning of the end-time—the whole world has witnessed the rebirth
of "national" Israel, as an independent, self-governing state among the
nations, identified by the old name "Israeli."

The cry of Israel's enemies throughout the ages has been: "Come,
and let us cut them off from being a nation; that the name of Israel may

be no more in remembrance" (Psalm 83:4); but they reckoned without Israel's God, who declared: "For as the new heavens and the new earth, which I will make, shall remain before me, saith the Lord, so shall your seed and your name remain" (Isaiah 66:22).

The Twelfth Chapter of Genesis

The unfolding panorama of Bible revelation now changes from interest in the general history of the race to the record of God's dealing with One Man, his Family, and the Nation that descended from him. The first eleven chapters of the Bible deal with the human family as a whole; but Chapter 12, and the following 1189 chapters of the Blessed Book, deal with One family—Abram. One nation—Israel. One theme—Salvation. One person—Jesus. And One purpose—". . . these are written, that he might believe that Jesus is the Christ, the Son of God; and that believing ye might have life through his name" (John 20:31).

After the death of Terah and the delayed years at Haran, Abram, with Sarai, his wife, started out for the promised land, this time leading his own caravan, according to God's command, yet still reluctant to leave all of his kinfolk; for, we read, ". . . Lot [his nephew] went with him . . ." and he took ". . . all their substance, . . . and the souls that they had gotten at Haran . . ." (Genesis 12:4-5).

The extent of "the substance and souls" of a patriarchal household was far greater than we imagine with a casual reading. Being at first a semi-nomadic people residing in tents, their wealth consisted of their flocks and herds and slaves, and the accumulation of personal wealth. ". . . he had sheep, and oxen . . . asses . . . menservants, and maidservants, . . . and camels. . . . And Abram was very rich in cattle, in silver and in gold" (Genesis 12:16; 13:2). The first time "a rich man" is mentioned in the Bible.

The maidservants mentioned in the inventory of Abram's wealth doubtless were the concubines mentioned in Genesis 25:6 as having borne sons to him. Both mothers and children were slaves with the right of freedom, but not to inheritance (Abram gave them gifts and sent them away—Genesis 25:6). Besides home-born slaves there were those bought with money (Genesis 4:14; 17:27). The extent of this great household can be surmised from the number "born in his own house," 318 men capable of bearing arms (Genesis 14:14); with the women, the many children, and purchased servants, Abram's "household" was indeed a great establishment over which he ruled with absolute power and patriarchal authority.

Called out from the land of his birth, where his people worshiped many gods (Polytheism), Abram centered his faith in one God (Monotheism). The outward expression of his faith was the witness of his inner spiritual life; erecting an Altar at every place of his dwelling; carefully obeying the Covenant sign and token, Circumcision (Genesis 17:9-14); by tithing, and intercessory prayer. In the unfolding panorama of spiritual history Abram's name was indeed "great," as God had promised. He was a channel of blessing to his posterity and to the whole world, through the Bible, the Redeemer and the Gospel of Saving Grace, "So then they which be of faith are blessed with faithful Abraham" (Galatians 3:9), "And if ye be Christ's, then are ye Abraham's seed, and heirs according to the promise" (Galatians 3:29). (The Mohammedans also claim Abram as their own; his name is mentioned 188 times in the Koran, more than any name except Moses.)

". . . leave thy kindred . . ."

Years again pass since the Command and the Covenant Promise were first given to Abram, but no great name, no sign of a nation in the making, for the simple reason—"no seed." Could it be because the obedience to God's Command is still incomplete? Pressed for pasture land for the combined flocks and herds of Abram and Lot, there was strife among the herdsmen. ". . . their substance was great, so that they could not dwell together" (Genesis 13:6). Although there was a family affection between them, perhaps Abram at last realized that in God's purpose it meant the parting of the ways. Abram graciously suggested that Lot take the first choice of direction. He unhesitatingly chose the well-watered plains of the east, a coveted prize, ". . . even as the garden of the Lord . . ." (Genesis 13:10), and he pitched his tents near Sodom. His covetous choice, however, was the beginning of sorrows; it was a tempting pasture land but with depraved neighbors. ". . . the men of Sodom were wicked . . . before the Lord . . ." (Genesis 13:13), and the outcome of Lot's choice is a sad chapter of sorrow and degradation for all of Lot's household (Genesis 19).

How often God's people make the sad mistake of pitching their tent too near to Sodom. Too near the borderline of separation—exposing their household to the contagious influence of a wicked world. Of a certain worldly pleasure a Christian mother said, "I see no harm, my daughter uses her head"; but Satan's concern is with the heart not the head.

It had taken Abram twenty-five years to cut loose the shorelines and to get to the place (according to the Covenant) where God could put the world in line for the promised Messiah. Now, we read, after ". . . Lot was separated from him . . .":

> . . . the Lord said unto Abram . . . Lift up now thine eyes . . . all the land which thou seest, to thee will I give it, and to thy seed for ever. And I will make thy seed as the dust of the earth [for number]. . . . (Genesis 13:14-16.)

*Look now toward heaven, and tell the stars, if thou be able
to number them: . . . So shall thy seed be. (Genesis 15:5-6.)*

Both Abram and Sarai were "well striken in age," and Sarai had long
passed the period natural to women, yet in the face of physical impossi-
bility Abram *"believed"* (Genesis 15:6). This is the first time the word
"believed" occurs in the Bible. What a history this one word of pure
faith opened in the unfolding purpose of God. Doubt, at first, said,
"How?—Impossible!" (Genesis 17:17), but when Abram's heart was
assured by Faith he "staggered not" at the impossible but "believed"
and it was "accounted . . . to him for righteousness" (Genesis 15:6;
Romans 4:20).

The Birth of Ishmael
It is well said that Human Desire cannot wait upon Divine Wisdom.
Sorely tried by the long waiting for the fulfillment of God's promises
with apparently no hope of bearing the child who should inherit the
Covenant blessings, Sarai planned the expedient of giving her personal
maid to her husband, Abram, "to be his wife," that is, concubine or
secondary wife, ". . . that I may obtain children by her" (Genesis
16:2). According to contemporary law and custom, a son born of this
union would be the free-born son and heir of Abram and Sarai. Thus,
it was the barren Sarai's plan (but not God's plan) that the son born to
Hagar by Abram would be the recipient of the Covenant Promise and
the beginning of the long delayed posterity. Hagar, the bondwoman,
thus bore the son, and Abram became the father of ISHMAEL, the
progenitor of the Arab race (Genesis 16; 17:20).

Ishmael, though a source of discord, remained the rightful heir
throughout the long interval of waiting for the God-promised son to be
born (a period of fourteen years), Abram being eighty-six years old
when Hagar gave birth to Ishmael. When Abram was ninety-nine, the
Lord again appeared to the patriarch and declared that Sarai would bear
a child in the following year; He also renewed the Covenant, and instituted Circumcision as a pledge of its certain fulfillment. On the strength
of the promise, Abram's name was changed to Abraham, "the father of
a multitude," and Sarai's name was changed to Sarah, "princess" (Genesis 17).

The Birth of Isaac
Fourteen years after the birth of Ishmael, "Isaac" (meaning "laughter"), the God-promised son, was born to Sarah. A supernaturally conceived child. Born of a barren womb! At Isaac's birth, the elder son
Ishmael, the son of the bondwoman, was disinherited and cast out by

God's command, but against Abraham's wishes which represented the law and custom of his day (Genesis 21:9-13). God consoled Abram with another promise, ". . . I will make him a great nation," ". . . twelve princes shall he beget . . ." (Genesis 17:20).

From the very beginning there was a natural enmity between these two sons of the same father, Abraham, and later between their seed, the Ishmaelites (Arabs) and the Israelites (Jews); a breach which to this day has never healed. The age-old conflict between the Jews and the Arabs is still "dynamite" in our touchy, turbulent world. The Arabs naturally claim the land of Palestine by right of the first-born of Abraham, their father Ishmael; the Jews claim the land by the right of "the everlasting covenant" given their father Abraham, repeated and confirmed in Isaac and Jacob (Genesis 15:18; 17:8; 26:3-4; 28:13-14). Thus, the contest continues, and will continue until again God intervenes and Israel is regathered and restored permanently to the land given to Abram and his seed as "an everlasting possession" (Deuteronomy 30:5).

Isaac had twin sons, *Esau* and *Jacob*. Esau was the first-born, therefore entitled to the Birthright, which, when they grew to manhood, he foolishly sold to his brother, Jacob (Genesis 25:27-34). After reaping the harvest of his own deceit, and being taught the lesson of dependence upon God (Genesis 32:24-32), his name was changed from Jacob to *Israel,* "Prince of God."

The Children of Israel (Jacob)

When we think of "the Children of Israel," we immediately visualize a mass multitude coming up out of Egypt at the time of the great exodus; this is true in the light of posterity, but *Israel* actually had only *twelve children.* These twelve sons became the fathers of the twelve Tribes called by their respective names: Reuben, Simeon, Levi, Judah, Issachar, Zebulun, Joseph, Benjamin, Dan, Naphtali, Gad and Assher (Genesis 35:23-26).

The fact that the original "children of Israel" were twelve is mentioned because of God's dealings with them as individuals. It will be noticed that although Reuben was actually the first-born, he did not receive the "Birthright" (the eldest son's blessing of the double portion). He was disqualified because of a grievous sin, defiling his father's bed (Genesis 35:22), recorded even an hundred years later in the Book of Chronicles (I Chronicles 5:1). Simeon and Levi, the next in line, were passed over because of their cruel and treacherous conduct at Shechem (Genesis 34). Judah, although he prevailed above his brethren (I Chronicles 5:2), was disqualified for a like sin as Reuben's (Genesis 38). The Birthright, in God's Sovereign Will, went to Joseph, the favorite son of Jacob's old age, who resisted the temptation wherein his brothers fell (Genesis 38:7-10).

The material blessings of the Birthright, the double portion of the inheritance, went to Joseph's two sons; Ephraim and Manassah, being counted as one, for the Tribe of Levi had "been taken by God" for service connected with the priesthood.

The Birthright was twofold, spiritual and material. The material blessing with its double portion went to Joseph and his two sons. The spiritual blessing, however, did not descend by primogeniture (the right of the first-born), but was given to Judah. This is another instance where the creature cannot say to the Creator, "What doest thou?" God gave the spiritual blessing to Judah according to His own Sovereign Will and purpose. Through Judah the promised Messiah was to come.

Egypt—Bondage—Deliverance

When Abram came out of Ur of the Chaldees, the great Covenant promise which God gave him was accompanied by a prophecy:

> *Know of a surety that thy seed shall be a stranger in a land that is not theirs, and shall serve them; and they shall afflict them four hundred years; And also that nation, whom they shall serve, will I judge: and afterward shall they come out with great substance. (Genesis 15:13-14.)*

The history of Israel's sojourn in Egypt must begin with the story of Joseph—the beloved son of Jacob. Joseph was the first-born of Rachel, whom "Jacob loved," and who died at the birth of her second son, Benjamin. Thus, Joseph was a motherless son among the sons of other mothers, and soon to feel the jealousies of the "family" situation. For Israel's twelve sons were born of two wives and two concubines (Genesis 35:23-26).

Jacob was partial to Rachel and her children, and upon Joseph, whom he loved, he put a coat of many colors (Genesis 37:3). It is believed the garment was in some sense ceremonial, or a token of rank. It might well have been so, for the Patriarchs of those days were all semi-nomadic sheiks, or princes. The brothers, seeing this gesture of favoritism, may have been suspicious that their father's intention was to give Joseph the succession as Chieftain of the Tribe. It it otherwise difficult to account for their insane jealousy, even to a conspiracy to slay him (Genesis 37:18).

After Reuben's appeal to "shed no blood," they compromised and sold Joseph to some traveling merchants on their way to Egypt. In the Egyptian slave market he was sold (in God's providence) to an officer of Pharaoh's household. Joseph's fine moral and spiritual character, plus the favor of God upon his life, gave him such prominence in the Egyptian court that Pharaoh elevated him (again in Divine providence)

from the slave market to the responsible position of Prime Minister—
this was an honor indeed—but an even greater honor was the personal
testimony of the pagan Pharaoh to his servants, "Can we find such a
one as this is, a man in whom the Spirit of God is?" (Genesis 41:38).

Thirteen years had passed since Joseph was sold into Egypt by his
brothers, and we read, ". . . all countries came into Egypt . . . to buy
corn; because that the famine was so sore in all lands" (Genesis 41:57).
Thus, because of the famine, all the souls of Jacob's household, "threescore and six" (sixty-six), went down into Egypt, making a total of "all
the souls of the house of Jacob—threescore and ten." Jacob himself
(1), all of his household (66), Joseph and his two sons (3) = 70
(Genesis 46:26-27).

Finally Jacob (Israel) died; fifty-four years later Joseph died; and a
Pharaoh that "knew not Joseph" came to the throne. This Pharaoh
suddenly awakened to the fact that the Children of Israel were "more
and mightier" than the Egyptians. (In less than four hundred years they
had increased from a company of "seventy souls" to a multitude of over
two millions.)

> And the children of Israel were fruitful, and increased abun-
> dantly . . . and waxed exceeding mighty; and the land was
> filled with them. Now there arose up a new king over Egypt,
> which knew not Joseph. (Exodus 1:7-8.)

Foreseeing national jeopardy in the amazing increase of the Hebrews,
and the fact that they dwelt "in the best of the land," and in days of the
famine they had bread when there was no bread (Genesis 47:11-13),
this new king decided to put a stop to their reproduction. He issued a
decree to kill all the male Hebrew babies in the land. This cruel decree
brings us to the familiar story of the Hebrew mother, who, when she
could hide her baby no longer:

> . . . took for him an ark of bulrushes, and daubed it with
> slime and with pitch, and put the child therein; and she laid it
> in the flags by the river's brink. And his sister stood afar off,
> to wit what would be done to him. (Exodus 2:1-10.)

The cradle was discovered by the daughter of Pharaoh while she was
bathing, and she claimed the baby as her son and called his name
"Moses" (Hebrew, Mashah—"to draw out") for, she said, ". . . I drew
him out of the water" (Exodus 2:1-10). Thus Moses, the Hebrew, was
kept and raised in the court of the Pharaoh until his manhood. During
which time, we read that he ". . . was learned in all the wisdom of the
Egyptians . . ." (Acts 7:22).

The Call of Moses

Now under severe subjection, their lives made bitter with hard bondage and the whips of the taskmasters, the Hebrews cried unto the God of Abram, Isaac and Jacob for deliverance.

> *And the Lord said, I have surely seen the affliction of my people which are in Egypt, and have heard their cry by reason of their taskmasters; . . . And I am come down to deliver them out of the hand of the Egyptians, and to bring them up out of that land unto a good land . . . flowing with milk and honey; unto the place of the Canaanites. . . . (Exodus 3: 7-8.)*

God now commanded Moses to go to Pharaoh and demand the release and freedom of His people; but it took ten national calamities and visitations of Divine Judgment before Pharaoh would let God's people go. These calamities or plagues were not primarily to discomfort the Egyptians, but to strike at Egypt's many gods, ". . . against all the gods of Egypt I will execute judgment" (Exodus 12:12).

(1) The Water Turned to Blood (Exodus 7:14-25). This plague struck at the Nile-god; the river was a sacred rival to the God of Heaven. According to the Egyptians, the Nile watered the land "without cloud or rain," it simply and majestically overflowed its banks. Now its bloody, stinking waters, before held sacred, were loathsome to the Egyptians.

(2) The Visitation of Frogs (Exodus 8:1-15). Another superstition of the religion of Egypt was the idolatrous veneration of animals, beetles, insects, frogs, etc. The so-called "sacred" frog itself became their loathsome plague. In their houses, their beds, their kneading troughs—frogs, frogs, everywhere, until the land stank.

(3) The Plague of Lice (Exodus 8:16-19). The dust of the ground was turned to lice in man and beast, bringing the conviction to even the magicians of Egypt that "This is the finger of God . . ."—but still Pharaoh refused to let God's people go.

(4) Swarms of Flies (Exodus 8:24). God added "a grievous swarm of flies" that filled all the houses, and ". . . the land was corrupted by reason of . . . flies."

The First Compromise

Pharaoh called for Moses and said, "I will let you go, that you may sacrifice to your . . . God . . . only ye shall not go very far away . . ." (Exodus 8:25-29). This compromise offer by Pharaoh is familiar to God's people in every generation. Be a Christian but don't go "too far," don't be narrow; such a compromise, however, always ends in conformity to the world. When we come out for God, it's best to come out for good.

God removed the flies, "there remained not one," but again Pharaoh hardened his heart, ". . . neither would he let the people go."

(5) A Grievous Murrain (Exodus 9:1-7). A fearful disease came upon the cattle of the Egyptians. This was a telling blow to Egypt's popular gods, for the calf was one of their important deities. The gods, whose souls were supposed to dwell within the sacred animals, were helpless to save the beasts. ". . . but of all the cattle of the children of Israel died not one. . . . And the heart of Pharaoh was hardened, and he did not let the people go."

(6) Boils (Exodus 9:8-12). Moses was commanded to sprinkle ". . . handfuls of ashes . . . toward the heaven . . ." in the sight of Pharaoh, and as he did so "boils with blains" (running, itching sores) broke forth upon man and beast. The magicians were helpless, they were having their own troubles, "for the boil was upon the magicians," so that none escaped the grievous itch. Here we read, for the first time, "the Lord" hardened the heart of Pharaoh, that is, He judicially gave him up to obduracy (unyielding stubbornness) of mind, as He threatened He would (Exodus 4:21). God did not actually interfere to strengthen and confirm the obstinacy of Pharaoh, but, moved by that obstinacy, He withdrew from him gradually all the restraints of His grace; thus, gradually the heart of Pharaoh was more and more hardened.

(7) Hail (Exodus 8:13-35). ". . . the Lord sent thunder and hail, and the fire ran along upon the ground . . ." (lightning bolts), destroying the barley and flax and trees, and every living thing not under shelter in the land. And, although this outpouring of destruction was the most violent hail storm "since Egypt became a nation," "Only in the land of Goshen, where the children of Israel were, was there no hail." The terror of the storm, and the failure of Isis and Osiris, Egypt's gods of water and fire, to protect the land, caused Pharaoh to confess "I have sinned," but when God stopped the storm he again refused to let the people go.

(8) Locusts (Exodus 10:4). God now sent a plague of Locusts to cover the land, filling their dwellings, and devouring all the vegetation and trees that had escaped the fury of the hail. And again Pharaoh cried, ". . . forgive . . . my sin only this once. . . ." And God sent a strong west wind to remove the locusts that the east wind had brought; but Pharaoh would not let the children of Israel go.

(9) Darkness (Exodus 10:21-23). Now the Lord caused a thick darkness to cover the land for three days; it is described as a darkness

that could be felt. This was a terrific blow against Ra, the sun-god of Egypt. The Egyptians "saw not one another," but all of God's people "had light in their dwellings." Fearful and confused by the appalling darkness, Pharaoh made another compromise offer to Moses, "You can go . . . take the people but leave your flocks and herds." Moses answered, "when we go, not a hoof will be left behind us"—and again Pharaoh refused to let God's people go.

(10) The Death of the First-born (Exodus 11:4-7; 12:29-30). This visitation of Divine Judgment was the terrible crisis that at last made Pharaoh yield to the Power of Omnipotence. Immediately before the visitation of the messenger of death—"The Passover" was instituted and observed for the first time by the Children of Israel (to be observed as a memorial in all their generations).

God instructed His people to take "a lamb for an house":

> . . . and the whole assembly of the congregation of Israel shall kill it in the evening. And they shall take of the blood, and strike it on the two side posts and on the upper door post of the houses, wherein they shall eat it. . . . in that night, roast with fire, and unleavened bread; and with bitter herbs. . . . thus shall ye eat it; with your loins girded, your shoes on your feet, and your staff in your hand; and ye shall eat it in haste; it is the Lord's passover. For I will pass through the land of Egypt this night, and will smite all the firstborn in the land of Egypt. . . . And the blood shall be to you for a token upon the houses where ye are: and when I see the blood, I will pass over you. . . . (Exodus 12:1-13.)

That night the first-born of all the families of Egypt was slain; from the humblest hut to the palace of Pharaoh ". . . there was not a house where there was not one dead" (Exodus 12:30). Under this crushing blow, at last, Pharaoh relented and said to Moses, "Get you forth, you and your flocks be gone." Moses immediately prepared the people for the greatest mass exodus recorded in the history of man. Over two million men, women and children, flocks and herds, jewels of silver and gold and all that the Egyptians heaped upon them in their eagerness to see them depart, lest the God of the Israelites should again show His wrath and His displeasure (Exodus 12:33-36), fulfilling the prophecy "they shall come out with great substance."

When Israel entered Egypt they were a small company of seventy souls, but now God's promise of "innumerable seed" and "a great nation" is well on the way to fulfillment. The great lesson of "God's providential love and care and purpose" is declared in the words, ". . . I will put a division [Hebrew, *peduth,* translated 'redemption'] between my people and thy people . . . ," literally, "I will put redemption," that is, "a sign that they are redeemed from bondage, and are 'My people,' not thine any longer" (Exodus 8:23). They were "in" the world but not "of it" (Galatians 6:14). The land of Goshen, where God's people dwelt, was to them as the Ark in the days of Noah. The fury of God's judgment swept around it, but those within were safe from the storm. How true are the words of the sweet singer of Israel, "Because thou hast made the Lord . . . thy habitation . . . There shall no evil befall thee, neither shall any plague come nigh thy dwelling" (Psalm 91:9-10).

The history of Israel's sojourn in Egypt, from Joseph to the Exodus, is a marvelous testimony of God's never-failing, providential and miraculous care. In the migration of Jacob's family to Egypt, God had a great, eternal purpose: that they might increase and be conscious of their calling as "a separate people unto God."

Here, we see the difference between the "directive" and the "permissive" Will of God. When God first said to Abram, "Get thee unto a land which I shall shew thee"—Canaan was the promised land, their dwelling place and their inheritance; but, God also predicted a time of servitude in a strange land, for four hundred years, out of which they would come with great substance (Genesis 15:13-14). In God's appointed time He spoke to Jacob in a night vision, saying, ". . . fear not to go down into Egypt; for I will *there* make of thee a great nation: I will go down with thee into Egypt; and I will also surely bring thee up again . . ." (Genesis 46:3-4). Had they remained in Canaan, at that time, their gradual increase may have been diluted by mingling with the inhabitants of the land, for let us remember they were but a company of seventy when they entered Egypt, whereas they came out of Egypt a "solidarity"—now to be organized and recognized as "a great nation"; disciplined by trial and suffering through which they learned to put their trust in the Living God.

The twelfth chapter of Exodus is the *Great Redemption Chapter*— The Redemption of the Children of Israel from the Bondage of Egypt— foreshadowing a greater Redemption for whosoever will from the Bondage of Sin and Death. Although there are no direct prophecies of Christ (the promised Redeemer) in the Book of Exodus, there are, perhaps, more types of Christ and the great Plan of Redemption than in any other Book in the Bible. Scenes and experiences in Israel's Redemption which pre-figure the Redemption of all mankind.

← ———————————————————————————— LAW

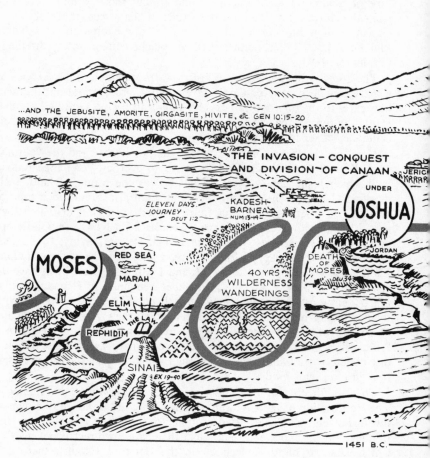

...AND THE JEBUSITE, AMORITE, GIRGASITE, HIVITE, etc GEN 10:15-20

THE INVASION - CONQUEST
AND DIVISION OF CANAAN

JERIC
KRRRR

UNDER

JOSHUA

ELEVEN DAYS
JOURNEY ·
DEUT 1:2

KADESH-
BARNEA
NUM 13-14

JORDAN

MOSES

RED SEA

MARAH

DEATH
OF
MOSES
DEU 34

40 YRS
WILDERNESS
WANDERINGS

ELIM

THE LAW

REPHIDIM

SINAI
EX 19-40

———— 1451 B.C. ————

RED SEA •   SINAI •   WILDERNESS

CONQUEST OF CANAAN

EXODUS   LEVITICUS   NUMBERS   DEUTERONOMY

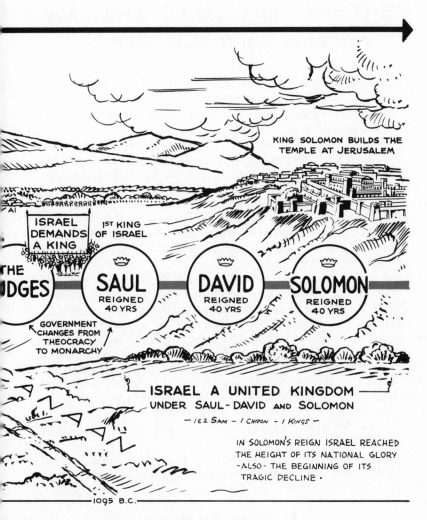

KING SOLOMON BUILDS THE
TEMPLE AT JERUSALEM

AI

ISRAEL
DEMANDS
A KING

1ST KING
OF ISRAEL

THE
JDGES

SAUL
REIGNED
40 YRS

DAVID
REIGNED
40 YRS

SOLOMON
REIGNED
40 YRS

← GOVERNMENT
CHANGES FROM
THEOCRACY
TO MONARCHY

ISRAEL A UNITED KINGDOM
UNDER SAUL - DAVID AND SOLOMON
— 1 & 2 SAM — 1 CHRON — 1 KINGS —

IN SOLOMON'S REIGN ISRAEL REACHED
THE HEIGHT OF ITS NATIONAL GLORY
- ALSO - THE BEGINNING OF ITS
TRAGIC DECLINE ·

— 1095 B.C. —

OURNEY · DEATH OF MOSES ·

HEOCRACY TO MONARCHY ·

OSHUA   JUDGES   1 AND 2 SAMUEL   1 AND 2 KINGS

THE DISPENSATION OF THE LAW

FROM MOUNT SINAI TO MOUNT CALVARY

AFTER ACCOMPLISHING the deliverance of His people from Egypt, ". . . the Lord went before them by day in a pillar of a cloud, to lead them the way; and by night in a pillar of fire, to give them light; to go by day and night" (Exodus 13:21).

On the third day of their deliverance the people were terrified upon seeing, in the distance, Pharaoh's chariots and horsemen pursuing them. With the Red Sea before them, the Egyptian chariots behind them, the redeemed people had nowhere to look for help but *Up*. Nothing is so uncertain as the minds of the multitude in the hour of panic, even turning upon the instrument of their deliverance (Exodus 14:11-12). Then, Moses lifted up his voice and spoke the assuring words which have been as a Rock of Gibraltar throughout all generations—"Fear ye not, stand still, and see the salvation of the Lord. . . ."

What a soul-thrilling experience of indescribable relief as they beheld "the cloud and the pillar of fire," which had gone before them, slowly and majestically **moving to the rear of them**—throwing a screen between them and their pursuers, while God rolled back the waters of the sea to make a pathway for their escape. When the last of the great multitude was safe on the Sinai shore, the pursuing host was trapped and destroyed in the fury of the returning waters (Exodus 14). Israel's experience is indeed a familiar type of the pursuing forces of evil that follow and fight relentlessly once a child of God has been redeemed from the bondage of Sin and Death. But God still "holds the reins" and has made "a way of escape" for all who dare to put their trust in Him (I Corinthians 10:11-13; Ephesians 6:12).

"Then sang Moses and the children of Israel" the great Song of Thanksgiving—the Song of the Redeemed, "The Lord is my strength and song, . . . my salvation; he is my God . . ." (Exodus 15:1-21).

At Mount Sinai

On the third month of the journey from Egypt (the actual route taken being 117 miles), the Children of Israel, led by Moses, pitched camp in a great plain in the immediate neighborhood of Mount Sinai. There, God's redeemed people encamped for *one year,* with the precipitous front of Sinai, like a great wall of granite, rising in frowning majesty before them. During this time Israel was "organized" into a great nation, thus, fulfilling the prophecy and the Covenant Promise given to Abram 430 years before his descendants stood before "the Mount of God" (Galatians 3:17). Called into being, in Abram, to be "a separate people unto God," they would have remained in bondage and servitude had not God intervened and sent His deliverer, Moses, to bring them out, "that they might worship and serve him." ". . . ye shall be unto me a kingdom of priests, and an holy [separate] nation," that is, a nation standing as a mediatory witness between God and the world (Exodus 19:5-6; I Peter 2:9).

This has been God's purpose from Creation—that He might have a company to love Him, to worship and serve Him, and to be "a people, a name, and a praise" unto His everlasting honor and glory. After the failure of Angels—Man, upon whom God had set His heart, was tested, and seduced to surrender the dominion with which he had been endowed; thus, all of his seed was plunged into a bondage greater than Egypt—a bondage to "the trinity of taskmasters"—the world, the flesh and the Devil. But God has sent a Deliverer—One greater than Moses, to bring whosoever will out of bondage, ". . . into the glorious liberty of the children of God" (Romans 8:21). In Abram, God put the world in line for the coming of the promised Saviour, "the Lord Jesus Christ," in and by, and through whom God's Eternal Purpose shall be gloriously, triumphantly and eternally fulfilled.

The Mosaic Covenant

(The Commandments, Judgments and Ordinances Given to Israel)

The arrival at Sinai and the great events that followed during their stay at "the mount of the law" marked *the* **Beginning of Israel's National History.** The Nation was here "consecrated" (set apart) as "a peculiar treasure unto God." A Theocracy, that is, God Himself would be their Sovereign Ruler, Guide, Provider, Protector and Sustainer. Set apart, unto Himself, God must ask for their part, Obedience: ". . . if ye will obey . . . then ye shall be a peculiar treasure unto me above all people: for all the earth is mine" (Exodus 19:5-8). "And all the people answered, . . . All that the Lord hath spoken we will do." Thus, Israel entered into a Covenant with the covenant-keeping God. The Covenant with Abram, confirmed in Isaac and Jacob, now becomes **a National Covenant.**

The Giving of the Law at Sinai

The giving of the Law was an important event in the establishing of "a New Nation." It was to preserve and identify Israel as a separate and peculiar people unto God. A Law that made them different from all other peoples of the earth. Just as "the law of love" in Christ Jesus should make the true believer distinctly different from the unregenerated world of men in which he lives. In the dispensation of Grace, all "born again" believers are unconditionally constituted a separate and peculiar people, "a kingdom of priests," with the wonderful privilege of access and intercession between a dying world and a living God (I Peter 2:9).

The Law was also given to provide additional spiritual light, that God's people might know the way of redemption and separation more perfectly; to impress and instruct them regarding the way of approach to God by "the sacrificial offering," and the sacredness of "the blood." The "token" of Israel's redemption was "the blood," and around this thought gathers the identity of a people *saved* by the blood—*sheltered* by the blood—and having *access* by the blood.

The first part of the Law was given directly to the people. God Himself declared "The Ten Commandments," that no place be left for the doubtful "Hath God said?" There was no soft, subtle voice of a tempter to misquote the Word of God as in Eden "in the beginning." The Voice at Sinai was attended with thunderings and lightnings, the trump of God, fire and smoke and a quaking mountain; and as they listened in awe to the naked Voice of God, the people, overcome with fear, entreated Moses, crying, "Speak thou with us, and we will hear: but let not God speak with us, lest we die" (Exodus 20).

Some day, sooner than we dream, a trembling universe again shall hear "the Voice of the Ancient of Days," echoing and re-echoing through the corridors of Heaven, and of a wayward world: "I am Alpha and Omega, the beginning and the ending . . . ," "I am he that liveth, and was dead; and, behold, I am alive for evermore, Amen; and have the keys of hell and of death" (Revelation 1:8, 18).

Why did God cause the very earth and the elements to bear such impressive witness to His unchanging Moral Law—The Ten Commandments? Moses gives the answer: "Fear not: for God is come to prove you, and that his fear may be before your faces, that ye sin not" (Exodus 20:20). To bring all generations to the realization that "The fear of the Lord is the beginning of wisdom . . ." (Psalm 111:10); but as Moses declared, we need not fear the fear of the Lord—it is but "to prove us," not to fear His wrath, but rather, reverently to fear that by our conduct we might grieve His heart of Love.

The Law

After the people's entreaty, and with solemn preparation, God called Moses to the Mountain top; and there, hid in "a clift of the rock," God communicated to him the instructions of His Divine Law in solemn and careful detail. The Ten Commandments were engraved upon "two tables of stone," written with the finger of God, signifying the permanency of

His Divine Law (Exodus 34:1). Exacting directions were given for the sacrificing of animals, and the minutest details regarding ceremonial offerings and of every religious duty.

God also gave Moses careful and detailed instructions for the building of a Tabernacle, or Sacred Tent. The central idea in the structure is given in the words, ". . . make me a sanctuary; that I may dwell among them" (Exodus 25:8). It was to be the dwelling place of the Holy Jehovah in the midst of His people. The details of the Tabernacle furniture, the garments of the attending priests, the Ark of the Covenant, which, with its Mercy Seat, was to be the Place of Communion between God and His people (Exodus 25:10-22)—all these instructions were given to Moses while on "the Mount of God."

"Thou shalt have no other gods before me"

First and foremost in the whole system of God's requirements and Man's instruction was written the Immutable Truth: *There is but One True and Living God.*

To appreciate more fully the unfolding panorama of Bible revelation and history, it is important that we have at least some understanding of the structure of the Mosaic Law.

No longer are God's people concerned with the minute details of the slaying and preparing of the animal or bird as a sacrificial offering for sin—for thanks be to God, our "Lamb of Sacrifice" has been slain "once and for all," and accepted of God as propitiation for the sin of the world. The details of method, manner, kind, ceremony, ordinance and sacrifice are, however, of vital interest and importance, for all are carefully designed "types" of "the better Covenant"—"good things to come"—"the True and Living Way."

The Hebrew word rendered "law" in our Bibles is *torah*, from a root meaning "to throw," "point out" (as the throwing out of the hand); hence, *torah* (the law) may be simply "human direction."

There are basic fundamentals in the Mosaic Law that are important factors in our study of the unfolding panorama of God's great Purpose and Plan. For a brief and interesting study of the Law, or the Mosaic Covenant, it is conveniently divided into three parts: **The Moral Law— The Ceremonial Law—The Judicial Law.** God's commandments, judgments and ordinances.

(1) The Moral Law, as expressed briefly in The Ten Commandments, is the expressed Will of the Righteous God in reference to Right and Wrong. Still the unchanging Rule of Life. The foundation stone of all civilized government in the earth.

(2) The Ceremonial Law had to do with sacrifices, worship and religious duties peculiar to Israel. An order of Priesthood was now instituted, instead of the head of the family, as before. Aaron and his sons were set apart for the duties of the priesthood, and invested with robes of office, as God had instructed Moses on the Mount. The Tribe of Levi was set apart to be assistants to the Priests. This honor was accorded them for their refusal to worship "the Molten Calf," which the people had impatiently and defiantly erected while Moses, their leader, was absent for forty days and nights on the Mount, communing with God (Exodus 32).

In the Ceremonial Law, the way of approach to God (the way Abel chose by faith in the beginning) was now definitely established by "Sacrifices and Priestly Meditation"; typifying the fullness and completeness of the way to God through Jesus Christ, who is both "the Sacrifice" and "the Great High Priest"—by whom alone sinners have access to a Holy, Righteous, Living, Loving God.

(3) **The Judicial Law** regulated administration of justice, the rights of property, punishment of criminals and offenders of the Law. Much the same as our civil and criminal Law today.

The Blood Covenant

After Moses had conveyed all of the words of the Law and all of the judgments to the people, the Covenant was made impressive as "a Blood Covenant." Moses was instructed to take "blood" from the sacrifice offerings and ". . . put it in basons; and half of the blood he sprinkled on the altar" (Exodus 24:6); the other half he sprinkled upon the people, saying, "Behold the blood of the covenant, which the Lord hath made with you . . ."—signifying that both God and His people had consented to the terms and conditions of the Covenant— obedience on the part of the people; the all-attendant blessings and Covenant Promises on the part of God.

And he [Moses] took the book of the covenant, and read in the audience of the people: and they said, All that the Lord hath said will we do, and be obedient. (Exodus 24:3-8.)

The Covenant was sealed with blood; but the sad part of the story is that the people so soon forgot their part of the contract, **obedience;** the history of Israel is one long record of the violation of the Covenant; but God remaineth ever faithful and true.

It is said that there are over nine hundred promises in the Word of God for those "who walk uprightly" (keep His commandments). In this Divine arrangement we see God's part—and the part of the Obedient Believer. The Covenant between the Redeemer and the Redeemed is sealed with the Blood of the Everlasting Sacrifice, and, like God's people of old, we too, in the fervor and ecstasy of our new-found freedom from the bondage of sin, declared, "I'll go where you want me to go, dear Lord—I'll say—I'll be—I'll do," but like Israel we so soon forgot our part of the Covenant, our vows, our promises of obedience, service and heart-felt devotion. "But God" (what wonderful hope and compassion in those two familiar words)—but God is a covenant-keeping God: His Mercy is from everlasting to everlasting unto those who with penitent heart seek His forgiveness with determination to do better, with the help and by the grace of God.

The Order of the Hosts

After Israel was Called—Consecrated—and Organized as a Nation, by the numbering of the people and the arrangement of the Tribes under their respective ensigns, all were ready to begin their long anticipated march to the Promised Land. (Numbers 1-10 describes in great detail "the Order of the Hosts.")

Upon arrival at **Kadesh-barnea,** on the very border of Canaan, their God-given inheritance, Moses sent twelve men across the border to report on the land. After forty days' absence they returned, bringing a sample of the productiveness of the Land of Promise. They all reported, "it is a good land"; ten of the twelve concluded that it could not be conquered; there was milk and honey and pomegranates, *but,* they said, ". . . we saw the giants, . . . and were in our own sight as grasshoppers . . ." (Numbers 13:26-33).

Fear and Unbelief barred the way to the Land of Promise, after God had so abundantly proven Himself Mighty to Deliver. Doubt is such a contagious infection that all Israel, with the exception of two men and their leader, refused to enter in and possess the land already given them by God as "an everlasting possession."

Our first reaction is, "They must have been crazy, after God had done so much for them"—but there are countless thousands of intelligent people, even today, who are doing the selfsame thing. All things are ours in Jesus Christ, the all-sufficient Saviour. Every need is abundantly supplied in Him, for Body, Soul and Spirit—for Time and Eternity; yet how few are really possessing their promised possessions. **Doubt is still the destroyer of Faith.**

As an act of disciplinary punishment for their ungrateful, stubborn unbelief, God declared: ". . . your carcasses . . . shall fall in this wilderness. And your children shall wander . . . *forty years* . . ." (Numbers 14:32-33), one year for every day the doubters searched out the land, viewing God's Providence but distrusting His Promises. Because of murmuring, disobedience and unbelief, Israel's entrance into the land which God had deeded to them as "an everlasting possession" was delayed for forty years. The only record we have of their fateful wanderings is a bare list of places at which they stopped (Numbers 33), showing that time spent **outside of God's Will and purpose** in our lives is lost both to God and to man. The generation that doubted, and refused to enter in and possess the land, died; every man over the age of twenty. But God patiently held the door ajar until those under twenty grew up, and the new generation was given the opportunity of believing God's promise, and in faithful obedience to possess the land (Numbers 14:29-34).

The sad part of the grievous episode is the fact that it was only *eleven days' journey* from Egypt to the Promised Land; but it took them forty years because of unbelief. As we follow the history of God's chosen people, what tremendous lessons should be learned—for ". . . all these things happened unto them as ensamples: and they are written for our admonition, upon whom the ends of the world are come" (I Corinthians 10:11).

The Church in the Wilderness

The wilderness journey must have been an impressive sight; over two million men, women and children carrying their pots and pans and kneading troughs, with their flocks, herds, tents and all their belongings. A Nation continually on the move like nomads of the desert.

When the great camp was pitched, it is estimated that its circumference must have measured over twelve miles. The Twelve Tribes arranged in their order in the camp. The Tabernacle in the midst of the people. Nothing left to self-will, every Tribe and every man in his place. A shadow of good things to come—Christ as the Center, the Life, the Glory, the Head of the marching, militant Church—with every member of the body in his appointed place (I Corinthians 12).

The idea of "the wandering Jews" as a disorganized body of stragglers is misleading and unscriptural. When they marched and pitched camp they moved with military precision and order. God guiding them by a great cloud that hovered over the Tabernacle by day, with the appearance of fire by night. When the guiding cloud was taken up from the Tabernacle, the Children of Israel journeyed, and in the place where the cloud abode they pitched their tents. God providing for their every·need (for they were far from any natural source of supply). When the people murmured for food, God set a table before them in the wilderness, saying: "Behold, I will rain bread from heaven . . ." (Exodus 16:4)— prefiguring the great discourse of Jesus on "The Bread of Life" (John 6:22-66).

For forty years there was no sickness, not even a swelling of their tired, marching feet; their raiment waxed not old upon them. (Think of it, Ladies—the same dress for forty years. Deuteronomy 8:4). Yet in spite of God's infinite love and abundant providence, Israel's ingratitude is one of the saddest pages in their tragic history. Their utter failure as a living testimony of the goodness of the only True and Living God, before an idolatrous world, can be traced to **murmuring and unbelief.** They murmured against the food, the way, the land, the leader; but God met their murmuring with patience, their ingratitude with abundant provision, their unfaithfulness with His faithfulness.

Finally, after forty years, as God had decreed, the New Generation now reached the border of Canaan for the second time. The older, unbelieving and rebellious generation having perished in the wilderness— all save two, Joshua and Caleb—who exercised faith and brought back a good report of the land, and assuring confidence in the Promises of God.

The Death of Moses

Upon arriving for the second time at the border of the Promised Land, Moses gathered the new generation together and solemnly reviewed the conditions of entrance into the land. The great Lawgiver himself repeated the Law to them firsthand, that it might make a lasting impression, for most of the new generation were not present when the Law was first given amidst the thunders and lightnings of Sinai. The Book of Deuteronomy is the record (*deuterous nomos*—meaning "second law"; that is, the law repeated). After reviewing God's patient dealings with their fathers, Moses reminded them of the Covenant, repeated the Ten Commandments, and admonished them "to be separate." The blessings for obedience, and the awful, far-reaching curse for disobedience are solemnly reviewed in Deuteronomy 27, 28 and 29. "Remember and obey" is the keynote of Moses' admonition.

The whole future destiny of the Hebrew Nation is foreseen in Deuteronomy 28. The Babylonian Captivity, and the destruction wrought later by the Romans, is vividly described. In both the Babylonian and the Roman sieges of Jerusalem, in desperate extremity, the besieged people ate their own children, as recorded by Josephus, the historian. Their dispersion, wanderings, persecution, trembling of heart, constant fear for their lives, even unto the diabolical plan of extermination by ruthless tyrants of our present generation, all is foretold with amazing and tragic accuracy.

The Palestinian Covenant

The reviewing of the Palestinian Covenant by Moses (Deuteronomy 30) was of great importance to those about to possess the land. It reaffirmed to the Children of Israel their title deed to the land of Canaan. A confirmation of the original Covenant made with Abram. And, as the review of Chapter 30 affirms, in spite of Israel's disobedience, failure and ultimate dispersion, the land is still theirs, and shall, according to the Covenant, ultimately be possessed by them in its entirety.

The Palestinian Covenant is an amazing summary of the history of Israel from their entrance into Canaan until the Second Coming of Christ, their long-rejected Messiah:

Verse 1. Dispersion for Disobedience. ". . . among all the nations, whither the Lord thy God hath driven thee."

Verse 2. Future Repentance. "And shalt return unto the Lord thy God. . . ."

Verse 3. The Second Coming of Christ. ". . . [God] will return and gather thee. . . ."

Verse 5. Restoration to Their Homeland. "And . . . will bring thee into the land . . . and thou shalt possess it. . . ."

Verse 6. The National Conversion of Israel. ". . . the Lord . . . will circumcise thine heart, and the heart of thy seed, to love the Lord thy God with all thine heart. . . ."

Verse 7. Judgment of Israel's Oppressors. ". . . curses upon thine enemies, . . . on them . . . which persecuted thee."

Verse 9. National Prosperity. ". . . fruit of thy body, . . . of thy cattle, . . . of thy land, for good. . . ."

Moses was 120 years old when God called him home. We read, ". . . his eye was not dim, nor his natural force abated"; he was still in the prime of his manhood, but his "mission" in God's great purpose was accomplished. The "great nation" entrusted to his guidance was now ready to enter in and to possess their God-given possession. So the faithful old warrior was called home, and God attended to the funeral arrangements personally, on the Mount where He had given His servant "a peek" into the Promised Land before He closed his eyes to the scenes of earth (Deuteronomy 34:1-8).

In saying farewell to the people he loved, Moses left one of the sublimest thoughts ever uttered by mortal man to encourage· and strengthen God's children in every generation in every corner of the earth: *"The eternal God is thy refuge, and underneath are the everlasting arms . . ."* (Deuteronomy 33:27).

The Appointment of Joshua

After the death of Moses, God appointed Joshua to lead the people into Canaan. *Joshua* is the Greek form of "Jesus." In the Hebrew, the name *Joshua,* a contracted form of *Jehoshua,* signifies "Jehovah is deliverance," or "salvation." Although born a slave in the brickfields of Egypt, Joshua was a prince of the tribe of Ephraim. A loyal, personal attendant of Moses, he rose in the ranks during the trying years of the wilderness wanderings. No word of adulation is spoken of him in his appointment; he is merely referred to as "Joshua, the son of Nun." His qualifications need no other endorsement than the fact that after the death of the grand old leader, Moses, God exalted Joshua to take command of His people, and to lead them on to possess their possessions (Joshua 1:1-9).

It was now well over four hundred years since God called Abram and commanded him "to go to a land which I will shew thee, to be an everlasting possession to thee and the generations of thy seed." Over four hundred years—and they are **not yet in the land.**

Thus, in the closing chapters of Deuteronomy, "the book of reviews," Israel faces the great crisis of their "Complete Redemption." True, they were redeemed from Bondage—but that is not Complete Redemption. **Redemption is twofold**—out of and into. "I will bring you out of the land of Egypt, into a land flowing with milk and honey." Redemption is still twofold. Out of Sin, into Christ; out of Death, into Life; out of the Bondage of Sin, into the glorious Liberty of the Sons of God; out of this World, into "a land that is fairer than day."

> . . . the Lord spake unto Joshua . . . saying, Moses my servant is dead; now therefore arise, go over this Jordan, . . . unto the land which I do give to them, . . . Every place that the sole of your foot shall tread upon, that have I given unto you. . . . (Joshua 1:1-3.)

That "have" I given you. It was already theirs (by the blood Covenant) for the possessing. What a beautiful simile of the believer's possessions "in Christ." There are over nine hundred promises in the Book for every blood-bought believer—yet hundreds of them are still lying in the "Unclaimed Blessings Department." In a spiritual sense the Book of Joshua is the Ephesians of the Old Testament. If you ever feel "low" or "licked" read "the Good Courage Chapter" (Joshua 1:1-9), then to make the blessing real and personal and up-to-date—read Ephesians 1.

There were three hundred cities, many of them fortified, and occupied by peoples who had settled in Canaan hundreds of years before the Children of Israel finally crossed its borders. The Hittites, Jebusites, Hivites, and a multitude of other "ites," plus the hostile and powerful Philistines—but God had given Israel a Covenant Promise—the land was theirs and needed now only to be possessed.

After crossing into Canaan and setting up twelve stones as a memorial, ". . . they did eat of the old corn of the land . . ."; God ceased to send Manna from Heaven, a token that their wilderness wandering was ended, and that He recognized their possession of the land, ". . . they did eat of the fruit of . . . Canaan . . ." (Joshua 5:11-12).

The Fall of Jericho

The first assault was upon the walled city of Jericho. Under Joshua, who proved to be a great military strategist, the people were obedient to God's instructions; although the method of taking the city undoubtedly looked foolish in the eyes of their enemies. Faith often looks ridiculous in the eyes of reason. The conquest of Jericho, however, is recorded in Hebrews 11, the great *Faith* chapter, because it took more Faith than Courage to march silently around the walled city thirteen times "til the walls came tumbling down" (Joshua 6).

Joshua proved his military genius by dividing the northern from the southern parts, marching a wedge through the center, thus, splitting the land and dividing the strength of the Canaanites. After seven years of conquest, Israel rested from war (Joshua 11:23). Joshua then divided the land, each tribe receiving its appointed allotment (Joshua 13-21). As long as Joshua and the Elders of his generation lived, "Israel served the Lord"; but after the death of the Leader and the last of the Elders, the history of Israel again takes a tragic turn to backsliding and utter disregard for the Law of the Lord.

Incomplete Obedience

Upon entering Canaan, God gave the people uncompromising instructions to destroy the Canaanites, root and branch (Numbers 33:52). But instead of complete obedience to God's command, they kept the likeliest to ". . . be hewers of wood and drawers of water . . ." (Joshua 9:21). This incomplete obedience brought the most tragic results upon the whole nation; the aftermath of which finally ended in their own destruction and final conquest. Just as habitually indulging in some besetting sin which, with a will, could be resisted and forsaken in the beginning—but petted and encouraged, it grows until its tentacles bind the will and weaken the moral and spiritual power of resistance. God had warned them that failing to destroy the Canaanites they would be ". . . pricks in your eyes, and thorns in your sides . . ." (Numbers 33:55), ". . . until ye perish from off this good land which the Lord your God hath given you" (Joshua 23:13).

"Canaanites" was a general term for all the inhabitants of the land; they were notorious idolators and their utter destruction was God's explicit command. The Canaanitish towns were destroyed and the people subjected to wholesale massacre. Such destruction of life seems inhuman unless we realize that. the object of God's command to exterminate the Canaanites was to execute a long-delayed judgment upon them, and to check the spread of universal Idolatry and corruption. God works at both ends of the line—Israel's delayed entrance of four hundred years into Canaan was four hundred years of mercy, long-suffering and de-

layed judgment for the Canaanites. The destruction of Sodom and Go-
morrah, God's judgment upon Egypt, the extermination of the two
kings on the other side of Jordan (Numbers 21:21-35), should have
been an unmistakable warning to the inhabitants of Canaan—had they
all, like the harlot Rahab, confessed their faith in the God of Israel, all
might have been spared even as she and her household (Joshua 2:9-11).

The Period of the Judges

With no God-appointed leaders since Joshua and the Elders, at criti-
cal periods when Israel was oppressed by the people of the land, whom
they failed to "drive out," God intervened by raising up a man from
the tribes through whom He would execute His judgments. These men
were called "Judges." The office was not hereditary, nor even in immediate succession, but by Divine appointment in times of desperation
and national jeopardy.

The history of the Judges was a repetitious cycle of *Backsliding,
Chastisement, Repentance, and Deliverance*. These four words have been
inseparably linked since the Fall of Man. Sin has always brought punishment—Repentance has always brought deliverance.

The turbulent history of this period of God's dealings with His people (a period of over three hundred years) is summed up in the oft-
repeated words: "Israel did evil in the sight of the Lord"—and the
Lord sold them (or delivered them) into the hands of their oppressors;
and they served them seven—twenty—eighty years (as the case may
be) until they cried unto the Lord and repented of their backslidings.
The object of the Book of Judges is to show that as often as Israel
sinned against God, He brought chastisement upon them at the hands
of their enemies; and when they repented and remembered their Covenant, God appointed someone from the ranks to deliver them.

The history of the period of the Judges ended with Israel in a state
of apostasy, confusion and spiritual darkness; told in the pathetic words,
". . . there was no king in Israel: every man did that which was right
in his own eyes" (Judges 21:25). Such a condition could but lead to
moral, spiritual and national bankruptcy. The tribes were at war with
the surrounding nations and among themselves, the national religion
had fallen into decay, the Priesthood was utterly corrupt, and the Heart
of God was grieved at the sins of His people.

The Call of Samuel

It was at this time of moral and spiritual declension that God raised
up the boy Samuel to be Prophet-priest of Israel; that He might again
make His Will known to His confused and wayward people (I Samuel
3). While still a child, God revealed to Samuel the judgment that was

to fall upon Eli, the failing old priest, and upon his evil sons who, though officiating as priests, "knew not the Lord." A terrible indictment in any generation against so-called "ministers of God" who know nothing of the personal experience of Regeneration.

The Priesthood of Eli and his sons was so badly corrupted that the people were afraid to bring their sacrifices. According to the Law ". . . when any man offered sacrifice, the priest's servant came, while the flesh was in seething, with a fleshhook of three teeth, . . . he stuck it into . . . the caldron, . . . all that the fleshhook brought up the priest took for himself. . . ." But the priests were not satisfied with "sodden flesh"; they took the best parts of the animal before it was put into the caldron, therefore the people feared to bring their offerings because of the sin of the priests (I Samuel 2:12-17).

From Theocracy to Monarchy

Until this time Israel had been a *Theocracy*. Twelve independent tribes under the immediate direction of God, a government of priests, or ministers, as His representatives. But consistently failing to obey His laws and leadership they had fallen prey to every evil agency throughout the land. Fearful of the aggressive nations around them, they demanded a King, that they might unify, as the other nations did, under a visible leader.

Samuel warned them of the consequences of rejecting God's direct and sovereign rule over them, and warned of man's lust for power, greed, oppression, and all of the evils that would beset them; but, nevertheless, the people said, "we will have a king over us," and the Lord said to Samuel, "Hearken unto their voice, and make them a king" (I Samuel 8).

Saul—the First King of Israel

The turning point in Israel's history was the changing of the government from a **Theocracy** (God-rule) to a **Monarchy** (man-rule). Saul, chosen from the tribe of Benjamin, the smallest and least of the tribes, was endowed with physical qualities which well fitted him to be the military leader the people desired. Physically he was great—Mentally, not so great—Spiritually, zero. He started well, humble and victorious over his enemies; but later became jealous, impulsive, stubborn and disobedient to God. His reign added little to national prosperity, and absolutely nothing to the spiritual welfare of the people. Sinking to a low ebb, he resorted to Spiritualism and died a suicide (I Samuel 31). Nevertheless, with all of Saul's failings, David, the man who perhaps knew him best, wrote an elegy to his more noble qualities, his great prowess in war, and his generosity in peace (II Samuel 1:17-27).

David—Saul's Successor

DAVID, the shepherd lad, was next chosen and anointed King of Israel—he was, circumstantially, anointed three times. Once by Samuel, when he was a shepherd lad; and, although, Saul still sat upon the throne, from that time on David was "the Lord's Anointed." The death of Saul, at last, removed the dangers that had made David an exile, and the men of Judah came and anointed him king over the one tribe. Saul's son, Ish-bosheth, was made king of the eleven remaining tribes, but was later murdered by two of his own officers. After the death of Saul's son, David was anointed king over all Israel: ". . . he [first] reigned over Judah seven years and six months . . . and . . . [subsequently] thirty and three years over all Israel and Judah (II Samuel 5:5).

The Reign of King David was without doubt the brightest era in the history of Israel. He fills more pages of history, poetry and prophecy than any other Old Testament character. The Book of Psalms (of which he wrote the majority) seems to be a poetic record of the whole range of his experiences; his ups and downs and varying emotions; from the depths of self-condemnation, to the heights of sublime faith and ecstatic adoration and communion with God.

Like a blot of utter darkness upon the brilliance and blessing of his God-anointed life, David's sin was deep, but his repentance was deeper, and God's love deeper still, revealing the encouraging truth to all generations, that: "The love of God reaches down to the deepest depths, and true repentance lifts the erring one into sweet communion and fellowship again by the Covenant Grace of God" (II Samuel 11-12).

The Davidic Covenant

The great, original Abrahamic Covenant embodied the Promised Land, and the promised seed of Israel. The Palestinian Covenant confirmed and enlarged the promise regarding the land. The next great covenant specifically concerns "the seed." The promise made by God to David is recorded in I Samuel 7:12-16:

> *And when thy days are fulfilled, and thou shalt sleep with thy fathers, I will set up thy seed after thee, which shall proceed out of thy bowels, and I will establish his kingdom. He shall build an house for my name, and I will establish the throne of his kingdom for ever. I will be his father, and he shall be my son. If he commit iniquity, I will chasten him with the rod of men, and with the stripes of the children of men: But my mercy shall not depart away from him, as I took it from Saul, whom I put away before thee. And thine house and thy*

kingdom shall be established for ever before thee; thy throne shall be established for ever.

The Davidic Covenant embodies **a House, a Kingdom, a Throne, Forever.** The provisions of the Davidic Covenant were: (1) David would have a son who would succeed him. (2) God would establish his kingdom. (3) He would build an house unto God. (4) The Throne of his kingdom would be established by God forever. Although the Covenant made with David was unconditional, disobedience in the Davidic "house" (posterity), would be punished by chastisement but not abrogation of the Covenant. History records the sad chapter of disobedience and apostasy, and the chastisement that followed. The kingdom was disrupted, divided, and finally dispersed—but the seed of David, by God's own oath, **shall never be destroyed.** The Covenant confirmed to David by the Word of Jehovah, and renewed to the Virgin Mary, by the Angel Gabriel, is *immutable.* The crucified, risen and ascended "seed of David according to the flesh," shall return, and God shall give to Him "the throne of his father David" (Luke 1:31-33; Acts 2:29-30; 15: 14-17).

The Reign of Solomon

David reigned for forty years, and upon his death he was succeeded by his son, *Solomon.* It was during Solomon's reign that Israel reached the peak of its National Glory. But, sad to say, it was also during Solomon's reign that the nation began its pathetic decline, which ended in ultimate division and dispersion to the four corners of the earth (Deuteronomy 28:63-68).

Solomon's reign was made famous by: (1) His Wise Choice, (2) His discriminating Wisdom, (3) His Building of the Temple, (4) the Growth and Splendor of his Kingdom.

(1) His Wise Choice (I Kings 3:5-15). When he came to the throne, the Lord appeared unto him and said, "Ask what I shall give thee." Realizing the magnitude of the task before him, and his utter insufficiency, Solomon said, "O, God give me an understanding heart," and his wise choice greatly pleased the Lord. In this, our day, when the whole world has seemingly lost its sense of direction and values, when gross materialism and ruthless intolerance has supplanted human compassion, surely there is no greater need than to pray earnestly that God will give us, above all things, an understanding heart, for even in the Christian realm there is far too much criticism and competition, and far too little compassion, love, patience and understanding.

(2) His discriminating Wisdom (I Kings 3:16-28; 4:29-34). Beginning well, Solomon's reign was marked by a devout spirit. He sought Divine guidance above everything else. It has been said, "If anyone sought first the Kingdom of God . . . and all these things were added

unto him, surely it was the youthful Solomon." The promise of God-given wisdom (James 1:5) is just as true today, and the need greater, to cope with the perilous problems that beset us—problems that can only be met with "that wisdom that cometh from above."

(3) The Building of the Temple (I Kings 5, 6, 7). David, Solomon's father, desired to build a house unto the Lord, but his incessant wars unfitted him to be the founder of a seat of peaceful worship. The Word of Jehovah came to him, saying, ". . . thou shalt not build an house unto my name, because thou hast shed much blood upon the earth in my sight" (I Chronicles 22:8). Nevertheless, for the purpose of the Temple construction, David bequeathed the equivalent of something like five billion dollars in gold, silver, brass and iron (I Chronicles 22:14). The name "Solomon" means "Peaceful," thus, when at last there was "rest in the land," David charged his son Solomon to build a house unto the Lord. Although he was a God-appointed King, David knew that death is no respecter of persons; realizing the end was near, he said, "I go the way of all the earth . . ." (I Kings 2:2); and so it was, after a reign of forty years, David died and was buried at Jerusalem.

The building of the Temple was the one magnificent achievement of Solomon's reign. It was accomplished in seven years, and dedicated with great joy and thanksgiving. After the building was finished and the Ark of the Covenant (a symbol of the very Presence of God) had been carried by the priests into the Holy of Holies, ". . . they drew out the staves. . . ." The symbolic beauty of this act had a very significant meaning. The staves were the wooden rods placed through the rings of the ark, that it might be borne upon the shoulders of the attendants when it was carried from place to place in the Tabernacle days; and God had given express command that the staves were not to be removed (Exodus 25:12-15). But, when the Ark was carried into the Holy of Holies, in the Temple (the place prepared for it, as an abiding presence), and they drew out the staves, it meant a final act—the Ark had found its resting place, the Holy of Holies had been surrendered to God as an everlasting possession and "they," the priests, went out. They did not remain to share the inner, "holy place" with the Divine Presence, for ". . . the glory of the Lord had filled the house of the Lord" (I Kings 8:1-11). When we surrender the Temple of our lives to God it should be for an "everlasting possession," a final act, and, like the priests of old, we must "move out," that the Glory and the Presence of the Lord might "fill the house," for ". . . know ye not that your body is the temple of the Holy Ghost . . . ?" (I Corinthians 6:19-20; Romans 12:1).

After the Ark had been brought in "unto his place" and the staves withdrawn, immediately, as a witness and an assurance of the Divine acceptance of His dwelling place, ". . . it came to pass, when the priests were come out of the holy place, that the cloud [the Shekinah] filled the house of the Lord, So that the priests could not . . . minister" (I Kings 8:10-11).

After Solomon's great prayer of Dedication, then the King and all the people offered sacrifices unto the Lord: "two and twenty thousand oxen, and an hundred and twenty thousand sheep," probably the greatest sacrifice (numerically) ever offered in the history of Israel.

(4) **The Splendor of Solomon's Court.** Following the example of other oriental kings, Solomon began to subject the people to heavy taxes and unbearable burdens to maintain his court in lavish splendor and sensual indulgence. The maintenance of his huge harem, seven hundred wives (foreign princesses) and three hundred concubines, necessarily entailed a heavy burden upon the state.

The provisions for one day, we read, were: ". . . thirty measures of fine flour, and threescore measures of meal, Ten fat oxen, . . . an hundred sheep, beside harts, and roebucks, . . . and fatted fowl" (I Kings 4:22; 23). He had forty thousand stalls of horses (his father, David, rode a mule [I Kings 1:33]). Solomon's annual income was about twenty million dollars. "So king Solomon exceeded all the kings of the earth for riches and for wisdom. And all the earth sought to Solomon, to hear his wisdom, which God had put in his heart" (I Kings 10:23-24). As God's Anointed, no man ever had a more glorious opportunity to bear witness to the goodness and greatness of the True and Living God. Delegates from all over the then known world came to see the splendor of his kingdom and to listen in wonder to his God-given wisdom.

With all of his wisdom, however, he gave himself to the pursuit of luxury and splendor, forgetting the interests of his people and the purpose of God in his life. His downfall was hastened by the building of shrines for the heathen gods of his many foreign wives, thus openly encouraging idolatry throughout his kingdom, and committing high treason against Jehovah. ". . . his wives turned away his heart after other gods. . . ." Under Solomon, idolatry struck its roots so deep in the land that all the zeal of the reforming kings that followed him failed to eradicate it. It was this climax that brought the judgment of a jealous God upon the house of Solomon. God declared, "I will surely rend the kingdom from thee, . . . not . . . in thy days, . . . for David thy father's sake: but I will rend it out of the hand of thy son. Howbeit I will not rend away all the kingdom, . . . for David my servant's sake and for Jerusalem's . . ." (I Kings 11:11-13). Solomon died, as Sayce expresses it, "worn out by excessive self-indulgence, leaving behind him an impoverished treasury, a discontented people, and a tottering empire." There is no repentant note in his life, such as his father, David's, 51st Psalm; he died as he lived, self-centered.

It is said, "the evil men do lives after them, the good is oft interred with their bones," but good once done and wisdom once spoken cannot be entirely forgotten. Solomon's reign of forty years is fittingly called "The Golden Age of Israel," and throughout the centuries to follow, men have read the Books of Proverbs, Ecclesiastes, and the Song of Solomon with thanksgiving for their God-given wisdom. Although the vessel may be imperfect, "Every word of God is pure . . ." (Proverbs 30:5).

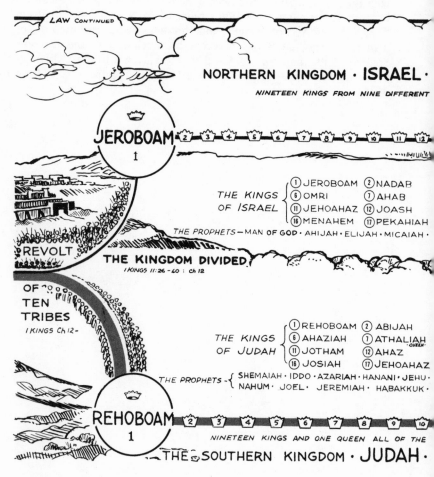

LAW CONTINUED

NORTHERN KINGDOM · ISRAEL ·

NINETEEN KINGS FROM NINE DIFFERENT

JEROBOAM 1

THE KINGS OF ISRAEL

- ① JEROBOAM ② NADAB
- ⑥ OMRI ⑦ AHAB
- ⑪ JEHOAHAZ ⑫ JOASH
- ⑯ MENAHEM ⑰ PEKAHIAH

THE PROPHETS — MAN OF GOD · AHIJAH · ELIJAH · MICAIAH ·

REVOLT

THE KINGDOM DIVIDED

I KINGS 11:26 – 40 : Ch 12

OF TEN TRIBES

I KINGS Ch 12 –

THE KINGS OF JUDAH

- ① REHOBOAM ② ABIJAH
- ⑥ AHAZIAH ⑦ ATHALIAH *QUEEN*
- ⑪ JOTHAM ⑫ AHAZ
- ⑯ JOSIAH ⑰ JEHOAHAZ

THE PROPHETS — SHEMAIAH · IDDO · AZARIAH · HANANI · JEHU · NAHUM · JOEL · JEREMIAH · HABAKKUK ·

REHOBOAM 1

NINETEEN KINGS AND ONE QUEEN ALL OF THE

THE SOUTHERN KINGDOM · JUDAH ·

–DIVISION OF THE KINGDOM 975 B.C.—— ——KINGDOM OF JUDAH SURVIVES ISRAEL BY OVER 135 YRS–

THE KINGDOM DIVIDED ·

CAPTIVITY AND END OF THE KINGDOMS ·

ISRAEL – 1 AND 2 KINGS · 2 CHRON ·

THE CAPTIVITY –

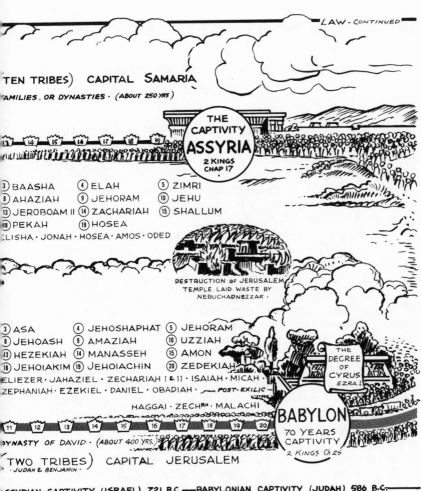

LAW - CONTINUED

TEN TRIBES) CAPITAL **SAMARIA**

FAMILIES. OR DYNASTIES · (ABOUT 250 YRS)

THE CAPTIVITY **ASSYRIA** 2 KINGS CHAP 17

③ BAASHA ④ ELAH ⑤ ZIMRI
⑧ AHAZIAH ⑨ JEHORAM ⑩ JEHU
⑬ JEROBOAM II ⑭ ZACHARIAH ⑮ SHALLUM
⑱ PEKAH ⑲ HOSEA
ELISHA · JONAH · HOSEA · AMOS · ODED

DESTRUCTION OF JERUSALEM
TEMPLE LAID WASTE BY
NEBUCHADNEZZAR ·

③ ASA ④ JEHOSHAPHAT ⑤ JEHORAM
⑧ JEHOASH ⑨ AMAZIAH ⑩ UZZIAH
⑬ HEZEKIAH ⑭ MANASSEH ⑮ AMON
⑱ JEHOIAKIM ⑲ JEHOIACHIN ⑳ ZEDEKIAH
ELIEZER · JAHAZIEL · ZECHARIAH I & II · ISAIAH · MICAH ·
ZEPHANIAH · EZEKIEL · DANIEL · OBADIAH · ⟶ POST-EXILIC

HAGGAI · ZECHᴿᴴ · MALACHI

THE DECREE OF CYRUS EZRA I

BABYLON 70 YEARS CAPTIVITY 2 KINGS Ch 25

DYNASTY OF DAVID · (ABOUT 400 YRS.)

(TWO TRIBES) CAPITAL **JERUSALEM**
· JUDAH & BENJAMIN ·

ASSYRIAN CAPTIVITY (ISRAEL) 721 B.C.——BABYLONIAN CAPTIVITY (JUDAH) 586 B.C.——

ISRAEL AND **JUDAH** ·

THE DECREE OF CYRUS - (EZRA 1)

JUDAH – 1 AND 2 KINGS – 2 CHRON · ISA · JER ·

JER – EZK – DANIEL ·

THE DISPENSATION OF THE LAW
(continued)

FROM THE DIVISION OF THE KINGDOM
TO THE CAPTIVITY

AFTER GOD HAD DENOUNCED Solomon's conduct and declared the disruption of his Kingdom, a series of revolts followed, during which God sent His Prophet to one of Solomon's officers, named Jeroboam, to reveal to him His intention of removing ten tribes from the king's jurisdiction and committing them to him, Jeroboam. When Solomon learned of God's intention he sought to kill Jeroboam, who fled into Egypt until the king's death (I Kings 11:26-40).

Solomon's reign began in a blaze of glory and ended in shameful disloyalty to God and His righteous cause in the earth. After a reign of forty years, beginning "in the spirit and ending in the flesh," Solomon died; and Rehoboam, his son and successor to the throne, went to Shechem to be crowned King of Israel. There, the people, discouraged by the heavy burdens imposed upon them to maintain the excessive splendor of his father's court, came respectfully with a justifiable petition asking that their burdens be lightened. The result was a defiant refusal by the newly crowned King, with an impulsive edict to impose even heavier burdens. "My father," he said, "made your yoke heavy, and I will add to your yoke." When the people heard the arrogant threat of the young king they revolted and renounced their allegiance to the dynasty of David. Rehoboam, fearful of his life, fled to Jerusalem.

The dominant mind and leader in the revolt was Jeroboam, who had returned from Egypt, and knowing what God had purposed for him, he encouraged the Ten Tribes to refuse to accept Rehoboam's edict; and just as God had decreed, only one Tribe (actually two; called one, because the tribe of Benjamin numbered so few compared with Judah's thousands), Judah and Benjamin, and later the Levites, followed Rehoboam of the House of David. The ten remaining Tribes rallied around the standard of Jeroboam.

When Rehoboam realized the extent of the revolution, he gathered an army of 180,000 subjects loyal to the Davidic dynasty and set out to regain the divided Kingdom. But God intervened by sending a prophet to restrain him. Realizing, at last, that "this was of God," he disbanded his army, and every man returned to his house (I Kings 12:1-24).

Thus, the kingdom which had been a united kingdom under the reign of Saul, David and Solomon, **was now divided.** With this rupture the powerful kingdom established by David had reached its end, and was now split into two kingdoms, each going their separate ways. From now on identified as **"the Kingdom of Israel"** (the Ten Tribes), with Samaria as its capital, and **"the Kingdom of Judah"** (the Two Tribes), with Jerusalem as its capital. This division and disruption was the beginning of the end of Israel's National Glory, for eventually both kingdoms, gradually weakened from within and without, were brought to a predicted and pathetic end by conquest and captivity.

The Kingdom of Israel

Jeroboam, the first King of Israel, began his reign by showing utter disregard for God as the source of protection, provision and blessing to the people. His first plan was to destroy the religious unity of the two kingdoms, lest in going back to Jerusalem (the center of Israel's religious life) for their traditional custom of offering sacrifices, the people might be influenced back to their old allegiance to "the house of David" (I Kings 12:25-33).

To accomplish his subtle plan he set up two golden calves, one at either extremity of the kingdom; and gathering the people he declared, "It is too much for you to go up to Jerusalem: behold thy gods . . ." (I Kings 12:28), and Jeroboam drove Israel from following the Lord, and made them sin a great sin, for ". . . he ordained him priests . . . for the devils [literally, 'hairy ones'] and for the calves which he had made" (I Kings 13:28; II Chronicles 11:15; probably referring to the Egyptian goat-god, or "satyrs" of Isaiah 13:21). Thus, an abominable and idolatrous system of worship, with its own order of priests, became the established religion during Jeroboam's reign, in opposition to the true and traditional worship at Jerusalem.

The Kingdom of Israel (the Kingdom of the Ten Tribes) lasted for 250 years, when it was overthrown, after repeated invasions, by the Assyrians. The siege and fall of Samaria, the capital, at last brought an end to the backslidden and idolatrous kingdom, while the people were taken captive and "colonized" in the vast Assyrian Empire.

The Kingdom of Israel had nine different dynasties in the two and one-half centuries of its existence (unlike the Kingdom of Judah, which had but one; all of the Kings of Judah being of the lineal descent of the House of David). The prevailing practice of the nations was common in the history of the Kingdom of Israel: plots against the reigning king, and the murder of all of his household. After a wicked reign of twenty-two years, Jeroboam left the crown to his son, Nadab, who followed the bad example of his father. After a short reign of two years he was murdered by a man of Issachar named Baasha, who seized the Kingdom—

thus it was throughout the turbulent and treacherous history of the kingdom.

Not one of Israel's nineteen kings was a godly man, in spite of the faithful pleading of the prophets of God. Elijah's fearless testimony, for instance, in the reign of the wicked King Ahab, stands out like a burning beacon in the darkness of his day (I Kings 18).

The history of the Kings of Israel is largely a record of gross idolatry, murder, profligacy and abominable practices so strongly denounced by God's prophets, yet increasing from reign to reign until at last in the days of King Hosea, Shalmaneser IV, a new King of Assyria, invaded and ravished the land, imprisoned King Hosea, laid siege to Samaria, and carried the remnant of the people captive to Assyria (II Kings 17).

The Kingdom of Judah

The Kingdom of Judah (the Two Tribes) lasted four hundred years after its separation from the Ten Tribes. During which time it was governed by nineteen kings—and for six years of wicked tyranny, one queen, Athaliah, the only woman ever to sit upon the Throne of David.

Successive massacres, culminating in the slaughter of all "the royal seed" of Judah by the wicked queen mother, Athaliah, reduced the descendants of David until only one representative was left—the little prince, **Joash,** who was hidden with his nurse "in the house of the Lord," and thus escaped the slaughter. At the age of seven he was brought out of hiding and proclaimed King of Judah, while the infamous Athaliah was slain by the sword (II Kings 11:1-16). Thus, the Davidic dynasty made a fresh start under Joash (the first Judean King to be assassinated by his own people (II Kings 12:20).

All of Judah's kings were the lineal descendants of King David, confirming the Davidic Covenant; ". . . an house, . . . the throne . . . his kingdom for ever" (II Samuel 7:8-17). Many of the Kings of Judah were godly men, others were not so godly. The religious life of the kingdom was a reflection of the spiritual influence and concern of the king who sat upon the throne at the time. There were religious revivals and declensions according to the spiritual attitude of the reigning ruler. But eventually the same Divine indictment was pronounced: "Judah also did evil in the sight of the Lord."

Associated with the Kings of Judah were such great prophets as Isaiah, Micah, Jeremiah, Ezekiel, Daniel, Haggai, Zachariah and Malachi (see scene, Study 7, *The New "Panorama" Bible Study Course*).

The Babylonian Captivity

Nearing the end of the history of the Kingdom of Judah, with its spiritual ups and downs and national conflicts within and without, came the first invasion of the land by Nebuchadnezzar of Babylon. Seizing the

Capital, Jerusalem, the invader was induced to spare the King, Jehoiakim, and be satisfied with taking tribute from the kingdom: a part of the Temple Vessels, and a company of chosen captives, including several of the young and godly princes, among whom were Daniel and "the three Hebrew children" whose names were later changed to Shadrach, Meshach and Abednego (Daniel 1:1-7).

Nine years later in the reign of King Jehoiachin (a youth who reigned but three months in Jerusalem), Nebuchadnezzar again invaded the land. This time he thoroughly plundered the city, carrying away all of the treasures, the young king, ten thousand nobles and artisans, including the Prophet Ezekiel, leaving only the poorest in the land (II Kings 24).

The invading king now made Mattaniah, an uncle of the young King Jehoiachin, puppet ruler over Judah, changing his name to **Zedekiah,** who proved to be the last King of Judah. It was in his reign that Nebuchadnezzar made his final attack upon Jerusalem. Attempting to escape from the besieged city, the King was overtaken by soldiers of the invading army. His terrible fate is written in one short sentence in the Book of Kings: "And they slew the sons of Zedekiah before his eyes, and put out the eyes of Zedekiah, and bound him with fetters of brass, and carried him to Babylon" (II Kings 25:7).

The siege of Jerusalem is one of the darkest chapters in the history of God's ancient people. The Temple was rifled and burned; the walls of the city reduced to ruins; and those who survived the cruelest of torture and massacre were carried away captive to Babylon. The diabolical cruelties suffered by the people during the destruction of their city, according to the Jewish historian, Josephus, were too terrible for words. When Nebuchadnezzar took the city he ". . . had no compassion upon young man or maiden, old man, or him that stooped for age . . ." (II Chronicles 36:15-21).

Famine had already done its work before the ruthless conqueror entered the besieged city. The ghastly sight of dying, hunger-stricken children, princes raking dunghills for a morsel (Lamentations 4:4-5), mothers eating their own babies (Deuteronomy 28:53; Lamentations 4:10)—witness to the terrible extremities to which the people were driven. Never before had such permissive evidence been given of God's wrath against the sins of His people.

The prophecies and lamentations of the faithful Jeremiah, whom they had scorned and persecuted, were now tragically and surely fulfilled. Even the prophecy of Moses, uttered in warning over eight hundred years before, had its first, though not final fulfillment—"the seed of Jacob" was indeed "scattered among the heathen" (Deuteronomy 28:49-68).

Before Judah's captivity the Prophet Jeremiah had repeatedly warned the King, and predicted the kingdom's coming doom. He also foretold that the captivity of the people would be of seventy years' duration (Jeremiah 25:11). The period of seventy years was determined by God for the disobedience of His people in not observing "the law of the land," the sabbatical year, as recorded in Leviticus 25: "Six years thou shalt sow thy field, and . . . vineyard . . . But in the seventh year shall be a sabbath of rest unto the land, . . . thou shalt neither sow . . . nor prune. . . ."

This meant that the land was to lie idle for one year out of seven; but thinking to get ahead of God, and be one harvest to the good, they disobeyed by disregarding "the law of the land"; they sowed and reaped in the seventh year. Jeremiah had warned them of the consequences of their disobedience, and at last God visited the kingdom with Judgment; permitting their downfall and captivity into Babylon, that the land might lie desolate for seventy years—ten years for every year they had disregarded "the sabbatic rest" for the land (II Chronicles 36:21). A solemn warning indeed for all generations; "Be not deceived; God is not mocked . . ." (Galatians 6:7). How solemnly this same truth is brought home in the New Testament object lesson of Ananias and Sapphira (Acts 5).

It was during the seventy years of Babylonian captivity that events now so familiar to us such as: Daniel in the lion's den, the story of Queen Esther, Nebuchadnezzar's forgotten dream, the Handwriting on the Wall, the Fall of Babylon—made spiritual history.

The Fall of Babylon

Just before the captivity of Judah came to an end, the great Babylonian Empire itself came to an end. Nebuchadnezzar, the proud and arrogant King of Babylon, was troubled by a dream, which upon awakening he could not recall. After the failure of his "wise men" to bring the forgotten dream to his remembrance, the King appealed to Daniel, the captive Hebrew prince, to make the dream known.

The now famous "dream of Nebuchadnezzar" took the form of a Great Image, the image of a man, representing four successive World-Empires, followed by a fifth, a kingdom far greater than all the previous kingdoms of the earth together. In the God-given interpretation of the vision, Daniel revealed to the King the sequence of these successive kingdoms, and the great purpose of God in the ultimate sovereignty of the earth (Daniel 2).

The Great Image represented the whole course and end of Gentile world-dominion, to be followed by a kingdom which shall never be destroyed—when "The kingdoms of this world are become the kingdoms of our Lord, and of his Christ; and he shall reign for ever and ever" (Revelation 11:15).

Daniel declared that the First World-Dominion, represented by the golden head of the image, was Babylon itself, which came to its predicted end in the reign of Belshazzar, a grandson of King Nebuchadnezzar. The Fall of Babylon was of great significance in the light of both history and prophecy, for the rise of Babylon, the first of the four World-Empires, marked the beginning of **"the Times of the Gentiles,"** spoken of by our Lord (Luke 21:24).

Surrounded by great walls, a veritable fortress, and having provisions enough to withstand siege for twenty years, Babylon was seemingly impregnable. Nearing the time of its overthrow, however, a time of feasting and drinking was going on within the city; while Belshazzar and his lords drank and desecrated the Sacred Vessels stolen from the Temple at Jerusalem, a mysterious hand was suddenly seen writing upon the palace wall. The panic-stricken King commanded his "wise men," but they could not decipher the strange and ominous words. Again, Daniel was sent for, this time to make known the meaning of the mysterious writing. The captive prophet ended the God-given interpretation by boldly announcing that Belshazzar had been ". . . weighed in the balances, and found wanting," therefore, his kingdom was to be taken from him and given to "the Medes and the Persians" (Daniel 5).

In the meantime, Cyrus, the ruler of the Persian Empire, was busy drawing off the waters of the River Euphrates, which ran through Babylon; diverting the stream and thus making it possible for his soldiers to enter the city by a way never dreamed of by the over-confident Babylonians, the way of the river bed. That night Belshazzar was slain, and the kingdom passed into the hands of Darius, the Mede, and Cyrus, the rising Persian invader. After the death of Darius, two years later, Cyrus was in undisputed possession of the consolidated Medo-Persian Empire. The Second World-Dominion was depicted, in Nebuchadnezzar's dream, as the shoulders and arms of silver in the great Image of Gentile World-Dominion (Daniel 2).

The Proclamation of Cyrus (Ezra 1)

Just before Babylon fell to the invader, Belshazzar promoted Daniel to be the third ruler in the kingdom (Daniel 5:29). There is no doubt that the Hebrew Prince, who had risen so high in the favor and the councils of the Kings of Babylon, sought an interview with the new Ruler, Cyrus. Not only to discuss his future, and that of his people, but particularly to bring to the King's attention the startling prophecy written more than 160 years before; foretelling that "one who knew not God" would be the instrument for setting His people (the Hebrews) free from their Babylonian captivity. Great must have been the astonishment of Cyrus to find himself (even mentioned by name) in the old Hebrew scroll, written well over a century before he was born.

> *That saith of Cyrus, He is my shepherd, and shall perform all my pleasure: even saying to Jerusalem, Thou shalt be built; and to the temple, Thy foundation shall be laid.* (*Isaiah 44:28.*)

In the prophecy that followed, the Lord promised that nations would be subdued before Cyrus, and the gates of brass (Babylon) would be open and broken before him; and God marvelously fulfilled His Word.

Deeply moved by the evidence of such overwhelming truth, Cyrus issued a proclamation: "Who is there among you of all his people? his God be with him, and let him go up to Jerusalem, . . . and build the house of the Lord God of Israel, (he is the God,) . . ." (Ezra 1:3). Cyrus put the proclamation in writing (an act, in God's providence, that later "saved the day" for the builders of the Temple long after the death of Cyrus (Ezra 6). Cyrus not only consented to their return to Jerusalem, but provided them with money and material for the rebuilding of the Temple, their National Sanctuary. He also put into their hands 5,400 gold and silver vessels that Nebuchadnezzar had taken from the House of the Lord in Jerusalem when he sacked the city (Jeremiah 28:2-3).

Strange as it may seem, the mass of the nation chose to remain in the land of their captivity. The generation born in Babylon had no firsthand memories of the plight of their fathers, and were contented to follow the advice of the Prophet Jeremiah: ". . . build ye houses, and dwell in them; and plant gardens, and eat the fruit of them . . ." (Jeremiah 29:28). The period of captivity, however, came to an official end with "the decree of Cyrus."

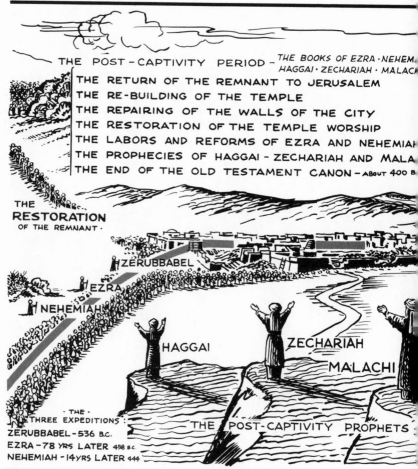

THE POST-CAPTIVITY PERIOD – *THE BOOKS OF EZRA · NEHEM.*
HAGGAI · ZECHARIAH · MALACI
THE RETURN OF THE REMNANT TO JERUSALEM
THE RE-BUILDING OF THE TEMPLE
THE REPAIRING OF THE WALLS OF THE CITY
THE RESTORATION OF THE TEMPLE WORSHIP
THE LABORS AND REFORMS OF EZRA AND NEHEMIAH
THE PROPHECIES OF HAGGAI – ZECHARIAH AND MALA
THE END OF THE OLD TESTAMENT CANON – ABOUT 400 B

THE
RESTORATION
OF THE REMNANT ·

ZERUBBABEL

EZRA

NEHEMIAH

HAGGAI

ZECHARIAH

MALACHI

· THE ·
THREE EXPEDITIONS:
ZERUBBABEL – 536 B.C.
EZRA – 78 YRS LATER 458 B.C.
NEHEMIAH – 14 YRS LATER 444

THE POST-CAPTIVITY PROPHETS

END OF BABYLONIAN RULE 539 B.C. — MEDIA-PERSIAN PERIOD ENDING 332 B

THE RESTORATION • REBUILDIN

• END OF THE OLD TESTAMEN

DANIEL   EZRA   NEHEMIA

=====LAW CONTINUED=====

HE END OF THE LD TESTAMENT ISTORY & CANON

FOUR HUNDRED YEARS FROM MALACHI TO MATTHEW

THE REVOLT OF THE MACCABEES

GREAT HISTORICAL CHASM of about four centuries stretches between the close of the Old Testament and the commencement of the New. Of this period of history the Scriptures are silent. From the writings of the Jewish historian, Josephus, from certain books of the Apocrypha, from many Greek and Roman writings, we gather our knowledge of these four hundred years of important history.

The history of Israel, during these centuries, was one of terrible oppression, invasion, and bloodshed. But in their darkest hours a faithful band of patriots guarded with their lives "The sacred oracles of God,"—the Old Testament Canon, which had been gathered together by Ezra as

one whole book, *The Law, The Prophets,* and *The Psalms.* To these, the faithful in Israel, clung desperately, together with the hope of the coming deliverer — the long promised Messiah. This period of history may be remembered for convenience, as: [1] The Persian period. [2] The Greek period. [3] The period of Jewish Independence. [4] The Roman period.

The Old Testament ending under Persian rule, the New Testament opening under Roman rule.

For the story of the revolt of tne Maccabees, and their brave struggle for Jewish Independence, turn to the notes found in the last pages of the "Panorama."

HE LAST OF THE OLD TESTAMENT PROPHETS

—GREEK PERIOD ENDING 167 B.C.—PERIOD OF INDEPENDENCE ENDING 63 B.C.—ROMAN RULE

AND DEDICATION OF THE TEMPLE

• MACCABEAN REVOLT •

ESTHER   ZECHARIAH   MALACHI

THE DISPENSATION OF THE LAW
(continued)
FROM THE RESTORATION TO THE END OF THE OLD TESTAMENT

THE RETURN OF the Jews from Babylon was accomplished in three separate expeditions:

(1) **The First Company** returned under Zerubbabel, a prince of Judah, and consisted of less than fifty thousand men, women and children. Those choosing to remain in Babylon were to contribute money for the restoration of the Temple in Jerusalem. It took the expedition four months to make the journey of seven hundred miles from Babylon to the beloved city of their homeland. From this time on, because the returning remnant were predominantly of the tribe of Judah, the people were commonly called Jews (an appellation used ever since for anyone of the Hebrew race or whose religion is Judaism).

Upon arriving at Jerusalem, the first thing the returning company did was to repair the Temple Altar and restore the regular form of sacrificial worship (for "unless God build the house it is built in vain"). In the second year of their return the foundation of the devastated Temple was laid (Ezra 1-3).

"The people of the land" (who were actually "strangers" in the land), being brought from various parts of the Assyrian Empire to occupy the province of Samaria, when the Ten Tribes were taken captive to Assyria (II Kings 17:24-41), upon being refused a share in the work of rebuilding the Temple, hindered and opposed the effort with such vindictiveness that they finally obtained an order from King Artaxerxes (the King of Persia) to cause the work to cease (Ezra 4).

At last, after an interval of sixteen years, the Prophets Haggai and Zechariah stirred the people; obtained a confirmation of the decree of Cyrus (which providentially he had put in writing), and the work was energetically resumed. After four years of building, the Temple was completed and dedicated with great joy (Ezra 5-6). It was now some twenty years since the work of rebuilding first began, and at last Isaiah's prophecy regarding Cyrus and the Temple's restoration was wondrously fulfilled (Isaiah 44:28), although written 160 years in advance of the momentous event.

(2) **The Second Expedition** was led by Ezra, a scribe, about seventy-eight years after Zerubbabel's return. Ezra gained permission from King

Artaxerxes to return to Jerusalem with a small but dedicated band of six or seven thousand exiles. Carrying a large number of the gold and silver vessels belonging to the Temple, it took the company four months to make the journey. Upon his arrival Ezra was overcome with grief when he heard of the abominations, abuses and unsound religious practices prevalent among the people of God who had returned from captivity and rebuilt the Temple—only to "mingle their holy seed" with the old enemies of the land.

For three months Ezra made a stirring appeal to the consciences of the people; and after praying, confessing and weeping before God, ". . . there assembled unto him . . . a very great congregation of men and women and children: for the people wept very sore" (Ezra 10:1). Ezra's prayers and God's gracious answer brought about a spiritual awakening and a great reformation among the returned but unsettled people (Ezra 9-10).

Ezra is called "a ready scribe in the law of Moses"; the burden of his heart was to teach the commandments and the statutes of Jehovah in Israel; to restore the vow of separation; and to inspire a reverence for God's Holy Word. The great danger to purity of religion was "mixed marriages," and moved by Ezra's intercession on their behalf the people confessed their sin and put away their "strange wives," the daughters of the idolatrous people of the land. The fruitage of Ezra's zeal for "the law of the God of Heaven" was a great revival that swept the land (Nehemiah 8).

(3) The Third Expedition was led by Nehemiah, a pious Jew of the Captivity who had found favor and position in the court of the Kings of Persia. A small group of those who had returned to Jerusalem with Ezra made their way back to the city of Shushan, to make known to Nehemiah the sad condition of the city of their fathers; although the Temple was rebuilt, the walls of the city were still broken down; the gates, burned with fire, had never been replaced, thus, the city was unprotected, the people discouraged and a reproach in the land. Nehemiah was deeply moved; for even though he enjoyed favor and position in Shushan, the city of his fathers held sacred memories and allegiance. As the Psalmist wrote, "By the rivers of Babylon . . . we wept, when we remembered Zion. . . . If I forget thee, O Jerusalem, let my right hand forget her cunning" (Psalm 137:1, 3).

Having obtained a leave of absence from the King, Nehemiah returned to Jerusalem (some ninety-four years after the return of Zerubbabel with the first company of Jewish exiles). Heartsick at the sight of the ruins, he was inspired to action without delay. Catching the contagion of his zeal and his appeal to their patriotism, nobles, rulers, priests and people said, "Let us arise and build." With enthusiasm, prayer and "faith with works," they finished the colossal task in fifty-two days. The

secret of the accomplishment was "united devotion to a sacred cause"—
"to every man his work." What great things could be accomplished
for the Kingdom of God if every believer found his place and had "a
mind and a will to work with united devotion" for the Cause of Christ.

The rebuilding of the city's defenses in so short a time was, in itself,
a gigantic task—but made the harder by bitter opposition; intrigues of
malicious neighbors on the outside and disgruntled ones on the inside,
a familiar pattern of any effort for the Glory of God. The work was
hindered by: ridicule, anger, discouraged workers, greed, selfishness and
graft—but "the faithful" continued to build, trusting in their God to
bring the "threatenings" to nought. Nehemiah's inspiring words, "I am
doing a great work, so that I cannot come down . . . to you . . ."
(Nehemiah 6:3), should be the unshakable testimony of every Christian
laboring for Christ's sake, amidst criticism, and the subtle attempt of
the enemy "to cause the work to cease." "So the wall was finished . . .
in fifty and two days. And . . . when all our enemies heard thereof,
and . . . saw these things, they were much cast down in their own
eyes: for they perceived that this work was wrought of our God" (Nehemiah 6:15-16).

Together, Ezra and Nehemiah labored; the forgotten Feast of the
Tabernacles was restored; the people separated themselves from their
foreign and idolatrous entanglements; "stood up" when the Book of the
Law was opened, marking a new reverence for the Word of God (Nehemiah 8:5); confessing and promising not to intermarry with unbelievers;
not to buy nor sell on the sabbath; to bring all the tithe into the store-
house; and not to forsake the House of God—with determined hearts
the people renewed, signed and sealed the "sure covenant" (Nehemiah
9). With such evidence of a great moral and spiritual awakening, with
the blessing of God upon the rebuilt city and its repentant people—
surely, at last, in the sight of God and man, Israel is ready to accomplish
its Divine mission to all nations, witnessing of the goodness, the long-
suffering mercy, and the greatness of the one True and Living God.

After accomplishing a great and noble work among his people, Nehemiah, after an absence of twelve years, returned to Shushan. Later, upon
his second visit to Jerusalem, he was again "sorely grieved" at the
spiritual chaos he found awaiting him. The record ends with Nehemiah
rebuking the people for violating the sabbath; neglecting their tithes and
offerings; forsaking the House of God; and their old sin of intermarriage
with the heathen, so that their children could not even speak the Jewish
language (Nehemiah 13:6-31).

The Order of the Prophets

(1) Before the Captivities:
    Jonah—prophesying to Nineveh.
(2) To the Kingdom of Israel (the Ten Tribes):
    Amos, Hosea, Obadiah, Joel.
(3) To the Kingdom of Judah (the Two Tribes):
    Isaiah, Micah, Nahum, Habakkuk, Zephaniah, Jeremiah.
(4) During the Exile (in Babylon):
    Ezekiel, Daniel.
(5) After the Exile (to the returned remnant):
    Haggai, Zechariah, Malachi.

The prophets of the Restoration were: **Haggai, Zechariah and Malachi.** Haggai was born in Babylon during the Captivity and accompanied the returning remnant under Zerubbabel. Zechariah also appears to have been one of the returning pilgrims with Zerubbabel; he was a co-laborer with Haggai, exhorting, prophesying and encouraging the people in the work of restoration. Haggai and Zechariah were sent to reprove the people for delaying to build the Temple. Malachi was sent to reprove them for neglecting it after it was built.

The End of the Old Testament Canon

Malachi was the last of the Old Testament Prophets. The name signifies "my messenger." He probably prophesied in the time of the spiritual chaos during Nehemiah's absence (Nehemiah 13:6). Little is known of the person Malachi, other than that he lived and labored during the times of Ezra and Nehemiah. His message was to admonish and encourage a backsliding and disheartened people who were still looking for the optimistic predictions made by Haggai and Zechariah a hundred years before to be fulfilled. The priests were indifferent to the inferior and blemished sacrifices being offered; the people were neglectful of their tithes; God's Covenant was ignored; divorce and idolatry went hand in hand, for men were evidently putting away their Jewish wives and marrying idolatrous foreigners—a flagrant violation of God's purpose to preserve unto Himself a "Godly Seed" (Malachi 2:15).

The doubters declared, "It is vain to serve God . . ."—to all appearances the wicked and the good prosper alike, but Malachi reminds the faithful that Jehovah knows them that are His, and "a book of remembrance" is being kept. He declared a Day of Judgment and a time of sifting, and of the faithful remnant he declared, ". . . they shall be mine, saith the Lord of hosts, **in that day when I make up my jewels . . .**" (Malachi 3:16-18).

With a concluding exhortation to repent, remember and obey the Law of Moses given to their fathers at Horeb, the Prophet announced **"a forerunner"** who would go before the Lord (the promised Messiah) in the spirit and power of **Elijah,** to avert, if possible, the threatened judgment by reconciling the heart of the fathers to the children . . . the children to the fathers. According to Isaiah 63:16, and Malachi's own admonition: "Even from the days of your fathers ye are gone away from mine ordinances . . ." (Malachi 3:7)—"the fathers" here were the patriarchs whom the Prophet regards as estranged from their degenerate "children," or descendants—"O generation of vipers, . . . think not to say within yourselves, We have Abraham to our father . . ." (Matthew 3:7-9).

Malachi begins his message with a declaration of the everlasting love of Jehovah for Israel, but by their disobedience and impenitence, continually provoking God to wrath, they had laid themselves open for the long-delayed curse—the uprooting of the tender vine of God's own planting. Thus, the last words of the Old Covenant were words of ominous warning: ". . . lest I come and smite the earth with a curse," literally "the" curse; referring to Deuteronomy 28:15-68, the predicted calamities that would befall the nation if they persistently followed the course of disobedience.

Before the curse should fall, however, Malachi declared that God would send "a forerunner" to preach repentance—**the last overlapping link where two dispensations were to meet,** the closing of the Old Covenant and the proclamation of the New. Had Israel, as a Nation, brought forth "fruit meet for repentance," the course of world history would have been changed. But, as a Nation, Israel not only rejected the Herald of the Coming Kingdom, but the King Himself, the Messiah, the Saviour of the world. The Curse fell upon both the land and the nation, bringing with it world-wide dispersion, affliction, persecution, and all of the multiplied sorrows that have followed the scattered nation throughout the centuries.

Thus, Old Testament History comes to a close. The unfolding panorama is almost entirely devoted to God's dealings with His chosen people—Israel. Chosen in the Divine purpose for three specific reasons:

(1) To be the Repository for the Divine Revelation.

(2) To be the Channel for the Introduction of the World's Redeemer.

(3) To be a Faithful Witness of the True and Living God.

Our study of the calling, the life and the development of "the chosen people" showed how the first two God-directed purposes were realized, and how completely Israel failed in the last, yet first, all-important purpose of their existence as a nation (Deuteronomy 4:5-8).

The Old Testament, with its Covenant promise to Israel, ". . . if ye will obey my voice, . . . ye shall be a peculiar treasure unto me above all people . . . ," ends with a rebuke and a burden for the sins of both priests and people in the light of the long-suffering Love of Jehovah. The Messenger, Malachi, closes his pleading admonition with two great promises—a "forerunner" in the spirit and power of Elijah ". . . before the coming of the great and dreadful day of the Lord" (Malachi 4:5); and **the great Messianic promise,** ". . . unto you that fear my name shall the Sun of righteousness arise with healing in his wings . . ." (Malachi 4:2).

From Malachi to Matthew

A Great Historical Chasm of four hundred years stretches between the close of the Old Testament and the beginning of the New. During this time there was no prophet or inspired writer among the Jews. Our knowledge of what took place during these centuries, of which the Bible is silent, is derived largely from the Jewish historian Josephus, from parts of the Apocrypha, and from many Greek and Roman writers.

The most outstanding days of Jewish history, between Malachi and Matthew, were the days of "the Maccabees," in their heroic fight for independence. Continually oppressed and massacred by every invader (it is reported that the sieges of Jerusalem have been twenty-seven in number), the spirit of revolt finally inspired the Jews to break the yoke of their oppressor.

The climax came under the cruel persecution of a tyrannical invader named Antiochus Epiphanes. This tyrant invaded Jerusalem, slaughtered forty thousand Jews in three days; he forced his way into the Holy of Holies, set up an idol altar, sacrificing a sow as a burnt offering. This blasphemous act of desecration was foretold in the prophecies of Daniel, that armed men would go forth and pollute the Sanctuary, and set up ". . . the abomination that maketh desolate" (Daniel 11:31).

In Daniel 9:26, the *future* abomination is graphically described, when the *Anti-Christ,* of whom this blasphemous tyrant is a pre-figure, shall again desecrate the Temple in "the end-time." It was to this passage that our Lord referred when answering the question of the Disciples, ". . . what shall be the sign of thy coming, and of the end of the world?" Christ answered, "When ye therefore shall see the abomination of desolation, spoken by Daniel the prophet, stand in the holy place. . . . For then shall be great tribulation, such as was not since the beginning of the world, . . . nor ever shall be" (Matthew 24:15-21).

At the height of the excesses of Antiochus, the Jews, forced to idol-worship and to eat the flesh of unclean sacrifices, revolted under the leadership of an old patriot named Mattathias. This man, with his five sons, under the name of "the Maccabees," became the valiant leaders of the great fight for Jewish independence.

In less than a year the old warrior died and his son Judas succeeded him in the struggle. Under his inspiring leadership, and restored faith in God, every army that was sent out against them was defeated until, at last, Judas Maccabeus was successful in throwing off the yoke of the foreign invader and establishing independence for the long-oppressed Jews.

The Maccabean family now governed for a period of one hundred years. They re-opened, cleansed, and re-dedicated the Temple, and some of the splendor of the old days of the kingdom was restored. The Maccabean leadership, however, became selfish and ambitious. Greed for position and material things overcame their patriotism, and party divisions weakened their cause; for this period gave rise to the three great parties of the New Testament history, the Pharisees, Sadducees and the Essenes.

The successors of Antiochus continued the fight against Jewish dominion, invading the land with a large army determined upon the destruction of the restored kingdom. After another year of hardship, discouragement and confusion, Judas made the first alliance with Rome. Rome was fast becoming a dominant world power, and although the alliance seemed likely to insure peace for Israel, the Jews were destined to find in Rome a persecutor beyond them all.

The end of the struggle came when the Roman army under Pompey besieged the city, storming the walls, utterly destroying the Temple, and ruthlessly slaying both young and old. Henceforth, Judea was declared a Roman Province.

Julius Caesar followed Pompey. Caesar appointed Antipator as ruler over Judea. Antipator appointed his two sons to authority, Phasel over Galilee, Herod over Jerusalem. Herod was about twenty years of age when his father appointed him as Governor over Judea, and after a few years of cruel events, he was appointed **King of Judea and the Jews.** It was during his notorious (both wicked and eventful) reign that **Jesus was born.**

It is here that **Matthew** takes up the story in the opening pages of **the New and Better Covenant.** The four hundred years of historical silence is broken by the Proclamation of the Gospel, or ". . . good tidings of great joy, which shall be to all people" (Luke 2:10-11).

Four Hundred Years of Changing World-Dominion

Great historical events had taken place between the Prophecies of Malachi and the Proclamation of Matthew. Malachi closes his ministry with the world under **Persian Rule;** Matthew opens with the world under

Roman Rule. Between these two periods of World History came the rise and fall of the great Grecian Empire of Alexander the Great. Thus, the Persian Empire of Malachi's day was overthrown by the Grecian Empire, which in turn was overthrown by the Roman Conquerors. It was at this particular God-appointed time in World History that **Christ and Christianity appeared.**

These great changing historical events contributed much, in God's foreknowledge, to the subsequent propagation of the Gospel throughout the world. There were now three great national groups involved in world affairs: **the Romans, the Greeks** and **the Jews;** and each was destined in its own peculiar way to prepare the world for the planting of the Gospel Seed in the hearts of men everywhere.

First, the rise and world-wide influence of the Grecian Empire gave the world a universally understood language; the Greek tongue becoming generally known throughout the world. Thus, the New Testament Scriptures, in God's purpose, were written in Greek.

Secondly, the rise of the Roman Empire, which established political and judicial unity in its far-reaching dominion, and built magnificent roads, making all of the territory of their conquests accessible, was a great contributing factor in preparing the world to hear and to receive the "good tidings of great joy," the gift of God to all peoples. For over the same roads that carried marching armies and banners of World-Dominion, there followed, in God's appointed time, the marching army of Christian witnesses. Faithful unto death—but not until Gospel fires had been kindled from the center to the circumference of the powerful, pagan, Roman Empire, and the ends of the then known world.

Before we leave the Old Covenant with its outstanding characters, both good and bad, whom we have come to know, it seems, almost personally, we should lift our hearts with gratitude to the faithful band of Israel's Patriots, who, in the darkest hours of oppression, invasion and bloodshed, guarded with their lives "the Sacred Oracles of God," the Old Testament Canon, which had been gathered together by Ezra the Scribe as one whole Book: The Law, the Prophets and the Psalms. To these, the faithful of Israel clung desperately, together with the hope of the Coming Deliverer, the long-promised Messiah.

The greatest tragedy, however, in Israel's history is the fact that **"He came unto his own, and his own received him not"** (John 1:11). While the greatest blessing, for whosoever will, is the glorious truth that ". . . as many as received him, to them gave he power to become the sons of God, even to them that believe on his name" (John 1:11-12).

The Old Testament, "the law was our schoolmaster to bring us unto Christ, that we might be justified by faith" (Galatians 3:24). "Schoolmaster" is translated "pedagogue," literally "child-leader," not a teacher, but the Roman slave whose duty it was to take the child to and from school. Necessary but irksome to the child, who was happy, no doubt, when the control of the pedagogue ceased. Thus, the law was our schoolmaster until the coming of Christ; then with our spiritual "coming of age" we are no longer under "a schoolmaster," but should enjoy spiritual liberty, as mature "sons of God." No longer under the law, but "justified by faith."

LAW

BEGINNING OF THE
NEW TESTAMENT
CANON

"THIS IS MY
BELOVED SON"

THE
BIRTH
OF JESUS

THE
BAPTISM
OF JESUS

CHRIST'S
EARTHLY
MINISTRY

BETHLEHEM

MATT Chaps 1-2

MATT Chap 3

MATT Chaps 4-25

BIRTH OF JESUS
'BEFORE THE DEATH OF HEROD'
PROBABLY B.C. 5 OR 4

BAPTISM
LUKE 3:23
"ABOUT 30 YRS OF AGE"

BEGINNING OF THE NEW TESTAMENT

AND ASCENSION

MATTHEW   MARK   LUKE

5TH DISPENSATION ENDS IN JUDGMENT OF SIN AT CALVARY

"IT IS FINISHED"

ASCENSION
ACTS 1:1-11

THE TRIUMPHAL ENTRY

BETRAYAL ARREST TRIAL

CRUCIFIXION

RESURRECTION

OLIVET

MATT 27:27-66

MATT 21:1-17

MATT Chaps 26-27:1-26

MATT Chap.28

A.D. (ANNO DOMINI) MEANING 'IN THE YEAR OF OUR LORD'.)————A.D.33

BIRTH - MINISTRY - DEATH - RESURRECTION

F JESUS CHRIST •

JOHN   ACTS 1:1-11

THE DISPENSATION OF THE LAW

(concluded)

FROM THE BEGINNING OF THE NEW TESTAMENT TO THE CRUCIFIXION

ALTHOUGH THE Old Testament Canon came to an end, the revelation did not cease. The Old Testament and the New are not two separate, opposing books; they both enshrine the Saviour, who is the Alpha and Omega, the Beginning and the End.

Why Four Gospels?

The Old Testament dealt, almost exclusively, with Israel, whereas, the predominating feature of the New Testament is to take the Gospel, or Good News, to *all the world*. With the ending of the Old Testament Canon and the four hundred years of silent history, followed at last by the Proclamation of the New and Better Covenant, Christ and Christianity must needs be presented and commended to four distinctly different and divergent phases of thought and influence in the known world; **the Roman, the Greek, the Jew,** and those who, with its inception, had embraced **the Christian Faith.**

Each of the great groups had their own panacea for the ills of the world, but neither the Power of the Romans, the Culture of the Greeks, nor the Rabbinical Law of the Jews satisfied the heart—the whole world was ready for its Spiritual King. Therefore, each of the four accounts of "the Gospel," has its own distinctive viewpoint and presentation of Christ as "the anointed one."

The Jews were looking for a long-promised Deliverer down the ages, and more definitely at about the time of the presentation of Jesus, and when He was announced as being the Christ, or Messiah, the rulers among the Jews refused to accept Him largely because both He and the method of His coming were so extremely different from their traditional ideas of what the Messiah was to be.

(1) The Message of Matthew. Although wonderfully presenting an "all-sufficient Saviour," and a complete plan of Saving Truth to a sinful world, Matthew's Gospel is written primarily to convince the Jews that Jesus of Nazareth is the Messiah, the King of Israel, promised in their Old Testament Scriptures. The writer uses about sixty references to Jewish prophecies, and traces the genealogy of Jesus back through David to Abraham, for the Jews would consider no claimant to the Throne of

Israel outside of "the Covenant line of Promise" given to their father Abraham.

(2) **The Message of Mark** was primarily written to converts from among both Romans and Greeks. He gives no genealogy of Jesus for it would be of little importance to prospective Gentile converts. He explains the Hebrew and Aramaic names and customs which would have been familiar to Jews (Mark 3:17; 5:41; 7:11; 7:34). The Gentile converts would not be interested in Jewish prophecies but in the immediate claims of Christ; therefore, Mark stresses the "doings" of Jesus more than the "sayings." For instance, he records nineteen miracles while only four parables.

(3) **The Message of Luke.** Although written essentially to both Jew and Gentile, Luke undoubtedly has the Greek primarily in mind. "Power and Authority" was characteristic of the ideology of the Romans, but to the Greek "Culture" was pre-eminent. The Greek philosophy was to elevate and perfect humanity by culture, wisdom and beauty. Thus Luke presents Jesus as the embodiment of perfection, as "Son of Man" and "the Son of God," interested in all men, both the cultured and uncultured. Luke traces the genealogy of Jesus back to Adam, the progenitor of the whole race.of which Jesus is "the perfect Saviour," come ". . . to seek and to save that which was lost" (Luke 19:10).

(4) **The Message of John** is for all Christians. The genealogy of Jesus is traced immediately to God. John's Gospel is the Gospel of Eternity, the dwelling place of "the Eternal Word" (Greek, *Logos*). Beginning with the mystery of the New Birth, John's Gospel radiates with the blessedness of Eternal Life. The purpose of John's Gospel is the purpose of **all Bible revelation:** ". . . that he might believe that Jesus is the Christ, the Son of God; and that believing ye might have life through his name" (John 20:31).

JESUS—the Mediator of the New and Better Covenant (Hebrews 8:6; 12:24)

The New Testament opens with a genealogy showing Jesus Christ, as the son of David, to be the Heir to the Throne of Israel; and as the son of Abraham, the One in whom "all families of the earth shall be blessed." Thus, Matthew, writing primarily to the Jews, gives the natural descent of Jesus through Abraham, and His royal rights through David. The oft-repeated expression, "That it might be fulfilled which was spoken by the Prophet so-and-so," indicates the writer's purpose to convince the Jews that **Jesus is the fulfillment of Old Testament Prophecy.**

The Fulfillment of God's First Promise
(Genesis 3:15)

Matthew 1 is "the book of the generation of Jesus, the son of David, the son of Abraham." In tracing the natural descent of Jesus, the word "begat" (which is the correct word for natural generation, or procreation) is used in "the account of descent." Abraham begat Isaac, Isaac begat Jacob, and so on until the record of natural generation reaches Joseph: ". . . Jacob begat Joseph the husband of Mary, of whom was born Jesus . . ." (Matthew 1:16). The word "begat" (Webster: to procreate as a sire, a male progenitor, father) stops at Jacob. "Jacob begat Joseph," whereupon (after a continuous record of forty-two generations, in "the register of families") the language suddenly changes from the seed of man "begat" to "the seed of a woman" (Genesis 3:15) —"Mary, of whom was born Jesus."

The Virgin Birth

"Now the birth of Jesus was on this wise" (Matthew 1:18-25). The Virgin Birth has been, and still is, the subject of both theological and scientific debate. Sad to say, it is disputed and denied even in the so-called "Christian" realm of modernistic theology. Yet, upon this cardinal truth the Christian faith must stand or fall. If Joseph was the natural father of Jesus, procreated by, and through, human seed, then the Redemption Plan of God—the plan of **sinless substitution** for "the sin of the world"—immediately loses its advocacy. If Joseph was the natural father of Jesus, no atonement has been made for Adam's fallen race and the wrath of God still rests upon us all. The Virgin Birth must be accepted **by faith,** not by reason; as the Angel declared to Mary in answer to her most natural question, "How shall this be?"—". . . *with God nothing shall be impossible*" (Luke 1:37).

The *Virgin* Birth is the only correct designation of the wondrous event. "Supernatural birth" would not be the correct designation, for there is no intimation that the actual process of birth (gestation, act or period of carrying the young in the uterus) was in any way exceptional. Neither can the term "miraculous conception" be completely adequate. (Conception, act of becoming with child; the birth of Isaac, and John the Baptist, by comparison, can be considered "miraculous conceptions" in that "fertility" was renewed to the barren mothers and the aged fathers, but in the conception of Jesus there is no comparison.) The *Virgin* Birth is the only key which fits the mystery of the Incarnation. The questioning *"How?"* of Mary, and of the ages, **was not answered**— the silence of God must be respected. The words of the Angel were not the explanation but "the Annunciation."

*The Holy Ghost shall come upon thee, and the power of
the Highest shall overshadow thee: therefore also that holy
thing which shall be born of thee shall be called the Son of
God. (Luke 1:26-38.)*

The Angel told Joseph, ". . . that which is conceived in her is of
the Holy Ghost" (Matthew 1:20). Not germinated from the life-stock
of the race; the origin of the body of Jesus is ascribed to God, ". . . a
body hast *thou* prepared me" (Hebrews 10:5). Not the origin of a
"new being," never before existing, as in all natural generation, but the
infinite mystery of a pre-existing, Divine Being implanted within the
realm of germinant life; ". . . the Word was made flesh . . . ," that
Mystic Union of Divinity and Humanity, passing through the successive
periods of natural gestation ("Mary, . . . being great with child"—
". . . the days were accomplished that she should be delivered"—
". . . she brought forth her firstborn . . .").

*. . . this was done, that it might be fulfilled which was
spoken . . . by the prophet [750 years before Jesus was
born], saying, Behold, a virgin shall be with child, and
shall . . . call his name Emmanuel . . . God with us.
(Matthew 1:22-23.)*

At last, after four thousand years of prophecies, promises and preparation—while Angels rejoiced and devils trembled, came the proclamation from the Glory World: ". . . behold I bring you good tidings of
great joy, which shall be to all people. For unto you is born this day
in the city of David a Saviour, which is Christ the Lord" (Luke 2:10-11).

Bethlehem (Matthew 1:18-25)
The New Testament opens under Roman sovereignty. In the reign of
Caesar Augustus a decree was issued requiring all people to enroll in
their own cities for Taxation. This decree brought Joseph and Mary,
now his espoused wife, to Bethlehem, the city of their fathers, for both
Joseph and Mary were lineal descendants of "the house of David."
Thus, it was that Jesus was born in Bethlehem (the name meaning
"house of bread") in fulfillment of the prophecy of Micah 5:2:
". . . out of thee [Bethlehem] shall he come forth unto me that is to
be ruler in Israel; whose goings forth have been from of old, from
everlasting."
There is usually privacy, sympathetic attention and tender understanding when God launches a little "eternity" into this world—but into
this village of a few hundred a multitude was crowded. People came

from everywhere to pay their taxes; and amid the busy, noisy confusion of an indifferent, preoccupied world; sharing the limestone grotto, or stable, with the crowded animals of other travelers; devoid of any semblance of convenience or comfort, "the Prince of Peace" was born.

The Incarnation—"God" becoming "man"—is indeed the mystery of mysteries. Leaving "the ivory palaces"—laying aside His robes of Majesty—while celestial messengers direct astonished shepherds watching their flocks by night, saying, "Ye shall find the babe wrapped, . . . lying in a manger" (Luke 2:12). The Lord of Glory "laid out for death" at His very birth. In the natural scheme of things every creature is born to live—that is the purpose of birth—but, here in Bethlehem, the miraculous difference and purpose is that **Jesus was born to die.** He was "the lamb slain" from the bosom of the Eternal—yet, **the birth of Jesus is the pivot of history.** It split the calendar of time right down the middle. Before the Birth of Christ (B.C.)—After the Birth of Christ (A.D.)—and an unbelieving world acknowledges the fact and adjusts its timetable of affairs by the light of a Stable Lantern—for "there was no room in the inn" on the momentous night that Jesus was born.

The Infancy—Boyhood—and Baptism of Jesus

Of our Lord's Infancy only four events are recorded in the Gospels, namely the Circumcision, the Presentation in the Temple, the Visit of the Magi, and the Flight into Egypt to escape "the slaughter of the innocents" by Herod.

Circumcision took place, according to Jewish custom, eight days after birth (Luke 2:21). The rite was one of the first ordinances that God made with His chosen people Israel. It was to be their physical sign, or testimony of separation unto God. But in the New Testament, on resurrection ground, Christians have the ordinance of Water Baptism as the outward and physical testimony of the inward work of fuller grace— nevertheless, the recorded event should have its solemn meaning to the Christian; here, Bethlehem is a prelude to the Cross, teaching the believer of "spiritual" circumcision. Christ came not to destroy the Law but to fulfill it, and we should practise "the circumcision of the heart," or that separation unto God of which Water Baptism is but a public and physical symbol.

On the day of Circumcision, Christ publicly received the name of *Jesus,* which the Angel Gabriel had already announced ". . . before he was conceived in the womb" (Luke 2:21). In reference to the name "Jesus" there is an interesting and somewhat amazing revelation. In the New Testament, where the name "Jesus" is recorded over six hundred times, as strange as it may be, *never once* was our Lord addressed directly as *"Jesus,"* except on two occasions, and then by demons (Matthew 1:24 and Mark 5:7). The names "Messiah" and "Christ" were names which represented His office as "the Anointed"; the name "Jesus" was His given, personal name—". . . and thou shalt call his name *Jesus* [Hebrew, *Joshua,* 'Saviour']: for he shall save his people from their sins" (Matthew 1:21).

The Presentation in the Temple: according to the Levitical Law, a woman having given birth to a male child was not permitted to enter the Sanctuary during the forty days before her purification (Leviticus 12:1-8), when she was to present herself to the priest with an offering for atonement and cleansing, according to her means. On the fortieth day Mary presented herself in the Temple at Jerusalem to offer a sacrifice, and to present her son to God, according to the Law "(As it is written, . . . every male that openeth the womb shall be called holy to the Lord) . . ." (Luke 2:23).

The details of the Presentation in the Temple are very brief, but the visit was made memorable by the Adoration and the Prophecy of a devout man, named Simeon, and an aged Prophetess, named Anna, who were expectantly "waiting for the consolation of Israel." Simeon had received a Divine intimation that he would not see death until he had seen the promised Messiah. When he saw the infant Jesus, inspired by Divine impulse, he took Him in his arms and burst into the Song of Adoration—the *Nunc Dimittus*—". . . now lettest thou thy servant depart in peace, . . . For mine eyes have seen thy salvation" (Luke 2:29-30).

The Boyhood of Jesus

Before the period of silent years in the life of our Lord, one more event of tender splendor is recorded. At the age of twelve, an important age for a Jewish boy, for He now became a *ben hat-torah,* or "son of the Law," Jesus accompanied His parents to the Feast of the Passover at Jerusalem. Suddenly missing Him in the crowded halls of the Temple, they found Him sitting in the midst of the great teachers of the Law, eagerly listening and calmly asking questions of the learned doctors. In amazement Mary, His mother, addressed Him in tender reproach—His answer, innocently simple and natural, but unfathomable in its depth of conscious meaning, furnishes us with the first recorded words of Jesus: "How is it that ye sought me? Wist ye not that I must be about my Father's business?" (Luke 2:49).

Mary had said, ". . . thy father and I have sought thee . . . ," but Jesus is now Divinely conscious of His parentage, and from now on He must give full recognition to the truth that "His Father" is the One which is in Heaven. By solemnly asking His mother the question, "Did

ye not know?" and declaring, "I must," He now revealed the consciousness of self-surrender and the life of self-sacrifice which He must walk.
Yet with humble and dutiful submission to His mother and foster-father,
He ". . . increased in wisdom and stature, and in favour with God and
man" (Luke 2:41-52).

The following years of Christ's life are passed in holy silence until
He presented Himself to John for Baptism, being "about thirty years of
age" (the age at which the priests and Levites began their public service,
and the Scribes had authority to teach [Numbers 4:3, 43, 47]). When
Jesus approached the banks of the Jordan where His great Herald and
forerunner, John, was baptizing converts "unto repentance," according
to the twice-repeated testimony John "knew him not." The Herald of
the Coming Kingdom, who fearlessly rebuked Kings, Pharisees, and
Hierarchs in uncompromising indictment, recognizes in this Presence a
serene majesty, a compelling purity that inspired him to confess reverently, "I have need to be baptized of thee, and cometh thou to me?"
The second recorded utterance of Jesus, and the first words of His
public ministry, is the answer, "Suffer it to be so now . . ." (Matthew
3:15).

We cannot resist the question, "Why should the sinless Saviour seek
'a baptism of repentance'?" Jesus Himself reveals the answer on the
ground of expediency. He did not say "I must," or "I have need," but,
"Suffer it to be so." In submitting to baptism He formally identified
Himself with the public expectation of the Kingdom, entering by the
same gateway as those who would follow Him in consecration and commitment. For thus, He said, ". . . it becometh us to fulfil all righteousness," ("to fulfill every religious duty"—WEYMOUTH)—to fulfill every
requirement to which God's will inclines (Psalm 40:7-8).

The significance, and the Divine approval of the Ordinance of Baptism as a public testimony is seen in what followed. The heavens were
opened, the Spirit of God descended like a dove upon Jesus, and a
Voice from Heaven declared: "This is my beloved Son, in whom I am
well pleased" (Matthew 3:13-17). Here, the Unity of the Godhead,
the Trinity, though dimly intimated in the Old Testament, is now clearly
revealed. The Father speaks from Heaven, the Son submitting to Baptism in the Jordan, the Spirit descending like a dove. Three distinct and
Divine persons active in the same scene in the same moment.

"And Jesus being full of the Holy Ghost returned from Jordan . . ."
(Luke 4:1). With Christ's public consecration of Himself to His Mes-
sianic calling, He now received the spiritual equipment to accomplish
His work. He went forth "full of the Holy Ghost"—**the seal of the
Father's pleasure, purpose and power.**

The Temptation of Jesus

Then was Jesus led up of the spirit into the wilderness to be tempted of the devil. And when he had fasted forty days . . . he was afterward an hungred. (Matthew 4:1-11.)

Realizing the meaning and magnitude of the task to which He stood committed, and conscious of a new inner power (being "full of the Holy Spirit"), there was need to wait upon the Father, and to meditate upon the way of approach to the popular hopes and expectations; and, we read, the Spirit led Him up to the wilderness—but, in the Father's purpose, to be tempted of the Devil.

The scene was Quarantania, a mountainous region full of barren rocks and caves where beasts of prey lurk even to this day—it was here that Jesus met Satan face to face. Three times the Adversary tried to turn Him aside from the path of consecration and complete confidence upon which He had entered.

The First Temptation Was to Distrust. After fasting for forty days, being very man, He felt the gnawing pangs of hunger, and was intensely vulnerable to Satan's challenge, "command these stones to become bread." The temptation was aimed to foster distrust, and to lead Jesus to exercise the powers entrusted to Him in an unlawful way, an act of self-indulgence. For if Jesus was in this position, it was the Father who brought Him there, in His own purpose, to be tried of the Devil. The temptation was immediately met by the word of His Father—God, "Man shall not live by bread alone . . ." (Deuteronomy 8:3). Man has a higher life than that sustained on bread, ". . . by every word that proceedeth out of the mouth of God" doth man live.

The Second Temptation Was to Presumption. Jesus is taken up to a pinnacle (literally, a wing, presumably more than 250 feet) of the Temple; from this great height the Devil suggests that He cast Himself down, trusting the promise ". . . he shall give his angels charge over thee . . ." (Psalm 91:11-12). This would be an easy and convincing way to demonstrate His Messiahship to the crowd below, with signs and wonders. An act of self-display. But again the Tempter is defeated by the Word: "Ye shall not tempt the Lord your God . . ." (Deuteronomy 6:16).

The Third Temptation Was World-Dominion, gained by a concession to the Devil. An act of self-aggrandizement. From some lofty elevation the kingdoms of the world and the glory of them—either seen, or flashed upon the mind of Christ—were offered to Him on condition of one act of homage and recognition of the Tempter's (usurped) authority in the world. It will be noticed that Jesus did not challenge the Devil's claim to the kingdoms of this world—it was a temptation to regain them by an easier way than the way of the Cross.

Jesus might well have answered, "Instead of my bowing to you for world recognition—when you have run your course of deception I am coming back to 'bruise your head'—take away your 'headship,' your usurped authority in the affairs of the kingdoms of this world—and every knee shall bow and every tongue confess that I am Lord of lords and King of kings." But again He simply answered from the Word: "Thou shalt worship the Lord thy God, and him only shalt thou serve" (Matthew 4:10).

The Tempter was real, the temptations were real, the purpose was real, the defeat of the Devil's intent was real. "The form" of the temptations, however, is still a question in the interpretation of many Bible scholars. Whether the struggle was an inward one (similar to our own experience), or whether Jesus was literally transported to a pinnacle of the Temple, then to a high mountain, and back again to the wilderness (cf. Ezekiel 41:1-2), actually matters not; the great object lesson remains—the Temptation of Jesus was typical of the whole realm of Satanic assault through the body, mind and spirit of man (I John 2:16), and the great object lesson to all generations—the most effective weapon in the hour of temptation is the Word of God—available to every child of His Love in the hour of trial.

Christ's Earthly Ministry

Before Christ's public manifestation of Himself as Messiah, by driving the money changers from the Temple and answering their challenge as to His authority (John 2:13-25), a more intimate and significant unfolding of His Glory and of His Mission was granted to His family and friends (showing immediately that His religion was by no means antagonistic to natural relations) at the marriage feast at Cana, where He first displayed His Deity by the miracle of turning water into wine. As the wine provided for the guests had given out, Mary, His mother, had suggested that Jesus supply the want—His startling reply, "Woman, what have I to do with thee? . . ." is not intended to convey disrespect or reproof (it is the same word as that addressed to her from the Cross) but intimating to Mary that His actions were henceforth to be guided by a rule other than hers, or even His own (John 2:1-12).

He was to be regarded thenceforth not as the son of Mary, but as the public servant of Jehovah—the Anointed One of God (Greek, *Christos;* Hebrew, *Messiah*). "This beginning of miracles" was followed by the healing of the sick; the calling of His disciples; teaching the multitudes; His parables and discourses; His demonstration of power over nature, over demons, and death. The Son of Man had now faithfully finished the work given Him by His Father to accomplish. He had shown Himself a spotless example as very man, ". . . in all points tempted like as we are, yet without sin" (Hebrews 4:15). He had reflected the image and nature of the invisible God, ". . . he that hath seen me hath seen the Father" (John 14:9). He had fulfilled the prophecies concerning the ministry of "the servant of Jehovah" (Luke 4:18-19). It remained now for Him to settle the Sin question; to conquer Death, and thus complete the work of Redemption. "For this purpose the Son of God was manifested, that he might destroy [undo] the works of the devil" (I John 3:8).

The Betrayal—Arrest—and Trial of Jesus
(Matthew 26:45-75; 27:1-26)

During the last year of the ministry of Jesus, the Jewish Leaders had become exceedingly hostile to Him, and had taken counsel together ". . . that they might take Jesus by subtilty, and kill him" (Matthew 26:4). Their determination was greatly intensified by His obvious popularity with the people, as evidenced by His triumphal entry into Jerusalem on the first day of the Passover week (Matthew 21:8-11). Their plans were expedited by Judas Iscariot (one of the twelve) approaching them with a bargain to betray His Master for money.

Fearing the influence of Jesus with the people, the Chief Priests and the Elders evidently appealed to the Roman authority for assistance. ". . . having received a band of men and officers [part of a Roman Cohort, four or five hundred men] . . . ," Judas led them to Christ's retreat in the deep shade of the olive trees in Gethsemane. There Jesus received the appointed signal, the betrayer's kiss; surrendered Himself without resistance; was bound and taken into the city—while even the closest of His disciples forsook Him and fled (Matthew 26:31)—"I will smite the shepherd, and the sheep of the flock shall be scattered. . . ."

It was about midnight when Jesus was arrested and hurried to the house of Caiaphas, the high priest, where, anticipating His capture, the Sanhedrin was already assembled. The travesty of the so-called "trial" of Jesus (actually it was not Jesus on trial—but **the world on trial**) was a twofold system—Jewish and Roman.

The whole procedure was a shameful and illegal mockery of Justice. Hustled by bribed agitators, angry passions and brute force into the courtroom at one or two o'clock in the morning; no counsel or witnesses for the defense; false witnesses and judges with inflamed minds for the prosecution—the night trial broken up to meet in the morning—

a shameful scene of disorder and abuse in which they spat in their prisoner's face, mocked Him and struck Him, as He stood bound, alone and helpless before His accusers.

The Verdict was Guilty! "He hath spoken blasphemy . . . ," the Judges declared, "He is guilty of death" (Matthew 26:47-68). The Jewish Sanhedrin, however, had no power to execute the sentence of death, nor had they any authority to try a capital offence. Judea was a Roman province, the Judicial authority was vested in the Roman Governor; therefore, it was necessary to invoke the aid of the Roman power in carrying out the sentence of death upon Jesus; therefore, ". . . they led him away, and delivered him to Pontius Pilate. . . ."

The Roman Governor, who was impressed from the first of the innocence of Jesus, the scheming of envious priests, and an angry mob thirsting for the blood of an innocent prisoner, made futile attempts to dissuade the Jewish Leaders and to acquit the accused, or, at least, to shift the responsibility of His condemnation—for, he said, "I find no fault in this man." But at last, in fear, when his loyalty to Caesar was challenged, he no longer had courage to resist.

To appease the mob who threatened his political security, he ascended the judgment seat and the fatal words which doomed Jesus to the Cross fell from his faltering lips. The trial was over and Jesus was led away to be crucified. We know that in the Great Redemption Plan ". . . he must . . . suffer many things . . . ," but why the ignomiy of such a malicious and unjust trial? That amid the injustices, the false accusations, insults and humiliation—we have a Divine sympathizer, "Who, when he was reviled, reviled not again; when he suffered, he threatened not; but committed himself to him that judgeth righteously" (I Peter 2:23).

Jesus was arrested after midnight—tried—condemned—and crucified before 9 o'clock in the morning. Nine hours of wretched infamy!

The Crucifixion (Matthew 27:26-66)

The world has witnessed some dark days, our history books are filled with them—but the darkest day since the world was made was the day they crucified our Lord.

The busy, preoccupied, thoughtless world sees the Cross as a pleasing feature in design and decoration, or in a haze of ritual and religious symbolism—in these last days of Grace may we make the message and the meaning of the Cross crystal-clear—". . . it is the power of God unto salvation . . ." (I Romans 1:16). All lines of Scripture in the Holy Book run to it and from it—and around it circles all history of ages past and ages yet to come. All the purposes, promises and judgments of God are gathered up here—all men must answer to the Cross.

"What will YOU do with Jesus?" is still the most important question in life.

Volumes have been written describing the things that were seen on that never-to-be-forgotten day—". . . sitting down they watched him there"—but the things that were *not* seen are infinitely and eternally more important than the things that were seen. They saw all the procedure of a common execution; soldiers, nails, a cross, the inscription written in Greek, Hebrew and Latin (for all the world to read): "JESUS OF NAZARETH THE KING OF THE JEWS" (John 19:19). The Sufferer has already hung for three hours on the nails—He is utterly in the hands of His crucifiers—it is man's doing, man's satisfaction, man's cross.

But at 12 o'clock the scene changes—**Darkness!** From now on man's cross of hate becomes God's Cross of "wisdom and power unto salvation." Although man pronounced the death sentence—and that "this man must die," Heaven and earth and Hell agreed—but, had earth and Hell but known, it was not possible to put **the Resurrection** to death (He laid down His life), so God took the Cross out of their hands—it now becomes *God's* place of execution—the execution of *judgment* against Sin; and the One hanging there, though sinless, is struck with the full lightning bolt of God's wrath.

Why should He be smitten, He has no sin? But—yes, He has, the Sinless One *became Sin,* and it is *Sin* that God is dealing with in judgment; therefore, the One upon the Cross receives the full stroke of its fury for He has taken upon Himself, voluntarily and vicariously, "the Sins of the World."

The Cross is now "God's Altar," where the Lamb must lay down His spotless life, a perfect and eternal sacrifice. "Without the shedding of blood"—without the life of an innocent victim being "given" in substitution for the guilty—"there can be no remission of sin."

"The Wages of Sin is Death," physical and spiritual death. Physical death is the separation of the soul from the body—Spiritual death is the eternal separation of the soul from God—that is the penalty of Sin—that is Hell—that is the death that Christ, man's substitute, must die before He can cry, **"It is finished."** He, who had just declared, "I and my Father are one," now cries, "My God why have you forsaken me?" How can we reconcile this paradox? What does this cry of abandonment mean?

It means that the God-man is now "as Man" dying Man's death. He has voluntarily allowed the veil of outer darkness to be drawn between the Glory of His Deity and His suffering humanity—leaving His human soul abandoned—separated—cut off. The cry, "My God why?" is the cry of a lost, forsaken soul tasting "spiritual death" for every man.

An **eternity** of utter abandonment is pressed into that one cry of a moment—for John, the revelator, declares, ". . . the smoke of their torment [the cry of the lost] ascendeth up for ever and ever . . ." (Revelation 14:10).

The wrath of God has broken over the soul of our Substitute—the claims of Divine Justice have been met—the price of Man's Pardon has been "paid in full." The veil of separation, which is spiritual death, has been withdrawn—the darkness passes and the Redeemer cries with a voice of triumph, **"It is finished."** And now—and not until now—He may bow His head and lay down His **physical life**—the purpose of the Cross has been accomplished, and we are brought to the realization that the real battleground was far removed from the eyes of men and the scene of earth and the physical cross. The triumphant cry, "It is finished," did not mean "physical death," the result of nails and spear and crucifixion; for no man could take His life—He laid it down. "It is finished" was the triumphant proclamation to a guilty world that Christ, our Substitute, had tasted SPIRITUAL DEATH, the penalty of Sin—once and for all—"That whosoever believeth in him shall not perish [shall not have to taste spiritual death] but have eternal life (John 3:15).

The truth that the cry, "It is finished," did not mean His physical death—but our spiritual death—is clearly revealed in the fact that "before" the darkness He was **not abandoned;** He was still in communion with Heaven, for He said, "Father, forgive them. . . ." But "during" the darkness **He was abandoned**—separated—cut off—no longer in communion with the Father—He is now paying the penalty of Sin— tasting death for every man, and He cries the cry of abandonment, "My God why . . . ?" "After" the darkness passes He cries, "It is finished" —He is no longer separated—He is again in communion with Heaven, crying, "Father, into thy hands I commend my spirit, . . ." and bowing His head, "he gave up the ghost" (Luke 23:46).

True, we cannot forget the suffering He received at the hands of wicked men; much has been written of what they did. They mocked Him, scourged Him, nailed and pierced Him—but the positive, powerful, Eternal Triumph of Calvary is **not what they did—but what He did:**

He offered Himself without spot to God.
He gave Himself for His own.
He laid down His life.
He poured out His Soul unto Death.
He dismissed His Spirit.
He declared, "the prince of this world is judged."
He cried with a loud voice, "It is finished."
He triumphed over all.

The Descent from the Cross

The Jews therefore, because it was the preparation, that the bodies should not remain upon the cross on the sabbath day, . . . besought Pilate that their legs might be broken, and that they might be taken away. . . . But when they came to Jesus, and saw that he was dead already, they brake not his legs. (John 19:31-33.)

Thus did they unconsciously fulfill and preserve the symbolism of the Paschal Lamb, of which Jesus, "the Lamb of God," was the anti-type. ". . . neither shall ye break a bone thereof" (Exodus 12:46).

Then took they the body of Jesus, and wound it in linen clothes, . . . as the manner of Jews is to bury. (John 19:40.)

The body of Jesus was taken down from Calvary's tree before sunset to meet the law of Deuteronomy 21:22-23: "And if a man have committed a sin worthy of death, . . . and thou hang him on a tree: His body shall not remain all night upon the tree, but thou shalt in any wise bury him that day; (for he that is hanged is accursed of God). . . ."

Christ hath redeemed us from the curse of the law, being made a curse for us: for it is written, Cursed is every one that hangeth on a tree. (Galatians 3:13.)

The Resurrection (Matthew 28)

Volumes have been written of the miraculous Birth of Christ, His miraculous Works and Resurrection, but the miracle of miracles is the miraculous **Death of Christ.** He who is the Resurrection—"who was, and is, and ever shall be"—the self-existent One, without beginning and without ending—Uncreated and Eternal life—*actually dies,* and dies the death of a lost, guilty Soul. Surely this is the most amazing miracle of all. That by His own Sovereign Will—the Author and Sustainer of life should reverse the very nature of His being—Eternal life to become Eternal death—that the claims of His own Eternal Justice might be met —is the marvel of the ages.

It was no marvel that He should rise again—for it is written, "it was not *possible* that he should be holden of it [death]" (Acts 2:24). We speak of the Resurrection as an "event"—but Jesus said, "I *am* the resurrection . . ." (John 11:25), and when He came forth on the third day, as He declared He would, it was the Victor returning with the spoils of battle, ". . . the Keys of hell and of death." "He arose a Victor from the dark domain and lives forever with His saints to reign!"

". . . the first begotten of the dead, . . . him that loved us, and washed us . . . in his own blood, And hath made us kings and priests unto God and his Father . . ." (Revelation 1:5-6).

During the forty days between the Resurrection and the Ascension, the Risen Christ was seen by many witnesses. Ten appearances of Jesus after His Resurrection are recorded or referred to; five on the day of Resurrection. During these appearances Christ taught His disciples concerning the Kingdom, and gave them the great commission to "Go . . . and teach all nations . . . ," with the assuring promise of His abiding presence ". . . unto the end of the world" (Matthew 28:19-20).

The Ascension

When He was ready to return to the Glory World from whence He came, He led them out to the Mount of Olives, where He gave them their last instructions and the promise of power from on high to carry on and accomplish their mission.

The story of the Ascension of our Lord could not possibly be told more beautifully, or more dramatically than by Luke, the writer of the Book of Acts:

> . . . being assembled together with them, commanded them that they should not depart from Jerusalem, but wait for the promise of the Father. . . . ye shall receive power, after that the Holy Ghost is come upon you: and ye shall be witnesses . . . unto the uttermost part of the earth. And when he had spoken these things, while they beheld, he was taken up; and a cloud received him out of their sight. . . . And while they looked stedfastly toward heaven as he went up, behold, two men stood by them in white apparel; Which also said, Ye men of Galilee, why stand ye gazing up into heaven? this same Jesus, which is taken up from you into heaven, shall so come in like manner as ye have seen him go into heaven. (Acts 1:1-11.)

The Dispensation of Law ended in the Judgment of Sin, on the Cross at Calvary. **"There is therefore now no condemnation to them which are in Christ Jesus . . ." (Romans 8:1).**

GRACE

THE DISPENSATION OF THE HOLY GHOST
(THE CHURCH AGE)
EPH 3:1-12

DESCENT
OF THE
HOLY SPIRIT
ACTS 2:1-21

I COR 11:23-26

PENTECOST

THE
LAST
DAYS

EARLY
CHURCH
FATHERS

GAL
3:29

APOSTOLIC
PERIOD

CONSTANTINE
EMBRACES
CHRISTIANITY
UNITES CHURCH
AND STATE
325 A.D.

THE
DARK
AGES

THE JUST
SHALL LIVE
BY FAITH

THE
REFORMATION
1500-1650

THE
GREAT
PERIOD OF
WORLD WIDE
EVANGELISM
"WHOSOEVER WILL
MAY COME"

BOR
AGA
BELIE

MATT 24:36-3

... THE DISPENSATION OF THE HOLY SPIRIT ...
FROM PENTECOST UNTIL THE "TRANSLATION"
OF THE TRUE CHURCH "THE CHURCH OF THE
FIRSTBORN WRITTEN IN HEAVEN" HEB 12:23

THE FIRST RESURRECTIC

DESCENT AND DISPENSATION OF THE HOLY SPIRIT

2ND COMING

ACTS OF THE APOSTLES

MATT Chaps 24-25

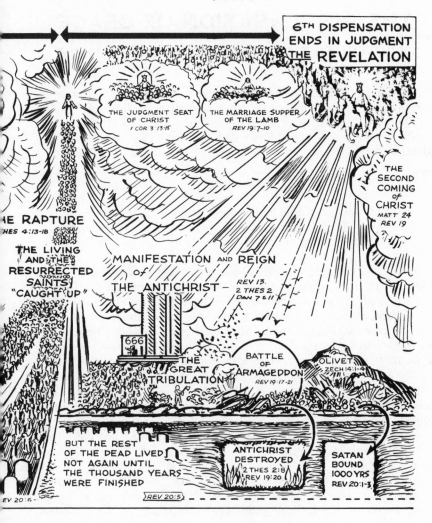

6TH DISPENSATION
ENDS IN JUDGMENT
THE REVELATION

THE JUDGMENT SEAT
OF CHRIST
1 COR 3:13-15

THE MARRIAGE SUPPER
OF THE LAMB
REV 19:7-10

THE
SECOND
COMING
of
CHRIST
MATT 24
REV 19

HE RAPTURE
THES 4:13-18

THE LIVING
AND THE
RESURRECTED
SAINTS
"CAUGHT UP"

MANIFESTATION AND REIGN
of
THE ANTICHRIST —

REV 13.
2 THES 2
DAN 7 & 11

666

THE
GREAT
TRIBULATION

BATTLE
OF
ARMAGEDDON
REV 19:17-21

OLIVET
ZECH 14:1-4

BUT THE REST
OF THE DEAD LIVED
NOT AGAIN UNTIL
THE THOUSAND YEARS
WERE FINISHED

ANTICHRIST
DESTROYED
2 THES 2:8
REV 19:20

SATAN
BOUND
1000 YRS
REV 20:1-3

EV 20:6

REV 20:5

HE RAPTURE • ANTICHRIST • TRIBULATION •

OF CHRIST

THESS 4:13-18   DANIEL AND REVELATION

THE DISPENSATION OF GRACE

FROM PENTECOST TO THE SECOND COMING OF CHRIST

WITH THE Death and Resurrection of our Lord begins the "Dispensation of Grace"—the present and personal ministry of the Holy Spirit—the "Church Age," symbolized by the "Table of Holy Communion"—for ". . . as often as ye eat this bread, and drink this cup, ye do shew [declare] the Lord's death till he come" (I Corinthians 11:23-26).

Pentecost

And, behold, I send the promise of my Father upon you: but tarry ye in . . . Jerusalem, until ye be endued with power from on high. (Luke 24:49.)

After the Ascension of the Saviour, the disciples returned to Jerusalem, as He had instructed them, to await the promise of the Father. One hundred and twenty souls seems to have been the entire assembly of believing converts who gathered in humble prayer and unity until the day of Pentecost, the fiftieth day after the Resurrection of Christ, when the Holy Spirit was poured out upon the infant Church—"And suddenly there came a sound from heaven as of a rushing mighty wind. . . . And they were all filled with the Holy Ghost . . ." (Acts 2:2, 4).

The Holy Spirit descended in answer to the explicit promise of the ascended, glorified Christ—". . . he shall give you another comforter" (Greek, *paraclete:* "advocate, counselor, called to one's side") clearly denoting the existence of the third person of the Godhead, and His direct and twofold ministry of "comfort" and of "power." Sent from Heaven, upon Christ's departure from earth, to occupy the place of Christ's physical presence, that He may make vital and actual Christ's spiritual presence, reproving the world of Sin, of Righteousness, and of Judgment. Pentecost marked the founding, or birthday of the Christian Church as a militant, witnessing, living organism, receiving its essential life from direct communion with its living Head and Lord. The outpouring of the Holy Ghost completely changed the minds, the hearts and the lives of the feeble but faithful band of believers in whom the Holy Spirit took up His abode as an abiding presence; to teach them "all truth"; to bring to their remembrance past revelations; and to shew them "things to come"; that through them Christ's mighty works should continue, to the glory of God (John 14:16; 16:7-15; Acts 5:12-16).

The Apostolic Church

While Christ's ministry was confined to a limited portion of Palestine, He made it clear that the scope of His vision was world-wide. Pentecost marked the dividing line between the personal, but geographically limited ministry of our Lord; and the dispensation of the Holy Spirit, with its multiplied channels—". . . as many as the Lord our God shall call" (Acts 2:39)—yielded to the same supernatural power, to accomplish the same eternal purpose, ". . . that the Father may be glorified. . . ."

May we remember that our Lord accomplished His earthly mission of living, teaching and dying, before the New Testament Scriptures, which we possess, were ever written. The Son of God came down from Heaven; proclaimed the glad tidings of Salvation; called and trained His disciples; breathed upon them the earnest of the outpouring of His Spirit, and went back to Heaven without leaving any written instructions or directions. He opened His mouth and taught them, and promised them the gift of the Holy Ghost, who would bring to their remembrance "all things" that He had spoken unto them (John 14:26).

Thus, the heritage that the Christ of Christianity left to the world was not a highly organized institution, or an elaborate priesthood of ecclesiastical trappings (ornaments, dress, superficial decorations); or volumes of written rules or dogmas—but a small handful of disciples (weak and imperfect vessels, until they received "power from on high") whom Christ Himself prepared to carry on the work that He came to set in motion.

Going forth with holy boldness and sublime faith, and, like their Master (Luke 4:1) ". . . being full of the Holy Ghost . . . ," in the short period of thirty years these first preachers of the Gospel, gathering converts to the growing cause of Christ as they went, shook the powerful, pagan Roman Empire, and kindled a Gospel flame from the center to the circumference of the known world, until even those in violent opposition declared of them, "These that have turned the world upside down . . ." (Acts 17:6).

This was called the "Oral Period" of propagating the Gospel; telling with their own lips and lives the story and purpose of Christ's Life, Death, Resurrection and Ascension, out of their own experience and knowledge as eyewitnesses of the truth. The "Oral Period" has been roughly placed between 30 and 50 A.D. The "Writing Period" between 50 and 100 A.D. The collecting of writings of the New Testament between 100 and 150 A.D.

The Apostolic Fathers

The early Church "fathers" were so named for their learning and piety, and for laying the foundation for theological literature. They were the immediate disciples of the Apostles (who were eyewitnesses) as the Apostles were the immediate disciples of the Master Himself. Their teaching and writings, so near the dawn of Christianity, gave them special importance as early witnesses of ". . . the faith . . . once delivered unto the saints (Jude 1:3).

The Pre-Millennial Coming of Christ

The Prophets of God in all ages have foreseen and foretold of a glorious age when universal righteousness shall triumph in the earth, and "The Kingdom of God" shall be established in visible glory. A time that shall be marked by the return of the earth's rightful King to gather in the final harvest of His Redeeming Grace, and to consummate the Father's eternal plan and purpose in the "Redeemed."

The Christians of the Apostolic Age, and of the early centuries of the Church, had no other view than that of Christ's Second Advent to usher in an era of universal righteousness. The oral witnessing of the Apostles, their later writings, and those of the Church fathers, were impregnated with the hope of Christ's imminent returning and called for vigilance, expectancy and preparedness.

The Apocalypse, "the revelation" or "unveiling" of Jesus, written by John twenty-six years after the destruction of Jerusalem, came as a conclusive testimony confirming the Prophets, and specifying the duration of "the Golden Age" to which their hopes aspired. Six times it is designated as "a thousand years," or millennium. Our word "millennium" comes from the Latin *mille,* "a thousand"; *annus,* "a year." The Greek word for "thousand" is *chilioi* (kil-i-oi)—thus, the early believers were called "Chiliasts" (kil-i-asts). These early Christians believed that the Lord's return would precede the Millennium; in fact there could be no millennium of peace and righteousness until Christ, "the seed of the woman," should first come to "bruise the serpent's head," and to consummate His redemptive work.

In the third century, Origen, one of the Church fathers, conceived the system of "allegorizing" or "spiritualizing" the interpretation of Scripture. This erroneous system of interpretation led to a rapid decline of spiritual vision and vigilance; together with the unholy union of Church and State under the Roman Emperor Constantine, who, although being instrumental in ending the diabolical persecution of Christians, influenced the Church into the beginning of its darkest hour of apostasy. John Wesley declared, "Constantine, calling himself a Christian and pouring a flood of wealth and honors upon the Church, particularly upon the Clergy, was productive of more evil to the Church than all of the persecutions put together."

With the gradual rise of Papal power, the avowed enemy of Chiliasm, failing to expunge the Book of Revelation from the Bible, it became a

sealed Book, and the era of torture, death and devilish darkness is now
a horrible page in the annals of history.

During "the dark ages" multitudes of "light-holders" were slain, but
the "light" could not be extinguished. A remnant of true believers dared
to preserve and propagate "the faith once delivered unto the saints."
The Reformation of the sixteenth century was, next to the early Apostolic Age, the most vital part of the history of the Christian Church. It
was a revival of Primitive Christian Faith against the tyranny of ecclesiastical corruption and the sinister influence of fear. Its protest gave
birth to "Protestantism," the beginning of the great evangelical move-
ments which again revealed the way of "Salvation by Faith"; and the
hope of the Coming of the Lord again became the inspiration of believing hearts; though during "the darkness before the dawn" millions
sealed their testimony with their blood.

The importance of the revelation of Christ's Second Advent is seen
in the fact that there is scarcely a prophecy in the Old Testament that
does not in some way bear upon the coming Kingdom and the promised
Messiah. In the New Testament it is mentioned 318 times, and it has
been declared by count and confirmation that one verse in twenty-five
makes direct or indirect reference to Christ's Second Coming and glorious presence on the earth in "the latter day."

The age in which we live—"the Church Age"—"the Dispensation of
the Holy Spirit"—began with the Birthday of the Church on the day
of Pentecost, and will end with the Translation, or Rapture of the
Church at the literal, visible, personal returning of the Lord Jesus
Christ (I Thessalonians 4:16-17). The verb "translate," as used twice
in Hebrews 11:5, has the sense of removing (transferring) one from
the earthly to the heavenly state without the intervening experience of
death (Hebrews 11:5).

In the portion of Paul's immortal chapter on the Resurrection (I
Corinthians 15:51-57, and in I Thessalonians 4:13-18), the Apostle
gives us a clear, complete and comforting description of the twofold
character of the one glorious event, namely, the Translation, or Rapture of ". . . the church of the first born, . . . written in heaven . . ."
(Hebrews 12:23). The resurrected dead "in Christ," and the living,
ready, born-again believing saints (without experiencing death) shall
be ". . . caught up together . . ." to meet their descending Lord
". . . in the air. . . ." In I Thessalonians 4:17, the Greek word
harpazo, which is translated "caught up," means "to snatch away." The
suddenness of the "catching away" is described by Paul as "In a moment, in the twinkling of an eye . . ." (I Corinthians 15:52), and in
the solemn words of our Lord, "As the lightning . . . so shall also the
coming of the Son of man be" (Matthew 24:27); and again, in the
words of Luke, "I tell you"—two shall be in a bed—two grinding at

the mill—two in the field—". . . the one shall be taken, and the other shall be left" (Luke 17:34-36).

The word "rapture" is not found in the Scriptures, but is used as a very significant expression of the nature of the event. Webster says "rapture" is "the fact of being transported"; and "a manifestation of ecstasy." Surely every expectant believer can say Amen! to Mr. Webster. Thus, "the Church of the firstborn," (born-again believers) shall be "caught up" that it might escape ". . . those things which are coming on the earth . . .". (Luke 21:26, 34-36), to be in attendance at the heavenly events, namely, "the Judgment Seat of Christ," and "the Marriage of the Lamb," just prior to Christ's returning to the earth ". . . with power and great glory" (Matthew 24:30).

In Christ's Discourses and Parables there is the constant admonition, "Keep watch," "Be ye therefore ready also: for the Son of man cometh at an hour when ye think not." Foretelling of His Second Coming, as recorded in Luke 17:22-37, Christ concluded with the solemn warning "Remember Lot's wife." The Divine command was "Escape with thy life; look not behind thee." Lot's wife did not go back to the condemned city; she obeyed in everything but the one command—she "looked back" —and in so doing missed "the catching away," the providential "escape."

Perhaps the question **"What becomes of those left behind?"** could best be answered by the perplexity of the rapt Apostle, John, when, in the apocalyptic vision, he beheld a great multitude ". . . clothed with white robes, and palms in their hands"—the Elder solved his mental questionings, and surely we should be satisfied with his answer, "These are they which *came out* of great tribulation, and have washed their robes, and made them white in the blood of the Lamb" (Revelation 7:13-14). That this company of white-robed palm-bearers "came out" of the great tribulation, they must, of necessity, have been upon the earth at the time of the manifestation of the Antichrist; caught in the snare of unpreparedness and consequently "left," when the translation of those "accounted worthy to escape these things" took place.

In spite of the constant forewarning that ". . . the day of the Lord so cometh as a thief . . ." (unannounced and unexpected) ". . . as a snare . . . on all them that dwell on the face of the whole earth" (Luke 21:35); a great multitude, not of the completely unregenerate only, but of the professing Church, will be overtaken by the pent-up fury of tribulation and judgment.

The Judgment Seat of Christ (The bema— II Corinthians 5:5-10)

". . . we must all appear before the judgment seat of Christ; . . . according to that he hath done, whether it be good or bad" (II Corinthians 5:10). This is judgment of the believer's works, not sins. The believer's judgment for sin is already passed; Jesus "bare our sins in his own body" on the cross—to be remembered against us no more forever; but every work must come into judgment. We must *all* appear; the pronoun "we" occurs twenty-six times in II Corinthians 5 and in every instance it means "the believer." The epistle was written "to the Saints at Corinth."

It is not a judgment based on "innocence" or "guilt"; it is for "the redeemed" only—those who have built upon the one foundation, Jesus Christ (I Corinthians 3:11-15). The Redeemed do not earn their redemption, it is a gift of God; but after being redeemed, the faithful and the overcomers receive rewards for service "well done." Some, evidently, will receive little reward, others great. Some will be saved "as by fire," others will have an abundant entrance. Every man's work will be manifest; the worthless works are represented as "wood, hay, and stubble" which will be consumed. There is much that passes for Christian service that is merely human effort, often prompted by self-righteousness, or even self-aggrandizement. Only the good and lasting works —even the "cup of cold water" given in humble devotion "as unto him," shall remain and receive its eternal reward.

The Marriage of the Lamb (Revelation 19)

The Marriage, of which no details are given, is a heavenly event taking place on the eve of Christ's returning to the earth to rule and to reign in righteousness. The Bridegroom is the Lamb, the Redeemer who ". . . loved the church, and gave himself for it" (Ephesians 5:25); the Beloved Son made incarnate for our salvation, and, in His twofold nature, now exalted, glorified and enthroned (Philemon 2:9).

In the Old Testament, Israel was the wife of Jehovah, but was repudiated (cast off as a wife) because of her unfaithfulness (Jeremiah 3; Hosea 2 and 3; Ezekiel 16); to be restored, however, forgiven, and identified with God's earthly glory in Christ Jesus (Ezekiel 36:17-36). In the New Testament, the Church is the Bride of Christ. The Marriage of the Lamb, the blessed and joyous consummation of God's purpose "in the beloved"; the most longed-for and looked-for event of the ages —is Christ, in the character of the Lamb, gloriously acknowledging and taking unto Himself, as co-heirs of His Throne, of His Dominion, and of His Glory, all those chosen ones who have been faithful in their betrothal. Paul speaks of those whom he begat in the Gospel as ". . . espoused . . . to one husband . . . ," whom he desired ". . . to present . . . as a chaste virgin to Christ" (II Corinthians 11:2)—now as the Lamb's Bride to reign with Him and to share His blessed inheritance forever.

This glorious event is the everlasting consummation of the Divine purpose **of this present age.** With the outpouring of the Holy Spirit at

Pentecost, the Counsel at Jerusalem announced that ". . . God at first [literally, for the first time] did visit the Gentiles, **to take out of them a people for his name**" (Acts 15:14). The "taking out of a people" is distinctly the work and purpose of the "Church Age." The mystery, ". . . which in other ages was not made known unto the sons of men . . ." (Ephesians 3). The Church is the "ecclesia," the "called out ones," the Bride of which Christ is the Bridegroom (Ephesians 25:27); the Body of which Christ is the Head (Ephesians 1:20-23); the New Creation of which Christ is the Firstfruits (I Corinthians 15:23; II Corinthians 5:17).

The out-calling of the Church, an assembly of hell-deserving sinners, "redeemed by the Blood of the Lamb," to be unto Him "a name" and a praise and a glory, will be the eternal manifestation of the infinite Grace of God, "That in the ages to come he might shew the exceeding riches of his grace in his loving kindness toward us through Christ Jesus" (Ephesians 2:7). For love He gave Himself for the Church, in love He is, even now, sanctifying the Church, and the great love affair is joyously consummated when He shall present the Church unto Himself in His own righteousness and flawless perfection—". . . a glorious church, not having spot, or wrinkle, or any such thing; but that it should be holy and without blemish" (Ephesians 5:25-27).

The Manifestation of the Antichrist

For the mystery of iniquity doth already work: only he who now letteth will let, until he be taken out of the way. And then *shall that Wicked be revealed. . . . (II Thessalonians 2:1-12.)*

Literally: He that hindereth the revelation of the Antichrist, will continue to hinder until he be removed. Then shall that Lawless One be manifested.

Paul made it clear that the consummation of Satan's program and purpose in the earth has been held in restraint until God's appointed time, and only by the removal of the restrainer can Satan's man of the hour, "that Wicked," that ". . . man of sin . . . , the son of perdition; Who opposeth and exalteth himself above all that is called God, . . . shewing himself that he *is God*" (II Thessalonians 2:3-4)—be removed. (This sinister world-power is personified as "the Beast" in Revelation 13.)

The Church, as "the salt of the earth," "the light of the world," is a great restraining influence in this corrupt and lawless world, but an "influence" would not be adequate to hold back the forces of evil; the indwelling Spirit of God, the third person of the blessed Trinity, is the empowering, personal presence that hinders the program and purpose of Satan in this age. **The Holy Spirit** is resident within the Church, the body of born-again believers who are, indeed, the "Temple of the Holy Ghost." Thus, when the Church is translated, the restraint or "hindering" will cease, by God's permissive Will, and "that Wicked" shall be revealed. The Translation of the Church does not mean that the operative ministry of the Holy Spirit will no longer be effective, for "the end is not yet." The Holy Spirit, the third person of the Trinity, is omnipresent and operative in the **eternal** plan and purpose of the Godhead.

With the manifestation of the Antichrist, soon to dominate the world scene, ominous clouds begin to gather that portent a time of unparalleled trouble for those left upon the earth, namely:

(1) The Jewish Nation—individual Jews who have accepted Jesus Christ as their Messiah and Redeemer become "New Creatures," members of the Body of Christ, in which there is neither Jew nor Gentile, but "all" one in Christ Jesus (Galatians 3:28).

(2) The Gentile Nations, or all unregenerate humanity (unregenerate, "not renewed in heart; remaining at enmity with God"), or, as designated in the Scriptures, ". . . them that know not God, and that obey not the gospel of the Lord Jesus Christ" (II Thessalonians 1:8). The same holds true, that individual Gentiles accepting Jesus Christ as Saviour and Lord will be "caught up together" with all born-again believers, before the Antichrist is revealed (Revelation 3:10).

From God's viewpoint there are only three classes, or divisions, that make up the whole of humanity: **Jews, Gentiles, and "the Church of the firstborn."** Or, in the final analysis: the Saved and the Unsaved, the Regenerated and the Unregenerated, the Redeemed and the Unredeemed. Thus, when the Church (a people taken out, from among both Jews and Gentiles, "for his name") is removed from the earthly scene, Israel and the Gentile Nations remain to be further dealt with, particularly in their relationship to the coming millennium of peace and righteousness in the earth.

The Great Tribulation

For then shall be great tribulation, such as was not since the beginning of the world to this time, no, nor ever shall be. And except those days should be shortened, there should no flesh be saved: but for the elect's sake those days shall be shortened. (Matthew 24:21-22; Daniel 12:1.)

Throughout the Scriptures, both Old and New, a period of unprecedented tribulation, in the nature of wrath, judgment, and Divine indignation before the end-time glory, is foreseen and foretold and repeatedly referred to as "the day of the Lord," or, "the day of Jehovah"—also referred to, seventy-five times in the Old Testament, as "that day" or "the great day." These passages, prophetic in nature, all "tell forth" of a consummate period of God's dealing with ". . . them that dwell [remain living] on the face of the whole earth" (Luke 21:35), after taking out a people "for his name" (Acts 15:14).

> *Because thou hast kept the word of my patience, I also will keep thee from the hour of temptation [trial], which shall come upon all the world, to try them that dwell upon the earth. (Revelation 3:10.)*

The Spirit of God alone could have guided John the revelator to use the exact language in keeping with the meaning and "the blessed hope" of the entire context. He uses the verb *tereso* ("will keep"), and the preposition *ek* ("from"), and *ek tes horas* ("from the hour"); that is, kept "from" the specific period of trial alluded to. Although "the Great Tribulation" is unescapably the outpouring of the wrath, enmity and hate of Satan and his unholy stooges upon Israel, and subsequently upon all who refuse to submit to his blasphemous claims, it is permissible only as God uses these instruments to execute His own judgments.

First to bring Israel to the place of utter dependence, recognition and acceptance of her long-rejected Messiah, and to prepare a sealed and saved remnant (Revelation 7:4-8) in whom all of the unfulfilled Covenant promises and millennial blessings will be fulfilled (Deuteronomy 1:10; Ezekiel 20:37-38; 37:1-14; Zechariah 12:9-10; 13:9).

God's judgment, and the numerous prophecies concerning the Gentile Nations, will also come to fulfillment in the Great Tribulation period and be consummated at the Coming of Christ "in power and great glory." With no righteous restraint left upon the earth, by the deceptive powers of Satanic agencies working with him (II Thessalonians 2:9), the manifested "Lawless One," the Antichrist, will soon dominate the minds and hearts of all that are subservient to him. Absolute authority will be given him, even to the control of buying and selling, the essential conditions of existence, until he will demand and receive Divine homage (Revelation 13 and 14). Multitudes who refuse to worship him and submit to his edicts will meet death by martyrdom (Revelation 20:4). The unregenerate and deluded world will acclaim him until the mask is dropped and he is revealed as the very embodiment of evil, tyranny and blasphemy. His short but diabolical reign will be brought to a climax of hate and bloodshed at the great gathering of the combined Armies of the Kings of the earth, under his deceptive dominion, to Palestine.

Armageddon

The Translation of the Church and the heavenly events that attend it are followed in terrible contrast by the treading of ". . . the wine-press of . . . the wrath of Almighty God," a scene of battle and blasphemy even now in preparation upon the earth. "And he [God] gathered them together into a place called in the Hebrew . . . Armageddon" (Revelation 16:13-16). "He" gathered them. It is God Almighty, in righteous retribution, who gathers them to this place of Judicial Judgment, employing the very Satanic trinity itself to carry out the Divine purpose. ". . . to gather them to the battle of that great day of God Almighty" (Revelation 16:14).

(1) The Dragon; that old serpent, the Devil (Revelation 12:9), the activating power behind the monstrous conspiracy of "War" against God and His Christ.

(2) The Beast; "the man of sin," "that Wicked," the Antichrist, the blasphemous leader of the last man-made, devil-inspired world-system (Revelation 13:1-10; II Thessalonians 2:2-13).

(3) The False Prophet (Revelation 13:11-18); who, by his deceptive propaganda, miraculous signs and lying wonders will cause the whole world (the Church having been taken out of the world) to worship the Beast, who, by the energetic campaign of his "ecclesiastical running mate," the False Prophet, will set himself up as very God (II Thessalonians 2:4). It has been well said, "The Dragon is Anti-God—the Beast will be Anti-Christ—the False Prophet Anti-Spirit." A Trinity of Hell!

And I saw the beast, and the kings of the earth, and their armies, gathered together to make war. . . . (Revelation 19:19.)

The greatest combination of the powers of Earth and Hell ever witnessed is gathered ". . . to the battle of that great day of God Almighty" (Revelation 16:12-16; 19:11-21). The nations, particularly those of the north (Ezekiel 38:15-16) and of the east (Revelation 16:12), seek first the total destruction of the Jewish nation (even now politically restored as the sovereign state of "Israeli"). This time of unprecedented persecution and wholesale slaughter of Israel is referred to in the prophetic Scriptures as ". . . the time of Jacob's trouble . . ." (Jeremiah 30:7; Isaiah 10:20-27; Zechariah 14:1-2). The result of the tyrannical onslaught (from which, evidently, only one-third of the nation escape) is tragically described in Zechariah 13:8-9. This invasion of Palestine, protested by freedom-loving nations (Ezekiel 38:13), is foretold in amazing detail in Ezekiel 38, 39.

All of this, however, is but the beginning of the great gathering at Armageddon in preparation for the boldest, maddest battle ever conceived in the minds of all the devil-inspired armies in history. **War against God and His Christ!** Take note again who is engaged in the battle. The Beast, acclaimed by the world as its invincible leader, with the combined armies of the Kings of the Earth (Revelation 16:14; 17:12-14). Their opponent—He that sitteth upon the white horse and His armies which were with Him in Heaven (Revelation 19:11-16). Should the question be asked "How did these armies get to Heaven, to accompany their descending Warrior-King?" the answer is, "Like all armies, they are mobilized"; the trumpet shall sound, the dead in Christ shall rise first, and the living, ready ones shall be "caught up" together with them, ever to be with the Lord (I Thessalonians 4:16-17).

This war, unlike all others, is not an array of nation against nation, race against race—but the gathering climax of the God-declared "enmity" of Genesis 3:15. "The seed of the serpent"—Antichrist and his armies—and "the seed of the woman"—Christ and those that are His.

The result of the battle is clearly determined. The Sovereignty of the earth, already declared in the mind and purpose of God (Luke 1:32; Daniel 7:14; Psalm 2; Psalm 72; Isaiah 9:7; I Timothy 6:15), is to be settled forever before three worlds, Heaven, Earth and Hell, by the complete overthrow of Satan's power and dominion, and the establishment of the Universal Kingdom of God and His chosen, already appointed King (Psalm 2:6; Daniel 7:13-14). No details of the battle are given—for there is no battle. We are simply told that ". . . the Lamb shall overcome them . . ." (Revelation 17:14); ". . . whom the Lord shall consume with . . . the brightness of his coming" (II Thessalonians 2:8). The word *parousia*, translated "coming," denotes personal presence, the literal, bodily reappearing of Christ. The word *epiphaneia*, translated "brightness," is, literally, "appearing." Emphasizing the truth that Christ will actually appear, be seen, and His glory manifested. ". . . out of his mouth goeth a sharp sword, that with it he should smite the nations . . ."; and the fowls of the air shall eat the flesh of kings, and their smitten armies (Revelation 19:15-18; Jeremiah 25:33).

The Binding of Satan

And I saw an angel come down from heaven, having the key of the bottomless pit and a great chain. . . . laid hold on the dragon, that old serpent, which is the Devil, and Satan, and bound him a thousand years, And cast him into the bottomless pit. . . . (Revelation 20:1-3.)

In the Authorized Version, the Greek word *abyssos* is rendered "the bottomless pit"; in the Revised Standard Version, it is rendered "abyss"; in Revelation, *abyssos* denotes the abode of evil spirits, but not final punishment; therefore it is to be distinguished from the "lake of fire" to which the Beast and the False Prophet are consigned, and in which the Devil will meet his final doom.

There is no mistaking the identity of the Dragon; he is declared, in the above passage, "the Devil and Satan" (*i.e.,* the Adversary). The word "devil" is not used of Satan in the Old Testament; it is *Abaddon* in Hebrew, *Apollyon* in Greek; that is, "destroyer"—the real instigator of the second daring, direct and open rebellion against the Almighty (already under sentence for the first unholy insurrection: ". . . thou shall be brought down to hell, to the sides of the pit" (Isaiah 14:12-17).

He is now "laid hold upon" (*ekratese*—the word denotes "quick seizure" by strength or force), for although Satan is a malignant "spirit," he is a personal devil. The key and the chain by which he is bound (even if, or though, symbolical) signify the sovereignty of God over the denizens of the pit and the nether regions. By one Angel (many eminent Bible scholars believe that this mighty Angel is no other than the Lord Jesus Christ Himself) the Devil is bound and cast into the "abyss." The other two members of the Satanic trinity are cast directly into "the lake of fire," Hell, the final Gehenna, the place of the eternally damned, into which none have yet entered (except these two in their appointed time), until the final judgment of the wicked dead at the Great White Throne (Revelation 19:20; 20:11-15).

With the eternal destruction of Satan's chief emissaries, the leaders of earth's deluded, God-defiant hosts, Satan, the malignant master-mind (bent on thwarting "the seed of the woman" from becoming "King of all the earth"), is seized and bound and cast into the pit, which is "sealed over him" (Revelation 20:3, RSV). **Thus ends the present world system.** The end of all *human* government with its misrule and maladministration. For no matter what "the label" may say, the Devil is the sinister power behind the scenes manipulating the strings, until, even in the "last days," noble-minded but deluded men shall cry "peace and safety"; but as we have seen in the unfolding panorama of the apocalyptic vision, ". . . then sudden destruction cometh upon them . . ." (I Thessalonians 5:3).

Watch ye therefore, and pray always, that ye may be accounted worthy to escape all these things that shall come to pass, and to stand before the Son of man. (Luke 21:36.)

KINGDOM

7TH DISPENSAT
ENDS IN THE
FINAL JUDGM

. REV 20:11-15

REV 1:5-6   I TIM 6:15   REV 11:15

KING OF KINGS AND LORD OF LORDS

THE MILLENNIAL
REIGN OF CHRIST
REV 20:6

FIRE FROM HEAVEN
CONSUMES THE ARMI
OF GOG AND MAGOG
REV 20:7-9

JUDGMENT
OF THE
LIVING NATIONS
MATT 25:31-46

HOLINESS
UNTO THE LORD

ISRAEL ZECH 8:23

ISA 11:6-9 · AMOS 9:13   JOEL 3:18   ISA 35:1
ZECH 14:9 · JER 25:5 · LUKE 1:32-33 · PS 98:9 · ISA 2:3 · ZECH 14:20-21
MICAH 4:1-4 · ISA 65:19-25 · REV 20:1-6 · ISA 25:7-9 · 2 TIM 2:11-12

SATAN
LOOSE
AFTER TH
1000 YRS
REV 20:7

MILLENNIUM (LATIN) MEANING 1000 YEARS

CHRIST REIGNING WITH HIS SAINTS

• NEW HEAVENS AN

2 TIM 2:12 · REV 5:10 - 20:6 ·   ESCHATOLOGY (THE STUDY OF LAST THING

— (MESSIANIC)

(ETERNAL AGES →   STUDY 11

REV 20:14 — "THEN COMETH THE END" I COR 15:24-26 — ETERNITY
AND WHOSOEVER WAS NOT FOUND WRITTEN IN THE BOOK OF LIFE WAS CAST INTO THE LAKE OF FIRE REV 20:15
THE NEW JERUSALEM
2 PET 3:7-13
THE HEAVENS AND THE EARTH PURGED WITH FIRE
"NEVERTHELESS ACCORDING TO HIS PROMISE WE LOOK FOR NEW HEAVENS AND A NEW EARTH WHEREIN DWELLETH RIGHTEOUSNESS"
"IT IS DONE"
"HE THAT OVERCOMETH SHALL INHERIT ALL THINGS AND I WILL BE HIS GOD, AND HE SHALL BE MY SON" REV 21:7
"I AM ALPHA AND OMEGA · THE BEGINNING AND THE END"
"BEHOLD! I MAKE ALL THINGS NEW"
THE LAKE OF FIRE eis tous aiōnas tōn aiōnōn
(THE FINAL GEHENNA) (FOR THE AGES OF THE AGES)
"THIS IS THE SECOND DEATH" REV 20:10-15
REV 20 11-15
RESURRECTION · JUDGMENT AND DOOM OF THE WICKED — "TIME NO LONGER" REV 10:6

FINAL DOOM OF SATAN AND THE UNBELIEVING

A NEW EARTH·

(THE PERFECT AND ETERNAL AGES →

THE DISPENSATION OF THE KINGDOM

FROM THE JUDGMENT OF THE NATIONS TO THE NEW JERUSALEM

The Millennial Reign of Christ

THE PROPHETS OF GOD throughout the ages have foretold of a glorious era when the Kingdom of God shall be established in visible glory and righteousness upon the earth. The light of the prophetic lamp clearly reveals the blessings and the Glory of the Coming Millennial Kingdom, when: "The kingdoms of this world are become the kingdoms of our Lord, and of his Christ . . ." (Revelation 11:15). The great prophecy of Daniel foretells the whole course and end of Gentile World-Dominion; to be followed by a kingdom which "the God of heaven . . . set up . . ."; a Kingdom which shall fill the whole earth, and shall never be destroyed (Daniel 2:31-45).

It is very evident that if this coming Kingdom of heavenly rule is to take the place of all previous dominions in the earth (Daniel 2:35), it must be a real, visible, tangible Kingdom; with a King, a form of government, and subjects over whom the King shall rule—just as real a Kingdom as those which preceded it, but with one wonderful difference: it will be *righteous* in character and in government (Psalm 72; Matthew 6:10; Isaiah 11:3-5). It will be, at last, the only truly Universal Kingdom in world history (Daniel 2:35; 7:14; Zechariah 9:10). Unity, Peace, and Prosperity, the ideal system of world government so coveted by every passing generation, is at last realized in the Kingdom of "the Prince of Peace" (Micah 4:1-4).

The Coming Kingdom of heavenly rule on earth will not only be Universal but Eternal, for the immortal King is ". . . he that . . . was dead; and . . . [is] alive for evermore . . ." (Revelation 1:18). It is readily understood why Christ taught His disciples to pray "Thy Kingdom come," for the Kingship of Jesus and the righteous government of God upon the earth is the paramount theme of Bible revelation. All lines of Scripture lead us to the King and the establishment of His Kingdom. "Thy Kingdom come" has been the unceasing prayer of the people of God throughout the ages.

Israel, chosen to be the repository of the oracles, or the Divine purpose of God, anticipated a literal fulfillment of the Kingdom promises on the basis of the Old Testament prophecies. Nurtured in the prophetical hope, they expected the promised Messiah to be the Ruler of Israel, the King who would break the alien yoke and restore the disrupted Davidic Kingdom. As the popularity of Jesus increased He seemed to answer to their expectations, and they purposed taking Him by force and making Him their king (John 6:15). His obvious claim to Messiahship was the basic charge that finally condemned Him to the Cross: that He said, ". . . he himself is Christ [Messiah] a King" (Luke 23:2); and when Pilate asked "Art thou a king?" He answered "Thou sayest that I am a king. To this end was I born . . ." (John 18:37).

The Claim to Kingship followed Christ to the Cross. The superscription (as customarily fixed to the cross upon which a criminal was crucified, bearing the charge of his condemnation) read: This is "JESUS OF NAZARETH THE KING OF THE JEWS," and Pilate, overruling the objections of the Priests, declared, "What I have written I have written" (the irrevocable testimony of the ages).

The references concerning the Kingdom and the Kingship of Jesus are far too numerous to record in a passing panorama. In Daniel 7:13-14, we behold a scene in Heaven—the investiture of the Son of Man with the everlasting Kingdom; while the Second Psalm is a foretelling of the order of the establishing of the Kingdom: The King rejected, and the Father's irrevocable decree, "Yet have I set my king upon my holy hill of Zion."

The New Testament begins with the genealogy of Jesus, with special prominence to His royal lineage, for both Mary, His mother, and Joseph, His foster-father, were of the royal house and family of David (Luke 2:4). The Angel in announcing the birth of Jesus declared, ". . . the Lord God shall give unto him the throne of his father David" (Luke 1:32). The Magi were searching for "the new born *king.*" Jesus took deliberate steps to fulfill the prophecy of Zechariah: ". . . behold, thy *King* cometh . . ." (John 12:14-15). Christ accepted, approved and justified the homage of the multitude (Luke 19:35-40). To summarize the conclusive testimony of the Kingship of Jesus: *He was born a King.* The Angel declared that He shall sit upon ". . . the throne of his father David: . . . and of his kingdom there shall be no end." *He died a King.* Nailed to His Cross was the irrevocable testimony "JESUS OF NAZARETH KING. . . ." *He arose a King.* The Sovereign Lord of a New Creation. *He is coming back a King.* "King of kings and Lord of lords."

The Subjects of the Kingdom

The subjects of Christ's Millennial Kingdom will include the remnant of tested, tried, converted national Israel; those surviving the refining fires of "the great tribulation," spoken of in the prophetic Scriptures as "the time of Jacob's trouble" (Jeremiah 30:7; Zechariah 13:9; Ezekiel 20:37); together with the spared, judged, sifted and saved Gentile Nations. Thus, the subjects of "the Kingdom" will be "the saved of Israel," the unsaved being "cut off from the land" (Ezekiel 20:37), and the saved of the Gentile Nations.

The Restoration of Israel is a major theme of Old Testament prophecy (Amos 9:14-15; Isaiah 43:5-6; Zechariah 8:13; also Matthew 24:30-31). Paul, an Israelite, by his own personal experience of salvation answers his own question, "Hath God cast away his people? God forbid" (Romans 11:1).

The Jewish question has long been the perplexing problem of the centuries. Israel, once ". . . a proverb and a byword among all people" (I Kings 9:6-9), shall not only be gathered and restored to her permanent homeland, but out of the refining process of affliction the remnant of Israel will experience a "national" conversion, a change of mind and heart and attitude toward their Deliverer, even He "whom they have pierced" (Zechariah 12:10; Romans 11:24-27; Ezekiel 11:19; Zechariah 3:20). From henceforth they shall call His name "THE LORD OUR RIGHTEOUSNESS" (Jeremiah 23:6). Thus, ". . . redeemed with judgment, and her converts with righteousness" (Isaiah 1:27), the unfulfilled Covenant Promises given to Israel will find fulfillment during the Messiah's reign.

As to the Gentile Nations

The host of the slain at Armageddon are not "the nations" in their entirety, but the confederated kings with their armies. After their destruction in the field of battle, follows "the rod of iron rule" of the Conqueror: that is, inflexible justice, moral discipline, and direction toward *a new world government* founded upon *righteousness*.

The Judgment of the Nations

. . . then shall he sit upon the throne of his glory: And before him shall be gathered all nations; and he shall separate them one from another, as a shepherd divideth his sheep from the goats. (Matthew 25:31-46.)

Those who share "the throne of his glory" and the administration of judgment and justice are the ransomed, glorified saints, returning with the King of kings to rule and to reign on the earth (Revelation 5:10; II Timothy 2:12; Revelation 3:21; 20:6). The basis of "the Judgment of the Nations" is not solely the rejection of "the Gospel of the Kingdom," but their treatment of Christ's "brethren," as to the flesh, the Jews.

"The brethren" of whom Christ speaks, in relation to the judgment scene, are undoubtedly the believing remnant of Israel; sealed for God against the blasts of tribulation. In Revelation 7 they are called "the servants [or messengers] of God"; and the fruitage of their witnessing, during "the hour of trial," is seen in a great multitude of Gentiles (the palm-bearers of 7:9) who accept "the gospel of the kingdom" and display an attitude of charity toward the persecuted witnesses. They feed, clothe and visit the sick, imprisoned and neglected messengers; and at the judgment of the nations they are called "righteous"—for the righteous Judge declared, "Inasmuch as ye have done it unto one of the least of these *my brethren,* ye have done it unto me" (Matthew 25:40). The Greek word translated "brethren" is *adelphos,* meaning, literally, "of the same womb"; brother, relative (Young's *Concordance*). Christ, the Jew, is speaking of His brethren, the Jews, in contrast to the Gentiles (*ethnos*) gathered before Him. In Joel 3:2, a prophetic picture of the same gathering and judgment of the nations, Jehovah speaks of pleading for "my people," and "my heritage Israel"; in Matthew 25, He calls them "my brethren."

Of the apostate nations, rejecting "the gospel of the kingdom," the last great witness, and refusing to give succor to the King's last witnesses, the Righteous Judge shall say, "Inasmuch as ye did it *not* to one of the least of these [my brethren], ye did it *not* to me."

Although the term "judgment of the *nations*" is usually used, it would seem that there must, of necessity, be an individual, personal aspect— for those surviving the Divine indictment are given the invitation, "Come, ye blessed of my Father, inherit the [earthly] kingdom prepared for you *from* the foundation of the world." The "heavenly" Kingdom; the ransomed, glorified "Church of the firstborn," was chosen in Christ *before* the foundation of the world (Ephesians 1:4).

The Earth, created a Paradise for the permanent abode of Man, was forfeited by *Sin* and brought under Sin's Curse; but with the returning of the rightful "King of all the earth" it shall be freed from the bondage of blight; its Edenic beauty restored; ". . . her wilderness like Eden, and her desert like the garden of the Lord . . ." (Isaiah 51:3; 35:1).

The gracious words "inherit the Kingdom" reveal the nature and purpose of the judgment: to determine those among the nations of the earth who shall enter the Millennial Kingdom of Christ; and those who shall not. To those who shall not, "the lion of the tribe of Judah," remembering the treatment of His brethren, shall say "Depart from me ye cursed." The sentence may well be the consummation of the oath of Jehovah to Abram in the beginning of the history of the chosen people: ". . . I will bless them that bless thee, and curse him that curseth thee . . ." (Genesis 12:3).

The Judgment of the Nations, which takes place at the beginning of

Christ's Millennial Reign, is often confused with **the Great White Throne Judgment** at the end of the Millennium, but a comparison is conclusive.

At the Judgment of the Nations (Matthew 25:31-46), no resurrection takes place; the subjects of judgment are living nations (*ethnos*). The word occurs 158 times in the New Testament and never in any instance is it applied to the dead or the resurrected. The scene is on the earth (Joel 3:2), while at the Great White Throne ". . . the earth and the heaven fled away . . ." (Revelation 20:11). No books are opened when Christ sits upon "the Throne of his Glory," and three groups are classified in the Judgment—"sheep" and "goats" (used as metaphors) and "brethren." The Judgment occurs at the personal returning of the "King of kings," therefore, at the beginning of the Millennium. The Judgment at the Great White Throne, a thousand years later, is marked by a resurrection, and those judged are the "risen dead." The books are opened, and one class only is mentioned—"the dead" (Revelation 20:11-15).

The Saved of the Nations

Witnessing the transforming conversion of Israel, ". . . I will be sanctified in you before the heathen" (Ezekiel 20:41), and the restoration of the remnant of the nation to their homeland as a permanent possession with the blessing of God upon them; "it shall come to pass" that representatives "out of all languages of the nations" in the Millennial Kingdom shall seek the Jew, saying, "We will go with you: for we have heard that God is with you" (Zechariah 8:23). The sifted and saved Gentile nations shall be brought into relationship with God through the witness of Israel. Once scattered to the ends of the earth to be ". . . trodden down of the Gentiles, until the times of the Gentiles [Gentile World-Dominion, from Nebuchadnezzar to the Antichrist] be fulfilled" (Luke 21:24).

At the coming, and the accepting, of their long-rejected Messiah, repentant Israel shall be exalted in Christ's Kingdom to be a witness of God's Righteousness in the earth; thus, saith the Lord, ". . . they shall declare my glory among the Gentiles" (Isaiah 61:9; 66:18-19; Zechariah 8:13; Zephaniah 3:20).

As to the Earth at Christ's Returning

The earth, which now groans with all creation under the thralldom of the curse (Romans 8:21-23), shall be delivered and restored to its former fertility and Edenic beauty. Delivered from blight and devouring, destructive hosts, the harvest will be so abundant that ". . . the plowman shall overtake the reaper . . ." (Amos 9:13). The millennial blessedness of God's good earth delivered from the curse of Genesis

3:17-19 is foreseen in such passages as: Amos 9:13; Joel 2:24-25; 3:17-18; Isaiah 35; 55:13. ". . . abundance of peace. . . . all nations shall call him blessed" (Psalm 72).

As to Human Life During Christ's Millennial Reign

It must be remembered that the subjects of Christ's earthly, Millennial Kingdom are not "glorified" beings (as the raptured "Church" of the Firstborn) but "natural" beings, inhabitants of the re-Edenized earth, with bodies of flesh and blood, begetting children and perpetuating the nations. Human life, however, will be free from the ravages of decay, pestilence and disease, which is part of the curse, the process of death; therefore, the life span, naturally, will be prolonged, until a man of a hundred years will be considered (age-wise) a child (Isaiah 65:20; Zechariah 8:4; Ezekiel 47:12).

Unlike all other ages, "death" will be the exception not the rule, and then, only as a punitive measure in dealing with flagrant violation of the "shepherdizing" administration of the Righteous King (Isaiah 11:4). Revealing the disquieting truth that although the character and environment of the Kingdom Age will be as near to perfection as all of the hopes and dreams of the ages have aspired, it will not be found perfect until the final purging of every trace of rebellion and enmity (Revelation 20:7-10). Death, "the last enemy to be destroyed" (I Corinthians 15:26; Revelation 21:4), will be finally, totally and eternally abolished after all of the works of the Devil have run their full and diabolical course—to the complete vindication and triumph of "God and the Lamb."

As to the Animal Creation

The nature of the animal creation shall be changed; losing its ferocity and venom, once again the animal kingdom (over which Adam was to have had dominion) shall be harmless and unharmed as in the original nature of Edenic harmony. We read "The wolf also shall dwell with the lamb, . . . and the lion shall eat straw like the ox. . . . They shall not hurt nor destroy . . ." (Isaiah 11:6-9).

Satan Loosed!

And when the thousand years are expired, Satan shall be loosed out of his prison. (Revelation 20:7-10.)

At the end of the thousand years of peace on earth, under the direct and righteous administration of the very "King of kings," Satan is loosed "for a little season," and immediately his evil influence is manifested among the nations. He quickly fans the age-old flame of revolt against God and His Christ, and finds willing rebels to join him in the four quarters of the earth. During Christ's reign all Israel shall become righteous, and multitudes of Gentiles shall also worship and serve the Lord; but with many (as a marginal reference in many Bibles suggests) it will, evidently, be "feigned" obedience (outward conformity to His Law) prompted more by fear than faith.

It must be remembered that those on earth (as already mentioned) are not "glorified" beings, like the Saints of the First Resurrection, but "natural" beings; therefore, those born during the Millennium will have the same inherent, Adamic nature as their fathers, but without the external sources of temptation; the evil power of Satanic suggestion. While Satan is confined to the pit, "man" is as a keg of dynamite without the spark to set it off—but once loosed from his prison, and gathering a still susceptible multitude about him, the spark of rebellious hate touches off the last desperately mad attempt to dethrone the King, seize the Kingdom, and still defeat God's purpose in the earth. But persistent rebellion against God is death! His answer to the rebel's last defiance is told in one short but terribly conclusive sentence: ". . . fire came down from God out of heaven and devoured them" (Revelation 20:9).

The question is often asked, "Why doesn't God destroy Satan and put an end to his infamy once and forever, instead of sealing him in the pit for a thousand years?" God is omnipotent, it is true, but not only God's power is challenged by the Adversary, but *all* of God's attributes: His justice, holiness, righteousness, His long-suffering mercy and undying love all have claims against the Devil and must be perfectly and eternally vindicated.

The purpose of God in the binding and loosing of Satan is the final display of the total depravity of the human heart apart from the sovereign grace of God. The philosophy that man is naturally good, if it were not for the Devil's influence and power, is put to the test by removing the Devil from the scene and sealing him in the pit, that man might live for a thousand years with no Devil to tempt him; in an atmosphere of absolute righteousness; on an earth redeemed from the curse and restored to Edenic serenity; yet at the end of the test the unregenerated heart of man is *unchanged*.

With the last rebellion put down, and the earth, for the first time in human history, populated with "the righteous" only, the great arch-enemy utterly and eternally foiled and defeated in his blasphemous ambition, now meets his final and everlasting perdition. The long-delayed sentence is swiftly executed. He is "cast into the lake of fire," already prepared for him and, sad to say, his blinded, and deluded followers (Revelation 20:10; Matthew 25:41). **Thus ends the last rebellion of a creature against his Creator.**

The Judgment of the Wicked Dead

Both the Old Testament and the New declare a day of judgment for every individual human being that ever lived and died, from the beginning of the world until the end. ". . . it is appointed unto men once to die, but after this the judgment" (Hebrews 9:27). This Divine decree is irrevocable in its nature, and will determine the eternal destiny of every mortal soul; either to everlasting blessedness or everlasting punishment.

The teaching, however, of one general resurrection at the end of the world, when all mankind collectively—saints and sinners, Jews and Gentiles, saved and unsaved, living and dead—shall stand before the Great White Throne in general judgment is certainly not the teaching of the Scriptures. The expression "general judgment" is nowhere found in the Bible.

There is a resurrection of both "the just and the unjust" (Acts 24:15). There is a "resurrection of life," and a "resurrection of damnation," *i.e.,* condemnation (John 5:29), and as we are assured, "There is therefore now no condemnation to them which are in Christ Jesus . . ." (Romans 8:1), these two resurrections could not possibly be one and the same. There is a resurrection "out from among the dead"; this is "the first resurrection," and it is necessarily eclectic (selective); some are raised, others are not (Revelation 20:5-6; I Thessalonians 4:16). Wherever the resurrection of Christ or His people is mentioned in Scripture (in the original Greek) it is always coupled with the preposition *ek,* "out of" or "from among." Thus, Paul assures us that ". . . the dead *in Christ* shall rise *first,"* clearly denoting a rising "out of" or "from among" those *not* "in Christ"; the unredeemed multitudes who died "without Christ and without hope."

In Revelation 20:5, they are referred to as "the rest of the dead"—those not taking part in the First Resurrection—they ". . . lived not again [were not resurrected] until the thousand years were finished." While those of the First Resurrection "lived and reigned with Christ" during the thousand years, "the rest of the dead" remained in their graves (Revelation 5-6); these are associated facts. The First Resurrection, therefore, is clearly a resurrection of saints only—those "in Christ," called "blessed and holy."

Not all the partakers of the First Resurrection, however (as already noted in our study), actually first taste death. Those who are alive and ready at Christ's coming shall be "caught up" without passing through "the Valley of the Shadow," but to be "clothed upon" with immortality. Thus, both the resurrected ones and the living ones ". . . shall all be changed, In a moment, in the twinkling of an eye . . ." (I Corinthians 15:51-54). "Caught up" ever to be with the Lord (I Thessalonians 4:15-18).

The Doom of the Unbelieving Dead

And I saw a great white throne. . . . And I saw the
dead . . . stand before God; and the books were opened: and
another book . . . , the book of life: and the dead were
judged out of those things which were written in the books.
. . . And whosoever was not found written in the book of
life was cast into the lake of fire. (Revelation 20:11-15.)

The subjects of the Great White Throne Judgment are "the rest of
the dead." Those who had no part in the First Resurrection. Now resurrected, "after the thousand years were finished" (Revelation 20:5), they
stand before the Judgment Throne; although physically alive they are
called "the dead," having never been made alive, spiritually, in Christ
Jesus. ". . . he that hath not the Son . . . hath not life" (I John
5:12). "For as in Adam all die, even so in Christ shall all be made alive"
(I Corinthians 15:22).

The basis of the judgment of the resurrected, unbelieving "dead," is
their rejection of the only Saviour and Mediator, God's own Son, who
loved them and died to save them from sin, death and the judgment
they now must face. "The books" are opened; these are the records of
all the deeds of the unregenerate (those who have died in their sins),
together with every evil thing entertained in the heart (I Timothy 5:24).
Everyone has such a searching biography set down to his account, for
". . . all things are naked and opened unto the eyes of him with whom
we have to do" (Hebrews 4:13). It is a sobering thought indeed that
before God's omnipresence every thought is conceived, every word is
uttered, every motive exposed, and every deed done. But—when a
sinner turns from his sin with a repentant heart and accepts the Salvation
made possible by the sacrificial death of Jesus Christ—who took upon
Himself the sins of the world, and tasted both physical and spiritual
death, sin's twofold penalty, for "every man"—the sinner's guilty record
is blotted out of "the books," and his name is written in "the book"—
"the Book of Life." The Book of Life is the record of *names* not deeds.

In the apocalyptic vision, as God swung back the curtain that veils the
future and eternal state, and gave John, the Seer, a glimpse of the
gathering crescendo of Divine wrath, the final and eternal Judgment,
John recorded the awesome consummation of the scene before him in
one terrible sentence of *Divine finality:* ". . . **whosoever was not found
written in the book of life was cast into the lake of fire**" (Revelation
20:15). Such is the eternal doom and destiny of "the lost."

A Review of the Ages

In reviewing the great panorama of God's patient dealings with man throughout the ages, and man's miserable response to God, we are brought to the realization of the truth that in spite of long-suffering mercy and undying love, man has failed God in every dispensation of time:

The Age of Innocence ended with willful disobedience; bringing its penalty of physical and spiritual death.

The Age of Conscience ended with universal corruption and the near obliteration of the race.

The Age of Human Government ended by ruling God out, and building for Self, with its inevitable confusion and disruption.

The Age of Promise ended with God's people out of the Promised Land, in slavery and oppression.

The Dispensation of the Law ended with the creature crucifying the Creator.

The Age of Grace ended with War against God and His Christ.

The Kingdom Age which follows under the personal reign of the Lord of Glory, the Devil's power paralyzed for a season, finds a multitude of unsettled souls again willing to believe the Devil's lie.

Thus, human history, as studied dispensationally, ends in continuing judgment. Truly we have learned the lesson of the ages, that men's hearts are "only evil continually"; that unregenerated human nature has not changed from Eden to Gog and Magog—but thanks be unto God, ". . . as many as received him, to them gave he the power to become the sons of God, even to them that believe on his name" (John 1:12).

The Eternal State

After the scene at the Great White Throne, a scene outside of "time" and beyond human history, we are ushered once again into the Eternal Ages, where, in our study, we were first introduced to *Elohim*, the Mighty Author and Cause—and now, **a new vision** opens before us. The Holy Spirit guide has led us from the first to the last of the unfolding panorama of the ages—through valleys of faith on to mountain tops of revelation, until we stand, spellbound, on the last pinnacle peak of "the Mystery of Godliness," looking out over the eternal vista of God's glorious "tomorrow."

The concluding chapters of the Revelation carry us out beyond finite understanding—we are on the threshold of the infinite. The Great White Throne in the pure, blinding whiteness of naked omnipotence spanned above by an emerald rainbow—the heavenlies and the elements melting with fervent heat—the Earth below ablaze with purging, purifying fire— above the blue, a city coming down out of Heaven bringing release from pain and sorrow, death and tears, forever (Revelation 21:1-5; II Peter 3:10-12). Surely this must be the grand and glorious consummation of all the cherished hopes and dreams of the Redeemed of the ages—but the seeming end is actually **the beginning**—God lets the curtain fall upon "time," and all things past, declaring, ". . . former things are passed away," and throwing open wide the portals of the Perfect and Eternal Age He announces the soul-thrilling declaration that the whole disturbed universe has been hoping, waiting, longing, striving, living, dying to hear—**"Behold, I make all things new"** (Revelation 21:5).

The Preparation for the Eternal Kingdom

The destruction of Satan and the last living rebellious earth dwellers; the judgment and eternal doom of the resurrected, wicked dead; the purging of every trace of sin, rebellion and discord in the universe; everything associated with the ruin and spoilation of the curse, ". . . melted and refined by that dreadful fire which shall burn up all the dross of the visible creation" (Matthew Henry). These are the momentous events which mark the preparation for the eternal state of the Redeemed; the Eternal Kingdom; God's everlasting rest; unchanging and absolute perfection; in this state, alone, can Righteousness *dwell*.

The Millennial Kingdom of the Son, with the ransomed, glorified saints sharing His blessed "reign" of righteousness on the earth, having fulfilled its purpose and object—"The exhibition of the restoration of Divine Sovereignty in the earth"—being triumphantly accomplished by the final overthrow of the kingdom of Satan, and the eternal destruction of the malign *Usurper* of ". . . all the kingdoms of the world, and the glory of them" (Matthew 4:8-9):

> *Then cometh the end, when he [Christ] shall have delivered up the [Millennial] kingdom to God, even the Father. . . . that God may be all in all.* (*I Corinthians 15:24-28.*)

New Heavens and a New Earth

> *. . . wherein the heavens being on fire shall be dissolved, and the elements shall melt with fervent heat?*
> *Nevertheless we, according to his promise, look for new heavens and a new earth, wherein dwelleth righteousness.* (*II Peter 3:10-13.*)

The "heavens" and the "earth" designate the respective spheres of the "Saved"—both the heavenly and the earthly peoples of God—wherein righteousness shall "dwell." The Millennial Kingdom of Christ is the thousand-year display of a righteous "reign," in contrast to all previous dominion in the earth. In the future Kingdom, righteousness shall "**dwell**"; the abiding, changeless, eternal state, in perfect harmony with what God *is*—"All in All"—Righteousness, Holiness, Perfection, Light and Love and Life.

Such passages which speak of the earth "passing away" (Greek, *parerchomai*), "having fled," "perishing," being "dissolved," never signify annihilation, or cessation of being; the idea is transition not extinction. The teaching of Bible revelation assures us that "The earth abideth forever" (Ecclesiastes 1:14; Psalm 119:90; Isaiah 66:22). Put in the crucible, to be sure, purged, changed, cleansed of old corruption and imperfections; made anew; that is, the state of things once present "to pass away," "perish," be "dissolved," to give place to a new, abiding, better, and eternal state. Peter writes that the world, once before, "perished," but the word translated world is *kosmos*, "order," "arrangement," "inhabitableness"; as a planet it remained, and still exists.

> The destruction of the present order being for the sake of that which is to usher in a new and better state. (Cambridge Bible.)

> "Melted and refined by that dreadful fire which shall burn up all the dross of the visible creation . . . purified, refined, erected and rebuilt" (Matthew Henry).

When a man becomes "a new creature," or "a new creation," he is not annihilated but changed, "old things pass away, all things become new." The word is "regeneration" (Greek, *palingenesia*), "re-creation," "making new" (Titus 3:5). The same word occurs in Matthew 19:28, referring to the re-creation of the existing order and the renewal of the earth. "The word signifies a renovation of all visible things when the old is passed away, and heaven and earth are become new" (*International Standard Bible Encyclopedia*).

The "dissolving" spoken of by Peter is the same word used by Jesus regarding Lazarus, "Loose him," and other instances where the idea of "loosing" is used as "setting free" (Matthew 21:2; Revelation 9:14; 20:7; I Corinthians 7:27), the idea being deliverance not destruction (Seiss).

While it is true that the ablest of Bible scholars still disagree as to the method and extent of the physical change in the universe implied in these dramatic passages, "a world 'wherein dwelleth righteousness' would be a new world, even without any physical change at all" (Cambridge Bible).

The New Jerusalem (Revelation 21)

And I . . . saw the holy city, new Jerusalem, coming down from God out of heaven, prepared as a bride adorned for her husband. (Revelation 21:2.)

This is the consummation, the everlasting Joy of the Lamb; "the Church of the firstborn written in heaven"; "the Bride, the Lamb's Wife," in her final completeness and eternal abode. Descending in her purity and beauty, the crowning gem to complete the blessedness of the re-Genesis of the world.

The New Jerusalem is the realization of that celestial city which Christ has gone to prepare, and to bring down from Heaven, to be the eternal home of His Glorified Saints. The faithful of all ages have been inspired by the promise of a dwelling place of heavenly blessedness; an enduring city built and prepared by ". . . the author and finisher of our faith. . . ."

These all died in faith . . . and confessed that they were strangers and pilgrims on the earth. (Hebrews 11:13.)

. . . [Abraham] looked for a city which hath foundations, whose builder and maker is God. (Hebrews 11:10.)

. . . [God] hath prepared for them a city. (Hebrews 11:16.)

. . . here have we no continuing city, but we seek one to come. (Hebrews 13:14.)

. . . [In anticipation they] are come . . . unto the city of the living God, the heavenly Jerusalem. . . . (Hebrews 12:22.)

In my Father's house are many mansions. . . . I go to prepare a place for you. (John 14:1-6.)

While some Bible scholars protest the idea of a literal, substantial, material city; declaring the apocalyptic scene to be "symbolic" of the Church in its final and beautiful triumph, when the whole world shall, at last, become a "spiritual kingdom"; those Bible-lovers, who are old-fashioned enough, and with simple, childlike faith believe that God means exactly what He says, have, in every generation, been blessed and inspired with the heavenly hope of a real, literal, God-built, enduring and eternal "home."

The City is called "the Bride, the Lamb's Wife." A city is a city only in the sense of those who inhabit it. Without residents a city would be an empty sepulchre. So it is that the heavenly city is the Lamb's Bride because of the ransomed, redeemed and glorified ones who dwell within its Jasper walls. The streets of transparent gold; the "many mansions"; the River, crystal-clear; the Trees of everlasting fruitage; the beauty of accommodation and arrangement; together with the immortal occupants, make it both "a city" and "a people"—thus, did the Angel describe it: ". . . the bride, the Lamb's wife. . . . that great city, the holy Jerusalem . . ." (Revelation 9-10).

John saw it "descending out of heaven from God. Having the glory of God. . . ." John's description of the heavenly city, built by the Almighty Architect who built the universe, is brief but breathtaking— "Having the Glory of God" is the *summum bonum,* the "all in all" of its transcendent splendor.

And the city had no need of the sun, neither of the moon, to shine in it: for the glory of God did lighten it, *and the Lamb is the light thereof. (Revelation 21:23.)*

The Holy Occupants

The Glorified Saints are the dwellers of the celestial city, the Tabernacle of God; yet John speaks of another company:

. . . I heard a great voice out of heaven saying, Behold, the tabernacle of God is with men [mankind], *and he will dwell with them, and they shall be his people, and God himself shall be with them, and be their God. (Revelation 21:3.)*

The living, undying "Saved of the nations"; the subjects of the Millennial Kingdom of Christ; now, the occupants of the New earth, and subjects of the Eternal Kingdom of God; dwelling even as Adam and Eve in Paradise when they walked in holy communion with their Maker —while everlastingly distinct from the Glorified Church of the First-born, the Lamb's Wife, which is the New Jerusalem:

. . . the nations of them which are saved shall walk in the light of it. . . . And they shall bring the glory and honour of the nations unto it. (Revelation 21:24.)

The unveiled presence of God and of the Lamb radiating in, and through, and from the celestial city shall illumine not only "the new heavens and the new earth," but the ransomed souls of a redeemed world, the new earth's happy and holy dwellers. "As in heaven, so on earth." What a blessed and eternal benediction!—no more tears, ". . . no more death, neither sorrow, nor crying, neither . . . pain: for the former things [of earth and time] are passed away" (Revelation 21:4).

Many scholars have tried to explain **the process** of transition and change from the Millennial Kingdom to the Eternal state of the dwellers of the New Earth, who bask in the glory and the light of the New Jerusalem; and the unveiled presence of the Eternal Godhead; but to explain *how* God will care for the loyal and righteous subjects of Christ's earthly reign during the great transition, the great purging, cleansing, changing conflagration described in II Peter 3:10-13—is futile when God is silent. We do not ask *how* He kept "the three Hebrew children" from being consumed in the fiery furnace, we rejoice in the assuring witness of omnipotence, omnipresence and omniscience—"Nothing is too hard for God"—His presence and concern is eternally everywhere—and "He doeth all things well."

All Things New

And he that sat upon the throne said, Behold, I make all things new. . . . It is done. I am Alpha and Omega, the beginning and the end. (Revelation 21:5-6.)

The Volume of "the Old" is eternally closed. The Cycle of Time, begun in Genesis, the book of beginnings, when *Sin* disrupted God's eternal and immutable plan of purpose, "Holy and Eternal Communion," has fulfilled the great circle and the course of history ends where it began, Eden lost now Paradise gained; and the two ends of "the cycle of the ages" are gathered and welded into the never-ending future, "the ages of the ages"—never again to be disrupted by a creature's will.

Cut off, because of *Sin,* from "the Tree of Life," whose fruit was the pledge of undecaying immortality for man's soul and body, the cycle of God's Redemptive Plan, with all of its attendant ministries of Grace, had but one objective: **Man's complete redemption and readmission to "the Tree of Life."** It is remarkably significant that "the Tree of Life" is mentioned but twice in God's Holy Word: at the beginning and at the end—in the *Genesis* of redemption, when the cherubim mercifully barred the way, lest man should eat of its Life-fruits and live forever in his sinful state—and in the *Revelation* of redemption's Glorious accomplishment in the person of the glorified Redeemer, Jesus Christ.

"All things new" and **"It is done."** God declares His Will and it is accomplished. All is eternally settled. Nothing short of what God *is* can be the measure of the Eternal state. Not the old order embellished and improved, but "All things new."

The great Panorama has passed before us—Creation, rebellion, promises and prophecies, mercy and grace, judgment and justification, complete redemption and the establishment of an eternity of uninterrupted righteousness. God "in the beginning"—God "all in all." The Alpha and the Omega—all, except Sin, had its origin in God, and all ends in and for His glory and honor.

"All things new"! Redemption has gone farther than the ruin. Repentant, regenerated, redeemed and glorified sinners "saved by grace" (The church of the first-born written in Heaven), those "in Christ" gain eternally more than they lost "in Adam"—becoming, by the infinite grace of God, immortal King-priests and co-regents with the Lamb upon His Throne in the heavenly city—". . . the throne of God and of the Lamb," ". . . and they shall reign for ever and ever" (Revelation 22:1-5).

And those with whom God tabernacles on the new earth, whom He declares "His people" and "He their God," gain all that Adam lost: the earth again as Eden—Communion with their Maker—Immortality, for "death is no more"; and in some manner, now veiled to our understanding, it appears that the fruit of the Tree of Life is the rewarding joy of those within the Jasper walls—while the leaves of the tree, as John records, ". . . were for the healing of the nations," the life-sustaining, health-preserving blessing of the eternal generations. God provided for the perpetuation of the race in Adam; "eternal generations" was God's plan had not *Sin* given birth to life's mortal enemy *Death* (James 1:15; Ezekiel 18:4).

Although to all knowledge no other planet is yet inhabited—when God declares "all things new," the perfect age is in its infancy. Surely the glorious and eternal Kingdom of God is not limited to one tiny planet, Earth—but **"a Kingdom without end,"** with "eternal" and righteous generations, over whom God and the Lamb and the glorified Saints shall reign for ever and for ever, carries us into the infinite vastness and immensity of God's Glorious Creation—surely such a Kingdom is commensurate with the Majesty, the Glory, the Omnipotence, the Omnipresence, the Infinity and the Eternity of our God. Then truly can we lift our voices with worshipful meaning and heartfelt adoration, with the words of the grand old hymn: "Then sings my soul my Saviour God to Thee, How great Thou art, *how great Thou art.*"

> *He that overcometh shall inherit all things; and I will be*
> *his God, and he shall be my son. (Revelation 21:7.)*

The Holy City—the Throne of God and of the Lamb—the River of the Water of Life, to ". . . make glad the city of God . . ." (Psalm 46:4)—the Tree of Life, yielding its abundant Life-fruits, the joyous, awarding privilege of glorified Saints the partaking of which is beyond our present finite understanding—no night to darken the crystal-clear brightness—the unveiled and effulgent Glory of God and the Lamb, the unity and embodiment of absolute Deity—the heavenly honor of participation, as celestial king-priests, in the reign of the eternal Godhead; not for a thousand years, or an eon, but to "the ages of the ages"— *"he shall inherit all [these] things"*—but the infinite grace of "he that sat upon the throne" is not yet exhausted—the fountainhead of all eternal blessedness is summed up in the tenderest, most precious words yet spoken, *"he shall be my son."* Sonship is the supreme joy, the most blessed and eternal relationship, the grandest inheritance.

"I will be his God." Inheriting "all things"—the deathless, painless, tearless, sinless, sorrowless, *endless* perfection of New Heavens, New Earth, New Jerusalem, New Name (Revelation 2:17; 3:12)—". . . an heritance incorruptible, and undefiled, and that fadeth not away . . ." (I Peter 1:4)—"all these things"—but, the crowning glory is the consummation of *God's own immutable purpose* **in** "all things"—the fulfillment of the longing of His heart—*Holy, Eternal, and Inseparable Communion*—*"I will be his God and he shall be my son."*

Out of the silence of the Eternal Ages God revealed "the longing of His heart" by Creating Angels, but the Holy Communion was broken by the self-will of a Creature. God then Created Man, and the Communion between the Creature and the Creator was *perfect* until, again, self-will shattered and marred the Holy Communion of Man and God. The Holy Communion of the Eternal Godhead was broken, this time not by *self*-will, but by the Father's Will; when the Son cried, "My God why hast thou forsaken me?"—but when He cried *"It is finished,"* the longing of God's heart, at last, was eternally satisfied—*A New Creation* "in Christ" His Beloved, whose prayer is now, after the Restitution of All Things, gloriously and eternally answered:

> *Father . . . that they all may be* one *. . . thou in me . . . I in thee . . . that they may also be* one *in us . . . I in them, and thou in me, that they may be made* perfect *in* one. *. . . (John 17:21-23.)*

"Even So Come Lord Jesus"